Toyota's Assembly Line

JAPANESE SOCIETY SERIES

General Editor: Yoshio Sugimoto

The 'Big Bang' in Japanese Higher Education:
The 2004 Reforms and the Dynamics of Change
J.S. Eades, Roger Goodman and Yumiko Hada

Japanese Politics: An Introduction
Takashi Inoguchi

A Social History of Science and Technology in
Contempory Japan, Volume 2
Shigeru Nakayama

Gender and Japanese Management
Kimiko Kimoto

Philosophy of Agricultural Science: A Japanese Perspective
Osamu Soda

A Social History of Science and Technology in
Contempory Japan, Volume 3
Shigeru Nakayama and Kunio Goto

Japan's Underclass: Day Laborers and the Homeless
Hideo Aoki

A Social History of Science and Technology
in Contemporary Japan, Volume 4
Shigeru Nakayama and Hitoshi Yoshioka

Escape from Work: A Lifestyle Choice of Japanese Youth
Reiko Kosugi

Social Welfare in Japan: Principles and Applications
Kojun Furukawa

Scams and Sweeteners: A Sociology of Fraud
Masahiro Ogino

Toyota's Assembly Line: A View from the Factory Floor
Ryoji Ihara

Social Stratification and Inequality Series

Inequality amid Affluence: Social Stratification in Japan
Junsuke Hara and Kazuo Seiyama

Intentional Social Change: A Rational Choice Theory
Yoshimichi Sato

Constructing Civil Society in Japan:
Voices of Environmental Movements
Koichi Hasegawa

Deciphering Stratification and Inequality: Japan and beyond
Yoshimichi Sato

Social Justice in Japan: Concepts, Theories and Paradigms
Ken-ichi Ohbuchi

Advanced Social Research Series

A Sociology of Happiness
Kenji Kosaka

Frontiers of Social Research: Japan and beyond
Akira Furukawa

MODERNITY AND IDENTITY IN ASIA SERIES

Globalization, Culture and Inequality in Asia
Timothy S. Scrase, Todd Miles Joseph Holden and Scott Baum

Looking for Money:
Capitalism and Modernity in an Orang Asli Village
Alberto Gomes

Governance and Democracy in Asia
Takashi Inoguchi and Matthew Carlson

Toyota's Assembly Line

A View from the Factory Floor

Ryoji Ihara

Translated by

Hugh Clarke

Trans Pacific Press

Melbourne

First published in Japanese in 2003 by Sakurai Shoten as *Toyota no rōdō genba: Dainamizumu to kontekusuto*

This English language edition published in 2007 by
Trans Pacific Press, PO Box 120, Rosanna, Melbourne, Victoria 3084, Australia
Web: http://www.transpacificpress.com

Copyright © Trans Pacific Press 2007

Designed and set by digital environs, Melbourne, Australia. www.digitalenvirons.com

Printed by BPA Print Group, Burwood, Victoria, Australia

Distributors

Australia and New Zealand
UNIREPS
University of New South Wales
Sydney, NSW 2052
Australia
Telephone: +61(0)2-9664-0999
Fax: +61(0)2-9664-5420
Email: info.press@unsw.edu.au
Web: http://www.unireps.com.au

USA and Canada
International Specialized Book
Services (ISBS)
920 NE 58th Avenue, Suite 300
Portland, Oregon 97213-3786
USA
Telephone: (800) 944-6190
Fax: (503) 280-8832
Email: orders@isbs.com
Web: http://www.isbs.com

Asia and the Pacific
Kinokuniya Company Ltd.

Head office:
Shin-Mizonokuchi Bldg. 2F
5-7 Hisamoto 3-chome
Takatsu-ku, Kawasaki 213-8506
Japan
Telephone: +81(0)44-874-9642
Fax: +81(0)44-829-1025
Email: bkimp@kinokuniya.co.jp
Web: www.kinokuniya.co.jp

Asia-Pacific office:
Kinokuniya Book Stores of Singapore Pte., Ltd.
391B Orchard Road #13-06/07/08
Ngee Ann City Tower B
Singapore 238874
Telephone: +65 6276 5558
Fax: +65 6276 5570
Email: SSO@kinokuniya.co.jp

ISSN   1443-9670 (Japanese Society Series)

ISBN   978-1-876843-36-6 (Hardcover)
ISBN   978-1-876843-42-7 (Paperback)

The National Library of Australia Cataloguing-in-Publication Data

Ihara, Ryoji.
  Toyota's assembly line: a view from the factory floor.

  Bibliography.
  Includes index.
  ISBN 9781876843366 (hbk.).
  ISBN 9781876843427 (pbk.).

  1. Toyota-Astra Motor – Management. 2. Factory management –
  Japan. 3. Industrial relations – Japan. 4. Assembly-line
  methods – Japan. 5. Employees – Effect of technological
  innovations on – Japan. I. Title.

331.0120952

Contents

Figures

Tables

Foreword

This book is a workplace study based on my own experience in an automobile factory. The Japanese economy, once lauded with slogans like 'Japan as number one,' is still struggling to extricate itself from a long period of stagnation and is, if anything, sinking deeper into recession. Throughout this period, Japanese companies have experienced violent fluctuations. In this climate, Toyota has been one of the few companies that have continued to be counted among the 'winners,' from the time of the bubble economy and its collapse to the present day. Through the 1980s up until the mid-1990s the 'Toyota Production System' attracted a good deal of attention in Japan and abroad as the source of Toyota's competitive edge. Even later, when other Japanese companies were struggling with the after-effects of the bubble economy and how to respond to globalization, Toyota continued to grow. In the 2001 fiscal year Toyota recorded its highest ever sales and profit figures (consolidated accounts) and became the first Japanese manufacturing enterprise to exceed one trillion yen operating profit and recurrent profit (*Nikkan Jidōsha Shinbun*, 14 May 2002). Its momentum has been unstoppable. In the nine months from April to December 2002 it had already exceeded the operating profit for the entire preceding year (*Ibid.* 6 February 2003). One gets the feeling that Toyota alone has come out on top.

But even Toyota has not necessarily grown smoothly throughout this period and it has not always been clear sailing for the company. As many researchers have pointed out, the 'reformation' has been pushed through within a climate of social change. From the end of the 1980s into the early 1990s, right at the zenith of the bubble economy, the company was plagued with serious labour shortages. Factory work was shunned as strenuous, dirty and dangerous, summed up in Japanese as the '3K's,' *kitsui*, *kitanai*, and *kiken*. Even those recruited, often ended up quitting immediately. Such was the severe management environment the company faced and it was in response to these problems that Toyota embarked on its drastic 'reformation.'

At the beginning of the 1990s, as a countermeasure to address the labour shortage, the company groped with the promotion of automation. But the measures taken at this time did not yield the results the company had been hoping for. A raft of new problems emerged – increased cost of capital investment, rises in salary costs with the increase in staff numbers and a deepening sense of alienation among assembly line workers stemming from the oversimplification of the tasks they performed. So Toyota tried another new 'experiment.' They changed direction, applied the brakes to over-automation and introduced the new concept of 'creating a people-friendly workplace.'

They changed the previous system of automation, which kept people and machines apart, and hit upon the idea of 'automation where people and machines co-exist' ('in-line automation'). By cutting the great long assembly lines here and there, they reduced the pressure of assembly line stoppages. In addition, they changed the system that had hitherto been nothing more than a succession of tedious, simple processes, to a focus on the function of the car as a whole, making it easier for workers to appreciate the significance of their labour ('independent completion process'). Further, by determining the degree of difficulty of the various tasks on the assembly line and refining the most difficult of them, they were able to increase the rate of retention of younger workers and strive towards creating a factory where older employees and women could work.

In this way, through a process of repeated trial and error, Toyota has always managed to make adjustments to its course. For the most part, scholars of management have been kind in their assessment of this 'reformation' from the viewpoint of its contribution to the company's competitive power. In the past, the various organizational processes of the 'Toyota Production System' were often cited as the source of the company's competitive supremacy, but in recent years, the focus of attention has been more on the company's capacity for 'total evolution.'

Among researchers of labour relations too, while it is true to say that some were less than enthusiastic in their praise of the 'reformation,' the majority tended towards a positive evaluation.

But before making an assessment one way or the other, clearly we must first have a good grasp of the actual situation in the Toyota workplace. To do this, we need to investigate matters from the viewpoint of the shop floor and carefully analyse the 'context' of the workplace, rather than just simply extrapolate work conditions from the explanations of management and deduce the facts from the model of the production system.

With this approach to the problem in mind, I observed the actual working conditions on the shop floor for a period of a little over three and a half months as a casual worker with Toyota from 24 July to 7 November 2001. In the area to which I was assigned, I was able to see the concepts I have referred to above at work all around me. Moreover, it seems that the factory I was in was regarded as a model Toyota workplace. In the short period that I worked there we had inspection visits from the Vice President of the company, the general manager and the factory manager (*kōjōchō*). As chance would have it, being assigned to this kind of assembly line gave me the opportunity to experience, to some small extent, a 'post-reformation' Toyota workplace.

In this book I divide my concrete research project broadly into three parts. First, establishing the facts of a Toyota workplace after (and during) the 'reformation.' Secondly, I examine some points of contention in previous research, and thirdly, I describe and analyse all aspects of work on the factory floor, an area that has received almost no scholarly attention to date.

Let me begin with a brief explanation of how this book is structured. In the introductory chapter, I set out the details, in the form of a diary, from my recruitment interview, through my job orientation training and entry into the company dormitory, to my workplace assignment.

Chapter 1 introduces an outline of the factory, my workplace and my mode of work. In Chapter 2, I strive to grasp the reality of labour on the factory floor in the 'post-reformation' era. I have sought to follow carefully each of the individual movements of the workers and to describe them in as much concrete detail as possible. In terms of content, I try to clarify the elements of the daily work, including standardized work, responses to 'change' and 'abnormalities,' and minor adjustments between the manufacturing processes. In addtion, I consider those activities outside the daily work routine, such as QC circles and long-term management strategies like rotation.

In Chapters 3 and 4, I pick up two themes on which there is still no general agreement, despite the great deal of attention both have attracted from those in the field of automobile industry research. The first is skill. According to the leading research since the 1980s, even the assembly-line workers acquire a high level of skill as they gradually carve out 'careers' within the company. So, in Chapter 3,

I examine two kinds of 'skill' – the 'skill' acquired in the course of building a 'career' and the 'skill' formed through the performance of 'standardized work' – in the light of the actual situation on the factory floor.

The other theme is the 'autonomy' of workers. It is said that Toyota workers acquire a certain degree of 'autonomy' through workplace management measures such as *kaizen* (improvement) activities and QC circles. Two differing assessments in regard to these various activities have so far emerged. On the one hand, we have those positive evaluations that see this as a system of 'human respect,' linked to 'industrial democracy,' 'bottom-up' policies and 'participation.' Others interpret it negatively, claiming that it is a system in which workers are forced to cut their own throats. In Chapter 4, looking at the specific processes of these activities, I want to focus on the connection between exercising 'autonomy' and the 'regulations' for 'workloads.' I feel that this approach also automatically leads to the conclusion that the positive and negative assessments are inter-related.

From Chapter 5 to Chapter 7, I take up an aspect of the workplace that can hardly be found in previous research. Putting it very simply, I would venture to say that perhaps past research has only portrayed those obedient, diligent workers who work in compliance with the aims of management. In this regard, I asked myself, why is it that workers do not abuse their 'autonomy?' Isn't it because there is a 'mechanism' that prevents them from doing so?

Past research has come up with two opinions on this simple question. The first is the view that the production system itself controls the workers. The other is that the elaborate system of personnel management exercises the control. It is certainly true that these kinds of management techniques play an important role in controlling the workers. But would these alone be enough? Would the workers, as it were, under indirect control, go ahead on their own, working in accordance with the wishes of their managers? In order to answer this question, in Chapter 5, I turn my attention to supervision on the factory floor and investigate the processes of workplace management. In Chapter 6, I describe the daily world of those being managed, looking at personnel labour management, not as a system, but in terms of how it is actually implemented on site. Through the analysis of Chapters 5 and 6, it should become clear that the workers are caught in a web of intricate control mechanisms that stretch out over the workplace and beyond.

But even though they are trussed up in a web of control, this does not mean that they are thoroughly imbued with the company's management ideology. Although it is a point that has received scant attention in previous research, if we observe the actual situation on the assembly line in detail, we come to understand that there is a constant stream of minor conflicts. However, the workers routinely deal with these, not through resistance, but by placing themselves at a distance from management ideology by re-interpreting the 'circumstances' and through this re-interpretation bring about change in the workplace. The 'context' of the workplace is extremely fluid. The dynamism of the workplace derives not only from those workers steeped in the company ideology, but also from the majority of workers, who, even though they do not openly resist it, maintain a distance from management ideology. In Chapter 7, I demonstrate the actual situation, giving as many concrete examples as possible.

The realities of the factory floor are also regulated by conditions of the labour market. This is one of the points I discuss in the final chapter.

Further, as a supplement to my research, I have compiled, from the standpoint of my own interests, a list of investigative research materials concerning assembly-line labour in Japanese automobile factories. I hope you may find this useful for understanding the thrust of my research.

The publication of this book was supported by a Grant-in-Aid for Publication of Scientific Research Results from the Japan Society for the Promotion of Science.

Finally but not least, I am indebted to Professor Hugh Clarke for his superb translation of my Japanese book.

Ryōji Ihara
December 2006

Translator's Preface

As a dedicated Toyota driver and admirer of the Toyota Production System, I was surprised – shocked might be a more appropriate word – to read of Professor Ryōji Ihara's experience as a casual worker in a Toyota factory. I had thought the company had long since addressed and put to right the appalling conditions for shop floor labourers so graphically described in Satoshi Kamata's 1973 account, *Japan in the Passing Lane: An Insider's Account of Life in a Japanese Auto Factory* (the English translation, published by Pantheon Books, New York, appeared in 1982). But it is clear that workers on the factory floor are still making sacrifices as the Toyota Motor Company continues on its inexorable march to become the world's biggest and most profitable carmaker.

It is not the role of the translator, however, to be moved by or to question the content of the material translated, nor to pass judgement on the views or literary style of the author. The translator's task is to adopt a detached, objective stance and transform the words of one language into those of another. In many cases this also involves translation of the cultural context, as for example, in Arthur Waley's translation of *The Tale of Genji*, in which one gets the impression that the manners, mores and physical infrastructure of the eleventh-century Japanese court have been transformed into those of Victorian England.

In this book I have been careful to let the cultural context speak for itself. On the surface it may appear that the circumstances Professor Ihara describes might as easily apply to Europe or the United States. Closer inspection, however, leaves us in no doubt that the protagonists of this saga – the workers on the factory floor – are indubitably Japanese, as is the Toyota Production System under which they are working. To remind readers of this different cultural context, I have made a point of leaving a number of Japanese terms, generally with an English gloss, in the translated text.

Some of these terms present a considerable challenge to the translator. Let me illustrate this point with just two examples.

The Toyota-coined term '*mieruka*,' which employs the suffix *-ka* '-ization,' usually only attached to Sino-Japanese nouns, on the Japanese verb *mieru* 'to be visible.' Elsewhere in the English literature on Toyota this term is translated as 'visualization,' but to me this implies a subjective mental process in which the individual imagines a situation not presently visible. Instead, I have suggested the neologism, coined along the same lines as the Japanese original, 'visibilization,' to convey the idea of 'making visible' or 'opening up to view,' a concept quite different, in my mind at least, from visualization.

My second example, '*jidōka*,' which sounds like the usual Japanese term for 'automation,' employs as its second element (*dō*), the Japanese character for 'to work' – itself a Japanese addition (*kokuji*) to the vast repertory of Chinese characters (*kanji*) – instead of the usual character meaning 'to move.' The idea behind the change is to convey the sense of the human element in automation under the Toyota Production System. This is applied variously to refer to machines with the in-built ability to react like human beings (i.e. to respond to the unpredicted) or to the concept of human beings and machines working together as an integrated whole. In the case of *jidōka*, I follow Toyota's own neologism 'autonomation.'

If I may be permitted once more to move out of my role of translator and into that of student of Japanese culture, I would like to make a few general comments on Professor Ihara's book.

Unlike Satoshi Kamata's journalistic exposé, Professor Ihara's book, originally published in 2003 under the title *Toyota no Rōdō Genba – Dainamizumu to kontekusuto* (the Toyota workplace – dynamism in context), is a meticulous academic study firmly situated within the context of the sociology of labour. Drawing on recent theoretical debates in Japan and internationally, the author challenges widely held views on the respective roles of skill, supervision and quality control in the car industry. Specialists in car industry research unable to access Japanese language sources should welcome this English translation, now with an additional chapter update.

The book clearly falls into two inter-related, yet thematically distinct, sections. The author's involvement as a participant observer on the factory floor necessarily means that he takes a subjective, personal view of the hardships of assembly-line labour. Particularly, in his diary entries and in his analysis of work intensification he becomes an activist for shop-floor reform.

On the other hand, in his analysis of theoretical questions, like the role of skill in career development or the debates over autonomy and control in Japanese industry, he is able to take an objective academic view, yet still basing his conclusions on the evidence drawn from his own experience working in a Toyota factory.

Since Professor Ihara's participant observation and the publication of the Japanese edition of this book, the Japanese economy seems to have finally dragged itself out of its long period of stagnation. Yet, despite the fact that Japan has enjoyed a long period of sustained, but unspectacular economic growth, that there has been a shift from a buyers' to a sellers' employment market and there are reports of severe labour shortages in some areas, the general working public has no real sense (*jikkan*) that their lives are improving. Quite the contrary, the mass media abounds with stories of the increased casualization of labour, not just in the car industry, but in the workforce across the board. There is much talk of the working poor. Yet, on the other hand, we hear of fierce employer resistance to increasing wages or the regulation of overtime working hours. There is no evidence to indicate that work is becoming more humane. Professor Ihara's additional appendix suggests that in the five years or so since his investigation there has been little improvement for workers on the shop floor in Japanese auto factories, indeed conditions may have grown worse. Certainly, his original findings remain vitally relevant to the situation today.

Yet, belying his book's academic intent, Professor Ihara writes in a relaxed, entertaining style that should appeal to any reader with an interest in car-making or Japanese society in general. His clear, fluent Japanese prose contrasts markedly with the turgid jargon of some of the specialists he quotes in his book. As translator, I hope my English version succeeds in capturing a little of the elegance of Professor Ihara's Japanese while removing the worst of the turgidity from the scholarly quotations.

I would like to acknowledge here the enormous assistance I have had from the author, Professor Ihara, in the preparation of this translation. Professor Ihara's excellent command of English and his experience in translating academic English into Japanese, meant that he was able to cast his meticulously discerning eye over my early drafts, not once, but several times. On each reading he picked up numerous errors in my use of sociological terminology, inconsistency in my translation of Toyota terms and even, occasionally, infelicities in my English expression. He was also largely responsible for the provision of the index, a feature that was lacking in the Japanese original. Finally, I would like to take this opportunity to thank Professor Yoshio Sugimoto of Trans Pacific Press for entrusting me with this very important translation project. Every effort has been made to ensure that the published version is free of errors. Any that remain are entirely my responsibility.

Hugh Clarke
March 2007
Tokyo

Prologue: Joining the Company

21 June 2001 (Thursday), the job interview

At 10 a.m. I am hurrying through the light rain, heading for Kokubunji station on the Japan Railways Chuo line. The interviews are from 9:00 to 11:00 in the morning and from 1:00 to 3:00 in the afternoon. The back cover of the employment magazine *Furomu Ei* (From-A) carries a full-page ad. calling 'for casual workers in Toyota – relaxed working conditions, no-experience necessary.' The previous day I had rung the telephone number for the Personnel Department in Nagoya that appeared in the advertisement and confirmed the time of the Tokyo appointment. Apparently, you could turn up any time within the hours given. I'm beginning to panic, worrying that I won't be in time for a morning interview. Fortunately, I arrive at the interview room a little before 11:00 a.m. The interview room is three floors underground in the building next to Yasuda Life Insurance by the west exit of Shinjuku station. The interviewer is sitting alone in the middle of a room with about twenty empty chairs. I'm a little disappointed. No one else turns up while I'm being interviewed. I wonder if this could be because people do not like to take on factory work because of the 3K's, *kitsui* (strenuous), *kitanai* (dirty) and *kiken* (dangerous), even though, in a recession like this, it is a buyers' market. The interviewer spends the first twenty minutes explaining very carefully about the wages and type of work to be done. In particular, he explains in great detail how the wages are calculated. For workers on a six-month contract the monthly wage ranges between 312,000 and 337,000 yen. This is certainly not bad at all.

There was, however, just one thing that made me feel uneasy. That was the day of payment. Payday was to be on the twenty-fifth day of the month following the month worked. That meant if, for example, you started work at the end of July, your July salary would be carried forward until 25 August, but since you had only worked a few days in July your wages for that month would be a negligible amount. In essence, you would have to wait until 25 September before you received a full month's pay. That is to say, you work the first two months for almost nothing. The interviewer was at pains to explain that, should I be employed, I would have to come along with enough money to tide me over that initial period.

When it came to the nature of the work I would be doing, I was initially relieved to learn that experience and academic record would not be taken into account. The only experience I had had of physical labour had been doing a bit of light work on a building site and in a job transporting parcels in the busy year-end round of gift-giving (*oseibo*). The interviewer told me, 'the job entails just very simple tasks, but you need to be a bit patient until you get used to it.'

After these various explanations we moved on to the interview itself. The interviewer checked through my *curriculum vitae*, and then went on to ask me two or three questions. First, after telling me that I did not have to answer if I didn't want to, he asked why I had decided to apply for a job with Toyota. As I was thinking how I should answer this question, the interviewer jumped in and answered it himself. 'I suppose it was because the pay is good, wasn't it?' Then he went on to ask, 'What are you planning to do with the money?' I thought of saying 'school fees' or 'living expenses,' but before I could get out an answer, he went on with his barrage of questions. 'Do you have any major debts?' 'Have you got any tattoos?' Finally, after assuring himself that I had five fingers on each hand, he tested them one finger at a time to make sure they all bent and straightened properly.

After this, he explained about the starting date and the period of the contract. As there were several possible starting dates, I was asked to pick one that suited me. My preference was for 24 July. The contract period could be from three to six months in monthly intervals. 'As this is your first time, it might be best to go for three months. It's hard work, you know.' As the interviewer had suggested, I decided on three months.

The interview was an extremely ritualistic affair. There did not seem to be any questions particularly designed to sort out the applicants, but there was one attribute the interviewer was concerned about. That was 'the ability to cooperate' (*kyōchōsei*). 'In your particular job you will be working alone, but the workplace is run by a group of from ten to twenty people, so you have to be able to get along well with others. What sorts of things have you done in your previous jobs to help you gain acceptance with your fellow workers in a new workplace?' I replied, 'I have always made a point, as far as possible, of engaging my workmates in conversation.'

The interview ended smoothly with no particular problems I could identify. I was told I would be informed of the outcome in about five days time, after the interviewer had discussed the matter with head office.

But, that same day, some time after 8 p.m., the interviewer rang me directly and told me unofficially I had got the job (*naitei*). He explained very briefly about the future procedures, and then said, 'You'll receive detailed instructions in the material I'll be mailing to you in the next few days. Read through it. We're counting on you.' With that he hung up. Funnily enough, I found this over-casual attitude quite concerning. After all, there was hardly anything written on my CV. In the past I had applied for factory work with several companies, but I had always been knocked back on the grounds that I had no experience. With this company, the thinking seems to be that anyone will do as long as they can keep up their headcount. At least they could pretend to be taking the interview process seriously.

23 July (Monday), Nagoya Station

On the day before I entered the company, I stepped from the Shinkansen bullet train onto Nagoya Station at 12:24 p.m. I still had a little time, as we were to meet between 12:30 and 1 o'clock. This was my first visit to Nagoya so I went out through the ticket gate to have a look at the area around the station. There were crowds of people sitting in front of a huge display screen. I gazed vacantly at the scene thinking this must be the spot at Nagoya Station where people meet.

Then, right in front of my eyes, a man in a suit began waving a little flag. At which all the people who had been sitting there stood up as one. Imagine my surprise when I realized they were all casual Toyota employees. The company name was emblazoned on the flag. About two hundred and fifty men followed along behind it, their heads slightly bowed. I had my name marked off and joined the queue. From my image of the poor turn-up at the interviews I would never have predicted that there would be so many applicants.

After the roll call had been completed we moved out of the station in single file. Perhaps because most of us had never met before, there was very little conversation. Even to my eyes, this long, silent queue snaking its way out of the station looked most peculiar. It was little wonder then, that others on the street cast furtive glances in our direction as they passed by.

We casual employees were then loaded onto six buses and driven off to No. II, SS Eastern Dormitory in T City. We arrived at the hostel a little after 2:00 p.m. On arrival, we were assembled in a vast, open floor area to clarify what we would be doing from that point onwards. We all sat there in the tubular chairs and listened meekly to the explanation of the first week's schedule provided by four or five education officers.

Although the hall was as hot and humid as a steam bath, there was hardly a word of idle banter spoken as we listened in silence. The meeting broke up at 3:30 p.m. and we carried our luggage off to the single room we had each been allocated. We were permitted only one cardboard box of luggage each and this had been sent on to the dormitory before we arrived. Then we had free time until 5 o'clock. When time was up, we gathered at the main gate and then walked fifteen minutes or so to the dining hall. We all finished our meals in silence and then, in twos and threes, returned to the dormitory.

While they were in training, casual employees had to live in the dormitory. Each man was provided with a four and a half mat room (an area roughly 9 feet square or $3m^2$). In the oppressive heat we felt very grateful for the air conditioning. The cicadas continued singing right through the night, falling silent briefly just before sunrise. Without the air conditioning it would probably have been impossible to get any sleep at all.

24 July (Tuesday), Medical check

All day today was taken up with medical checks and physical fitness tests. We had to assemble in the education hall by 7:40 a.m. Then we were bussed to the Health Center and T Factory where we were given exhaustive medical tests – height, weight, body-fat ratio, eyesight, hearing, grip, dorsal muscular strength, X-ray, urine test, blood test, electro-cardiograph, medical interview, manual dexterity, sense of balance, the soles of the feet. I wondered whether it was really necessary to examine us in such detail. A long line of mature-aged men standing there in just their underpants going in one at a time to receive their medical examinations. Unconsciously, I let out a word of complaint. 'What do they think we are, primary school kids?' Someone heard me and laughed out loud. 'That's just what I was thinking. It's really pathetic, isn't it? I'm Yamano.[1] Pleased to meet you.' From that moment Yamano and I were friends.

But, casual employees don't have the luxury of worrying about things like that. If the results of the tests were unsatisfactory, even though you'd come all this way, you would miss out on the job and have to go home. It is only when you have cleared all the medical tests that you are finally accepted into the company. The glum expressions of the poor applicants undergoing their medical examinations contrasted starkly with the smiling faces of the company doctors as they performed their work.

After the medical examination they collected the 'migrant workers' logbooks' (*dekasegi rōdōsha techō*). Of the roughly eighty men who had been examined with me fifteen to twenty handed in logbooks. It seems that even today there are still considerable numbers of migrant workers from Hokkaido, Northeast Honshu, Kyushu and Okinawa.

In the change room of the bath I overheard some young labourers, around twenty years old, expressing their dissatisfaction. 'I couldn't stand living like a prisoner in this place. It's bloody ridiculous!' Apparently I had gained some immunity from my experience living in a dormitory when I was a *sarariiman* ('salary man') in a company. The idea did not worry me particularly. Does that mean even I have finally 'grown up,' I wonder!

25 July (Wednesday), Induction

Hot again today. Cruel, oppressive heat! Mercilessly the mercury tops thirty-nine degrees. One hundred and two men are called up for re-examination as a result of problems picked up in yesterday's medical checks. The rest of us spend the day being trained in the hall with almost no relief from the air conditioning system. The morning is taken up with an overall explanation of Toyota. First we have an overview of the company – its history, the creative suggestion system, quality control etc.

We casual workers are not really listening to the explanations. In this heat it takes a concerted effort just to sit there in your chair. But you can't very well doze off either. If you fall asleep, one of the supervisors watching from the back of the room runs up immediately and wakes you up.

In the afternoon, we filled in documents detailing the bank account into which our wages were to be paid, our superannuation numbers and so on. The procedures took an inordinately long time as many of the workers had forgotten to write in their employee numbers or had not added their seals to the documents.

When the training had been underway for some time, an education officer would came in, quietly have a word in the ear of one of the casual workers and then the two of them would disappear together through a door at the back of the room. This scenario continued, occurring once every few minutes. At first I did not pay much attention to what was going on, thinking that they must be filling in gaps in the documentation or something. But none of the men who had gone out through the back door came back again. Gradually, the men left sitting there started to become a little restless. After a while, there would be a buzz of conversation right across the floor of the hall every time an education officer came into the room. We had all begun to feel that those who had been called out had failed their medical checks and been prevented from joining the company. If that were the case, then all this training was really no more than a distraction.

Our premonitions proved correct. At the end of the training session, we had an explanation from the education officer. Last time there had been about fifty and this time thirty men who had missed out on joining the company, because they had failed the medical. About one in ten of the applicants left Toyota without even setting foot in the factory. The seat next to me on my right was now vacant.

At 6 p.m. they announced which of us were to go to Plant T and which to Plant K. It was determined that I, along with forty-two others, was to go to Plant K. Apparently it was unusual for so many to be assigned to this factory. I wondered whether the reason they needed all these casual workers in such a hurry was because of the increased growth in car sales.

26 July (Thursday), Assigned to the factory

I had to take my luggage to the area in front of the office between 6:30 and 7:30 a.m. and between 7:30 and 8:00, my room key and sheets.

I got up at five, packed my bags and before eight o'clock I had completed my preparations to leave the dormitory.

In the morning we continued the training we started yesterday. There was a very detailed explanation of 'the work rules for casual employees,' but I had great difficulty staying awake. In the afternoon, we had another introduction to the company. Then we each received a printout of the results of Tuesday's medical examination, a cap, overalls and safety work boots. In the factory we all changed into our safety boots and put on our caps with the Toyota logo, but stayed in the jeans or cotton pants we were wearing. The overalls were optional, you could wear them or not, as you pleased. We were told that if we felt hot we could work in just a T-shirt.

Just before three in the afternoon, the forty-three of us who were to work in Plant K went off by bus to our new dormitory. We arrived there about an hour later. Nearby there is a little fishing port. The town as a whole has a run-down feel to it, despite the considerable volume of through traffic. In contrast to the streetscape in town, this dormitory is a modern complex; certainly superior to the training dormitory we left this morning. It consists of four blocks, two each of five and seven storeys. It turns out that ten of us, myself included, are to live in No. 1 Block. Each room is 6 mats (9ft x 12ft) with air conditioning, a television and an electric pot for boiling water. Today we just had an explanation of the dormitory before we broke up.

27 July (Friday), Assigned to duty

7:20 a.m. we all assemble in the ground floor lobby of the dormitory. We arrive at the factory after a five-minute bus ride. The morning is again taken up with training. We get an overall introduction to Plant K, warnings about driving under the influence of alcohol; learn about each of our assigned tasks and what problems require extra attention. In particular, we are given strict instructions regarding accidents on the assembly line. Just the other day there had been a major accident. Apparently the whole assembly line had come to a standstill. 'Just one person's minor mistake can cause the company unimaginable damage. An injury at home may cost several hundred dollars in medical fees, but an accident at work can result in hundreds or even thousands of times the damage. If things go badly it can run into millions.'

The education officer preached his sermon in a very solemn tone of voice. In the end he added, 'Accidents are no fun for the person injured either.' But I thought he had got his priorities the wrong way around. This education officer often seemed annoyed that none of us casual workers answered his questions, but who would blame us for not responding?

In the afternoon we were assigned to our various work sites. Mine was the No. 3 Factory machine shop. In this workplace the tasks performed were sub-assembly, inspection and packing. There were six of us newly recruited casual workers assigned here. We all went on a tour of our workplace together. The assembly workers run around working in a confined space like dormice. Compared to the assembly lines I had seen on television the workers' hand movements seemed extraordinarily fast. Looking on from the side, it was hard to tell what sort of work they were doing. Their feet too seemed to be constantly in motion. The carrying staff were incessantly lifting and putting down heavy looking parts. The inspection and packing staff were packing one part after another at intervals of less than ten seconds. All look very serious as they work and do not even give us a sidelong glance.

Whatever task we are allocated it is not going to be easy. Today it is just one week since I came to Toyota. It has been a long time. But we still have only received training. In reality, our first day of work will be next Monday.

1 Factory, Group and Mode of Work

Overview of the factory

We had learnt in our training sessions that Plant K began operation in August 1978. It was fourth newest of Toyota's twelve factories. The factory incorporated all the processes from moulding, forging and sintering, to processing, heat treatment, sub-assembly and so on. It handled the whole process from raw materials to unit product. The products produced were drive components for transmissions and the like. Ours was a unit product factory making parts to be sent to vehicle assembly plants in Japan and abroad where they were fitted into car bodies. At Plant K (Factories 1-4) there were approximately 2,500 employees.

Overview of groups

Characteristics of the production line

After we had been assigned to our workplace, our group leader gave us a brief rundown on the assembly line. Here (an assembly line in No. 3 Factory) they perform tasks ranging from machining and assembly to inspection and packing to produce transaxles and transmissions.

The finished parts are exported to Toyota factories in America from the port immediately adjacent to the plant. This assembly line was set up in January 2001 and really only started full-scale production in July, just before I was assigned to the factory.

Its major distinction lies in the way the machinery is positioned. The machines are arranged in a continuous line, two hundred metres long (*ippitsugaki rain* – one brush-stroke line). An overall view of the whole line reveals that it is actually two lines arranged in the form of the letter 'S' (see figure 1.1). Arranging the production infrastructure like this, keeps the workplace orderly and looking neat. In addition, new slim-line machines have replaced the bulky

Figure 1.1: S-shaped assembly line

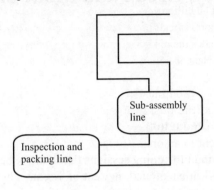

models of the past. A range of measures has been taken to prevent the machinery from becoming too complicated.

In the past the machines were enveloped in steel safety covers to stop workers putting their hands into them. By contrast, here, the machinery is shielded by clear plastic panels rather than the old-style metal covers. The steel covers hide the inner workings of the machine, so the operator has no idea how it functions. This meant that even very minor problems could not be addressed on site. So, it was decided, on the new line, to increase factory workers' awareness of the machines they were using, by letting them see how they were structured inside. Management calls this process '*mieruka*' ('visiblization').

Further, whereas formerly machines had been fitted with numerous safety sensors, on the new line, these had been kept to a bare minimum. The number of actuators had also been greatly reduced. If *autonomation* (*jidōka*)[1] in the installation of safety sensors and such is carried too far, workers tend to rely on them and this results in lower levels of safety awareness. In these circumstances, there is always the fear of a major accident, so the management decided that, as far as possible, automatic devices should be removed. The effect of this policy could be clearly seen in the statistics. I have taken the figures I cite below from a poster display, prepared for the visit of the Vice President of Toyota.

By avoiding excessive automation we have been able to greatly reduce our initial investment costs. In the past, the rate of automation of the assembly line was 71%, but in the new line this figure has been reduced to 17%. The original budget estimate of 80 billion yen dropped to an actual cost of 60 billion yen. In addition, the reduction in automation resulted in improvements in the rate of conversion of machinery, from a mere 2% under the old system to 58% on this assembly line. The versatility of plant also increased dramatically.

According to our group leader, Morita (with 20 years experience), the idea behind the design of this assembly line was to make 'human beings central to the production process' rather than have them subservient to automated plant. In addition, he says, the line is designed around the concepts of 'safety first' and providing an environment in which 'anyone can work.'

Operational flow

The group to which I was assigned was responsible for the processes of sub-assembly, cleaning, inspection, packing, transport and shipment.[2] We assembled parts manufactured in previous processes, inspected and packed them and finally shipped them out. These are the final processes on the S-shaped assembly line illustrated in figure 1.1.

Now let us look at the operations in more detail, dividing the flow of work into sub-assembly on the one hand and inspection and packing on the other.

The sub-assembly line
The sub-assembly line consists of 4 independent assembly machines. One worker is positioned by each of the machines and each assembles different manufactured parts (see figure 1.2). These are, from right to left, DIFF (differential), UD, REAR units and FRONT units

Figure 1.2: The sub-assembly line

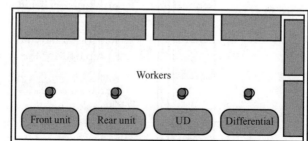

(Note: the terms used for the various parts, here and throughout the book, are those used by workers on the factory floor). When there is a need for increased production, two workers are assigned to each machine with one assembling and the other assisting. By adjusting the number of workers in this way the line can easily respond to requirements for increased or decreased production. Around the assembly line there are always two or three off-line workers. They restart any machines when they stall or supply additional parts for the assembly line as they run out. I was mainly in charge of the carrying of parts around the cleaning process on the inspection and packing line, but I also worked several times on the sub-assembly line. Let me begin by explaining the flow of work I performed at the UD station (See figure 1.3).

The assembly assistant would first take the job (the body to which parts are to be added) out of its tray and hold it in his hands. The tray had been conveyed from the previous process to the upper level of the chute (a shelf with rollers to facilitate the moving of the trays). The parts we made were of two kinds. Depending on the directions we had received, the assembly assistant would take out either a medium capacity (①) or a high capacity (②) unit. As in other factories, the medium capacity units were for small and middle-sized vehicles and the high capacity units were for large vehicles. In this factory we made twice as many medium capacity units as high capacity units.

After taking out the job, the assistant assembly worker picks up three small gears that are to be attached to it. He chooses medium

Figure 1.3: UD

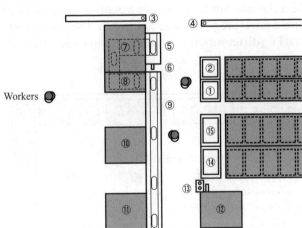

Workers

capacity gears (③) for the medium capacity units and high capacity gears (④) for high capacity units. He fixes the job and the gears to a plate in front of the cleaning machine, and when a lamp on the upper right of the cleaning machine comes on, the operator can move the plate into the machine (⑤). If the plate or the operator's hand goes into the machine before the light comes on, the machine stops automatically. This precaution is necessary to prevent serious injury. If the machine stops, we call the off-line worker and get him to restart it.

To insert the plate into the cleaning machine, the operator pushes the plate to a fixed point with his right hand and, moving his body to the left, lightly brushes his right hand against a bar on the left-hand side of the machine (⑥). Whereupon the job, and the plate on which it rests, automatically enter the cleaning machine (⑦). At the same time, the plate that had been inside the cleaning machine emerges (⑧). The operator takes the three gears from the plate and, with his right hand, gently pushes the plate, still with the job on it, to the assembly worker. There is a two-level conveyor belt, installed between the cleaning machine and the assembly machine. The plate with the job attached, sitting on the upper level of the conveyor belt, moves along automatically to the next stage (⑨).

The assembly assistant, taking care not to collide with the assembly worker, places the three gears he has in his hand in a designated basket. If they are medium capacity gears he places the basket in front of the medium capacity assembly machine (⑩). Any high capacity gears he places in front of the high capacity assembly machine (⑪). While the assembly assistant is performing these tasks, the assembly worker is attaching small parts, such as gears, washers and pins (the pins are about one centimetre long) to the job. (The plate, from which the job and the gears have been taken, is automatically returned, on the lower level of the conveyor belt, to position ⑤).

After that, either the assembly assistant or the assembly worker, places the job in the caulking machine (⑫). Which one performs the task depends on how quickly each is working, but it is generally the assembly assistant. In that case the assistant has the assembled work handed to him by the assembly worker. As was the case with the cleaning machine described above, the operator confirms that the lamp is on before he places the job and small parts used for the caulking process into the machine. These parts, about one centimetre in length, are taken from a small box in front of the machine. At the same time, the job that has just been caulked (i.e. the job which had been placed in the machine in the previous cycle) is removed from the machine. Then, the operator lightly touches the starting bar with his right hand (⑬). (When the assembly worker performs the caulking process, at this point he hands the previously caulked job to the assembly assistant). Next, the caulked job is inspected. We check three things, namely, whether the two washers (one gold, one black) are attached, whether the job is firmly caulked and whether the ball bearings roll smoothly. To indicate the job has been checked, we mark the caulked area and each of the bearings with a white marker pen. When the inspection is over, so there is no confusion between the medium capacity units (⑭) and the high capacity units (⑮) we place the job in an appropriate empty box.

What I have described above is one work cycle. It is carried out in a little over thirty seconds (or about one minute when one worker is performing the tasks alone). This sequence of tasks is repeated over and over again, as between six hundred and seven hundred units are produced each day.

Further, since each tray holds six units, as soon as a tray is full, the assembly assistant sends it on to the lower level of the chute. As the boxes start to pile up on the chute the post-manufacturing-process transport worker takes them, four boxes at a time, to the inspection and packing line.

Inspection and packing line

The inspection and packing line comprises the processes of cleaning, transport, inspection, packing and shipping (figure 1.4). When the inspection/packing worker has finished packing the parts, he sends the empty tray back on the bottom level of the chute (①). The worker around the cleaning line, loads these empty trays (the cleaning trays) onto a trolley (②) and takes them to the chute used for storing the spare parts, putting them on the lower level of the chute (③). At the same time, he loads onto the trolley the cleaning trays on the upper level of the chute, which contain the new spare parts (④). It is important to be careful here to load onto the trolley the same number and the same kind of trays as the empty trays that have been returned. There is a total of sixteen different parts. Each is in a different tray and each tray is loaded into a different chute. The part numbers and names are; 1 *dorapin* (drive pinion) – high capacity, 2 front ring gear – high capacity, 3 front unit – high capacity, 4 C1, 5 ring, 6 C2, 7 rear unit, 8 drive pinion – medium capacity, 9 front

Figure 1.4: Inspection and packing line

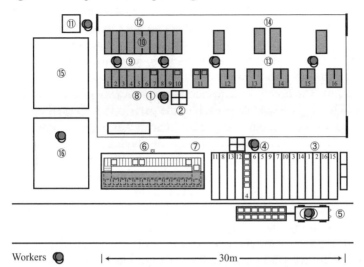

Workers ● |←——————————————— 30m ———————————————→|

ring gear – medium capacity, 10 front unit – medium capacity, 11 ring gear – medium capacity, 12 drive – medium capacity, 13 driven gear –medium capacity, 14 ring gear–high capacity, 15 drive – high capacity and 16 driven gear –high capacity. These are displayed on the right of the diagram in the order, 15, 16, 2, 1, 14, 3, 10, 7, 9, 5, 6, 4, 12, 13, 8, 11. The transport worker (*unpangakari*) from the previous process comes and places the cleaning trays containing the new parts on the top level of the chute and returns with the empty trays he has taken from the lower level of the chute (⑤).

Next the worker on the cleaning round begins preparing a new cleaning tray. He pushes a trolley with the trays on it up to the cleaning machine and places them four at a time on the pallet attached to the cleaning machine. Then, when he presses the start button, the cleaning pallet automatically enters the machine and the parts are cleaned (⑥). Inside the cleaning machine, the parts undergo, dip washing, tumble-washing, air-pressure cleaning and hot air treatment. It takes about ten minutes to go through all these processes. Of course, the worker in charge of the cleaning process does not remain idle all this time. He takes the cleaning tray that has emerged from the machine and places it on his trolley (⑦). Then, he carries it up to the front of where the packing is being done and slips it onto the upper level of the cleaned-parts chute (⑧). Here, too, each of the parts has a separate fixed chute, numbered from one to sixteen from the left.

The inspection and packing worker picks up one of the parts from the cleaning tray carried along on the cleaned-items chute. Then he checks a number of predetermined points and, if the item is not faulty, packs it into a cardboard box (⑨). This is performed in less than eight seconds. Possible faults include, dents, scratches, rust and extrusions (small fragments of metal remaining on the edges of the item). The order of the inspection and packing of parts is fixed. There is a light fixed where each of the parts is to be picked up and the work is carried out in the order indicated as the lights come on. Or, there is a screen behind the worker displaying the order in which the inspection and packing is carried out. When he has finished packing one box-full, as I mentioned at the beginning, the empty tray is sent back on the lower level of the chute. When a cardboard box has been packed with the designated number of parts, it is placed on the packing chute behind the worker (⑩).

The top level of the chute carries the cardboard boxes to be packed. A different worker assembles the cardboard boxes (⑪) and passes them on from behind the packing chute (⑫). The inspection and packing worker uses these for packing the parts.

Parts 11 to 16 are not packed in cardboard boxes, but are arranged unwrapped on a rack (⑬). The four chutes arranged opposite the rack are for the assembled parts (the differential and the UD) (⑭). The transport workers carry these parts to the chutes. (As I mentioned at the end of the explanation of the sub-assembly line. I should add that there are two transport workers, one carries the medium capacity parts and the other the high capacity parts and these assembled parts). There are two people each in charge of the boxed parts (1 to 10) and the rack parts (11 to 16) making a total of four workers.

The parts packed in boxes and arranged on racks are taken to an area to await shipping by a transport worker (different from the two I have just mentioned) (⑮).

Next, the workers assigned to shipping make a final check of the number of boxes and racks and pack a predetermined number of these onto the large racks provided (⑯). Finally, another group member using a forklift truck delivers the racks to a specified location to await shipment.

Group composition

I have summarized the group composition at the time of my assignment in Table 1.1. In total there were twenty employees, sixteen regular employees and four casual workers.[3] Of these, eighteen were

Table 1.1: Group membership (at time of my assignment)

Name	Age	Sex	Years service	Mode of appointment	Position	Responsibility
Supervisors						
Morita	38	Male	20 years	High school	Group leader	Overall
Shiraishi	43	Male	19 years	Outside appointment	Section leader	Assembly
Shimada	40	Male	21 years	High school	Section leader	Assembly
Yamashita	37	Male	19 years	High school	Section leader	Cleaning/transport
Regular Employees						
Nishiyama	35	Male	17 years	High school	Regular staff	Transport
Ōki	41	Male	16 years	Outside appointment	Regular staff	Packing
Takenaka	35	Male	15 years	Outside appointment	Regular staff	Cleaning/transport
Nagata	32	Male	13 years	High school	Regular staff	Inspection
Maejima	41	Male	12 years	Outside appointment	Regular staff	Shipping
Ogawa	28	Male	10 years	High school	Regular staff	Assembly
Shiroki	26	Male	8 years	High school	Regular staff	Packing
Kawakami	29	Male	8 years	Outside appointment	Regular staff	Packing
Tsuda	20	Male	2 years	High school	Regular staff	Packing
Murase	21	Female	2 years	High school	Regular staff	Assembly
Enoki	19	Female	1 year	High school	Regular staff	Shipping
Kuramoto	19	Male	< 1 year	High school	Regular staff	Assembly
Casual Contract Employees						
Tabata	22	Male	< 1 month		Contract staff	Assembly
Jōjima	32	Male	< 1 month		Contract staff	Assembly
Naganuma	18	Male	< 1 month		Contract staff	Assembly
Ihara	29	Male	< 1 month		Contract staff	Cleaning

Note: With the exception of Ihara all names are fictitious.

men and two were women. We had one 'support worker' seconded from another group, and one more seconded from a different factory. Of the regular employees, eleven had been recruited directly from high school or technical school and five were outside appointments from other employment.

The top manager of the group is the group leader (*kumichō*) or GL for short. Beneath the group leader there are several section leaders (*hanchō*), sometimes addressed as Ex (expert). The section leaders and above perform the role of supervisors of the group. Above the group leader comes the factory foreman (*kōchō*), who is addressed as chief leader (CL). Above the CL come the section head (*kachō*) and the division head (*buchō*). The top position in the factory is that of the factory manager (*kōjōchō*).

Mode of work

The mode of work is in two consecutive shifts. Our group and the backup (the group on the other shift) take responsibility for each of the shifts on a one-week rotation basis. The hours of work are from 6:25 a.m. to 3:05 p.m. for the first shift and from 4:00 p.m. to 12:40 a.m. for the second shift. As there is no fundamental difference between the shifts in the mode of work, let us consider here the operation of the first shift.

At each workplace a prefabricated hut has been erected and it is here that workers gather before they start work in the factory. At 6:20 a.m. all the workers come out in front of the prefab to do their morning exercises and chant the safety slogan. When this is over they move into the hut for the morning meeting. The meeting deals with issues such as confirmation of instructions from the night shift, reports of accidents from other factories, discussion of the proceedings of the previous day's cost committee meeting and reallocation of the duties of those on annual leave to workers off the assembly line.

After the meeting, a bell sounds to indicate the start of work. Rest-breaks are also signalled by the ringing of a bell. The following routine is repeated over and over again. When the bell sounds we walk at a brisk pace to our assigned positions and begin work immediately. Similarly, when the bell rings for a break, we stop work at once. We never stop work early – not a minute, or even a second, before the bell. After working two hours and five minutes from 6:25 a.m. to 8:30 a.m. (first period) we have a short ten-minute break. Then we work two hours from 8:40 a.m. to 10:40 a.m. (second period) and then take a break of forty-five minutes for lunch. A chime sounds five minutes before the end of the lunch break at which time we begin to move off to our posts. Work continues for a further two hours from 11:25 a.m. to 1:25 (third period) followed again by a ten-minute break. Then work resumes at 1:35 p.m. and continues for an hour and a half until 3:05 p.m. (fourth period). This is the end of a standard working day (7 hours 35 minutes) but there is usually overtime work that follows on directly from this period. With the first shift overtime is limited to a maximum of one hour, as the second shift is waiting to come on. With the second shift, however, depending on the progress of work during the day, overtime may be longer. Further, there are differences in the mode of work from one work place to another and some places even operate on a three-shift system.

2 Work on the Factory Floor

In the past, most commentators pointed out just how harsh work on the assembly line can be. But in recent years, it is said that work on the Toyota assembly line has been 'improved' (*kaizen sareta*) through the 'reformation' (*henkaku*).[1] Is this in fact the case? Can we really say from the standpoint of the labourer on the factory floor that things have improved? First, let us look at the situation from the realities of standardized work.

Previous research has shown that assembly line workers carry out, not only their daily 'routine work,' but also 'non-routine work' (e.g. responding to 'change' and 'abnormalities').[2] As we shall see in the next chapter, these studies have approached the question from the angle of 'skill acquisition,' but just what kind of 'change' and how much of the 'unexpected' do workers actually encounter? In this chapter we consider these questions in detail.

Besides, in this case, the assembly line is not completely co-ordinated into a kind of single conveyor belt. So, the workers carry out 'minor adjustments between manufacturing processes' in the course of their daily work. This is another area I would like to discuss here.

In addition to their daily work, assembly line workers also participate in non-daily *kaizen* (improvement) activities and QC (quality control) circles. There is a considerable body of research on these areas, but, to the best of my knowledge, there have been no previous studies detailing precisely how these processes work or the content of the activities concerned. Here, I focus on the reality of QC circles from the inside.

Further, most past studies have taken up the question of work rotation in the context of 'multi-skilling.' But the majority of these, it seems to me, have merely adopted the textbook definition of rotation and carried the analysis no further. I conclude the chapter by examining how closely, or otherwise, rotation, as it actually occurs in the workplace, follows the model of the textbooks. Let us now see what light we can shed on these questions from the reality of work on the factory floor.

Daily Work

Standardized work

Assembly line work is fundamentally a standardized, repetitive operation. Regardless of whether you are on sub-assembly or cleaning, as a production line worker you are obliged to repeat the same fixed motion over and over again.

When I was assigned to the cleaning round, the first thing I did was gain an understanding of the content and the flow of the work. Walking through my assigned position with the section leader I learnt each of the actions I was to perform in order. I learnt how to carry the cleaning trays, as they came back from the inspection and packing workers, to the chute where the spare parts were placed and move the same number of new trays into the cleaning machine. Then, as they emerged from the cleaning machine, I took the trays and placed them into the cleaned items chute. That was all. I performed each task just as the section leader, standing right there at my side, told me to. Whenever anything at all went wrong he would come to my assistance. In this way, I was able to carry out my job satisfactorily within less than half a day. However, as the carrying of the parts for the high capacity engines was a little more complicated, it took me longer to completely understand this process. But even so, from the third day after being assigned to my workplace I was able to perform the work by myself. As I later discovered when I had the task of 'educating' Kitamura (a casual employee who joined us in September) it took only three days to master the job. The same was true with Yada and Nonaka (both casual workers who started in September) who had been assigned to inspection and packing. Here, on their first day on the job, they spent the morning being trained by Kawakami and Shiroki, regular employees each with eight years consecutive work experience, but by the afternoon they were able to manage, after a fashion, to work alone. It took less time to train the assembly assistants. In my case, it took me less than an hour to grasp the work process and reach the point where I could work alone. It was the same on other assembly lines too. Yamano (a casual worker who joined at the same time as me) was apparently also able to manage the whole of the assembly process he had been assigned, in less than one day. No doubt there are some minor variations according to the type of work to be performed, but, in general, assembly line work is of such a simple nature that it can be learnt in a relatively short time.

This is not to say, however, that the work is easy in the sense that 'anyone can do it.' Even simple repetitive tasks can become difficult when they must be performed at a fixed constant rate. The *takt* time for sub-assembly work is a little over thirty seconds, while the time allocated for inspection and packing is a mere eight seconds. It is certainly not easy to complete the tasks within these time limits. The same applies to the cleaning round and the transport of assembled parts. For some time after I had been assigned to my post, because I was working too slowly, I found that the returned empty trays tended to accumulate on the cleaned-item chute. With transport work there is not only the matter of speed, but also the need to cope with heavy weights. It takes a considerable time to get used to all of this.

What then is the labour load of the tasks in the cleaning round? Let us now attempt to calculate it in concrete terms. A pedometer reading, averaged out over a thirteen-day period, indicated that I walked 20,137 paces per day. That is equivalent to walking 15 kilometres per day for a person with an average step of seventy centimetres or roughly 17 kilometres for someone with an eighty-centimetre step span.[3]

But it is the upper body not the legs that bears the greater load. The weight of the tray varies according to its contents, but it ranges between 10 and 20 kilograms. For each cleaning round approximately ten of these trays are loaded onto the trolley then unloaded from the cart into the cleaning machine then carried from the cleaning machine and placed into the chute. The time of the cycle is not strictly fixed, but when I timed it, it was approximately three minutes. This means that the process is repeated twenty times an hour, or 160 times in an eight-hour working day. (The distance walked in each cycle is about one hundred metres. 100m × 160 = 16km. This figure falls in line with the earlier pedometer calculations).

1 August (Wednesday)

The cleaned-parts chute is divided into two levels. The upper level is where the trays of cleaned parts are placed. This upper level is itself further divided into upper and lower shelves and you can put the cleaned-parts tray on either one. The trolley is just over one metre high and the upper shelf of the upper level of the chute is between 1.3 and 1.4 metres high. It requires a great deal of effort to lift the cleaned-parts tray up onto the chute. I imagine it would be particularly difficult if you were short in stature. Towards the end of a day's work, my grip becomes so weak that I can hardly feel that I am holding anything. I also begin to lose my ability to concentrate. Once, when I was trying to lift a tray up onto the top shelf, I could feel it starting to slip out of my fingers. Fortunately, I realized in time what was happening and managed to save the situation, but if I had dropped the tray it could have easily broken a bone in my foot.

It is not as if the management is entirely oblivious to this problem of workload. In front of the cleaning machine there is a lift called an 'easy-hand.' If you use this you can move the cleaning tray from the trolley onto the pallet of the cleaning machine without too much effort. When I first started work I relied on this a lot, but I soon found that it slowed things down and made it difficult for me to keep up with the pace of the assembly line. Within a week I had stopped using the easy-hand lift. I was not the only one. Now nobody at all uses this lift.

Lower-back pain comes as part of the job for those working on this process. Hashimoto, a short-term casual worker on the opposite shift, was moved on to another task because he had injured his back, but even so, his condition did not improve greatly and he was compelled to leave the company at the end of October before the term of his contract was up. His replacement, Sawada, was also unable to stand the physical pressure and left the job during his contract period.

1 November (Thursday)

My body is still aching all over, long after I have returned to the dormitory. My hands are hot and my fingers are swollen. Because I always have to return to work before they have had time to go back to normal, the joints of my fingers have become thicker and my hands increased in size. At first my hands became very red. With time this redness has disappeared, but to this day my hands are hard and rough. But my hands were the least of my worries. I soon got used to them, but the back problem has troubled me till the end. Sometimes while I was working I would feel a sudden shooting pain and I was in constant fear that I would end up with a slipped disc. Everyday when I got out of the bath I would rub my fingers and lower back with liniment. Come to think of it, Sawada used to bind his fingers with tape like a volleyball player.

The safety-first manual, (at Toyota we called it the 'zero-injury handbook') carried the statement, 'under no circumstances should a single worker attempt to lift loads in excess of 20 kilograms for men and 12 kilograms for women.' But to follow this instruction would bring work to a standstill. The zero-injury handbook serves as both a means of facilitating smooth communication with management and a guide to help new staff, including trainees, workers transferred from other factories, short-term casual workers and support staff from inside and outside the company, become accustomed to the new working environment. The handbook has a blank column that is to be filled in by the end of the week and handed to the group leader on the morning of the first day of the next working week. This routine continues for two or three months after a worker joins the company. Let me show you the entries for the first week.

1. This week's safety target.

At the beginning of each week everyone is required to fill in 'this week's safety target.' My target for the first week was, 'to acquire an overall understanding of the job and remain free of injury.' At the end of the week you are required to tick one of three boxes, namely,

① I was able to achieve my target
② I mostly achieved my target
③ I failed to achieve my target.

2. Please comment on the training you received in the post to which you were assigned.

① Is your work dangerous?
   a. Yes.
   b. Not particularly.
If you answered 'yes,' please give details.

② Explanation of type and purpose of safety equipment used.
   a. Explanation given (list safety equipment used).
   b. No explanation given.

③ Explanation of type and efficacy range of safety devices.
   a. Explanation given (give two or three examples of the safety devices used).
   b. No explanation given.

④ Explanation of the importance of the procedure performed and critical safety issues.
   a. Explanation given (list two or three examples of critical safety issues).

(following section omitted).

There were a further eight questions along these lines. Within two or three days of my handing it in, the handbook was returned with comments from my superiors (including the seal of confirmation from the group leader or section leader and advice from my seniors on the factory floor). This exchange continued for eight weeks. Three days before the end of the period, I undergo a 'health check.' The group leader records the results in the handbook and sends it on to the Safety and Hygiene Unit. Some of my casual worker colleagues found this exercise a nuisance and stopped handing in the handbook well before the end of the specified period. Apparently nobody even mentioned it. No doubt the managers find the whole exercise a burden too.

Another particular burden workers on the cleaning round face, is the excessive heat of the area. As it is the cleaning machine's function to apply heat treatment, naturally the parts produced are subjected to very high temperatures. When the parts first emerge from the cleaning machine they are still hot enough to give you a serious burn. And the whole area around the cleaning machine is unbearably hot from the ambient heat.

14 September (Friday)

This summer we've been having a heatwave. But the heat outside is nothing compared with the temperatures on the cleaning round. The humidity too is extremely high. Even well into September the humidity is over 70%. It feels just like being in a Turkish bath. The moisture clouds our goggles. The humidity is even more unbearable than the heat. I regret that I chose to work through the summer. They tell me that on the cleaning round you can work in a short-sleeved shirt even in mid-winter. The heat is so excessive that I find myself guzzling large quantities of soft drink every time we have a break. Without keeping up a copious intake of fluids you run the risk of heat exhaustion. Our daily wage is ¥9,000 for seven and a half hours work. That works out at ¥1,200 an hour. It takes about six minutes to drink a ¥120 bottle of juice. Five or six bottles a day costs us thirty minutes of hard labour. After discussing this fact with my workmates, we all began to rue the money spent on soft drinks and, sadly made do with water.

In contrast to this, the inspection and packing area is very cool. This is because it is surrounded by vinyl sheeting to keep out the dust and is air-conditioned to cool down the parts. It is set to maintain a constant temperature of twenty-two degrees Celsius, but in reality it is probably closer to twenty-five or twenty-six degrees. Even so, the more than ten degrees difference in temperature inside and outside the enclosure must take a lot out of the workers.

24 August (Friday)

Perhaps those working inside the inspection and packing area find the cool temperature pleasant, but for me, after working in the cleaning round, it feels positively cold. It can't be good to move suddenly from being in a lather of sweat in the cleaning round to freezing in the packing area. After lunch I began to feel nauseous and I was hit by a bout of diarrhoea. Lately, I've been feeling twinges of neuralgia in my knees and lower back.

In the sub-assembly operation you are hardly called upon to lift heavy loads or tolerate excessive heat. On the other hand, you have to work extremely quickly. A team of two working together can assemble about one hundred units per hour. A skilled pair can get up to about one hundred and twenty. When I was roped in to help out on the sub-assembly process, I could only manage around ninety units, even though I was working flat out the whole time. The task I was performing was that of assistant assembler, which is considerably easier than that of the main assembly worker. Even so, despite two weeks in the job, I was unable to keep up with the speed of the sub-assembly line.

It takes very little time to understand what is required and to perform the work to a minimal degree, but it is a long time before you can keep going all day at a constant rate, lifting heavy loads in the blistering heat. These facts illustrate the extraordinary physical burden the assembly line workers face in their daily work.[4] This is also clearly reflected in how much weight you lose performing these tasks.

10 August (Friday)

Just as I am beginning to feel my body is about to give out, we have a very welcome week-off for the mid-summer break (to celebrate the Japanese All-Souls festival). This will give me the opportunity I need to recover my strength. Recently, I have hardly had the energy to eat lunch. I know I need to eat to stay healthy, so I have been forcing down a bowl of cold noodles, but my weight has been dropping alarmingly. I was seventy-seven kilograms when I took my medical on joining the company, but I had dropped to seventy-four kilograms after the first week and seventy-two after ten days. In the early days, I had the energy to joke with my workmates about my weight loss, blaming it on the Toyota-style diet. But as time goes on, I am beginning to feel very apprehensive about it and have taken to eating chocolate, something I have never done before.

6 November (Tuesday)

My last day with the company. My weight has dropped to below seventy kilograms. All the casual workers who joined with me have also 'slimmed down' considerably. Yamano and Kimata each lost five kilograms and a casual worker on Yamano's opposite shift lost an astonishing fifteen kilograms, dropping from sixty-two to forty-seven kilograms. His appearance is so changed you can hardly recognise him. The physical changes in the body are also apparent in the fingernails. Since I came here I have developed rough ridges on the surface of my fingernails.[5]

Responding to change

Change occurs in the normal daily work. There is frequent change in the parts being manufactured and there are also slight fluctuations in the quantities produced. How do the assembly line workers cope with these changes?

Variety in manufactured parts

The sub-assembly line produces parts for both medium capacity and high capacity engines (only one type for rear-ends), but the change in the size of the parts we handle makes very little difference to the work pattern.

On the inspection and packing line they handle more parts (20 different items) and there are slight variations in the basic movements for each item. For example, there are different chutes for the cleaning trays. As the front and rear components do not need to go through the cleaning process, they are taken directly from the parts-storage chute and placed in a specified area. The high-capacity parts and the assembled components come in by different routes. The mode of inspection is also different. All this can introduce changes into the basic work pattern on the inspection and packing line.

But, it is important to remember, that even though there might be variations in the basic movements, these operations themselves are simply part of the standardized work process. Even though your work process may involve different parts coming through, it is not as if you are being asked to perform 'non-standardized' work or anything complicated.

You may wonder whether workers face similar differences in producing a single item as against multiple items. When producing a number of different kinds of items, the worker needs to make an instant 'choice' regarding the item he is about to handle. To take an example from the sub-assembly process, a worker on the line has to decide immediately what job to pick up, which gear to place on the mount and into which box he should pack the job. Making these choices is very stressful.

You would naturally think that choices of this kind do not demand much effort. But I can assure you that actually making these decisions on the assembly line is really a considerable mental burden. Put around the other way, you might say that the '*takt* time' is so strictly fixed that even simple decisions like this feel very stressful.

In the sub-assembly process there are only two kinds of parts, but there is a big difference in terms of pressure on the worker between just one type of part and two types. Perhaps that is why the female workers are assigned only to the rear-end assembly where there is only one type involved. In addition, high levels of concentration are required for the production of multiple parts, as the more different parts there are, the more likely it is for mistakes to occur.

If the worker on the cleaning round just happens to place some parts into the wrong chute, it is a very serious matter. Unless the inspection and packing crew notice the mistake, the product will be shipped off to America in the wrong box. Mistakes of this kind can happen quite easily, as the medium and high capacity versions of the same part look very similar and are packed into virtually identical boxes. Workers on the cleaning round need to concentrate constantly to avoid making mistakes like this, so there is considerable nervous tension in addition to the physical stress.

From the above, I think you can understand that variety in the types of products produced results in greater physical and mental pressure on the workers on the line.

Variations in product quantity
In the short period I was working in the factory there were frequent changes in the numbers of products we produced. When I first joined

the company we were producing parts for 613 vehicles a day, but that figure increased gradually to 630, then 700, then 705 and, finally, to 725 by the time I left. To cope with these fluctuations in production numbers, jobs are reassigned, staff are either taken on or laid off and work organization is rearranged.

At first, there had been only one person on the sub-assembly process, but as the number of vehicles increased, a second worker was added. When there was a major leap in the number of engines we were producing, the company considered taking on additional staff and, if necessary, pushing through a major reconfiguration of the factory. By about August or September, they were saying that they might move to a three-shift production system to cope with the large increase in vehicles planned for November.

But there was no sudden large increase in the number of engines produced, and the company was able to cover the small growth in production without taking on extra staff, but by increasing overtime work. Seen over a long period, there has been a considerable growth in the number of vehicles, but hardly any increase in the number of staff. At the time I left the factory, there was only one more member of staff than there had been when we were first assigned to our positions.

In this way, variation in the product types meant an increase in the intensity of our work, and variation in the number of products produced, required regulation of our overtime working hours. Through these 'variations' the workers were compelled to accept an increased workload, through both intensification of labour and extension of their working day.[6]

Coping with the 'unexpected'

Let us now consider responses to abnormalities. When we talk of coping with abnormalities, we are covering a great range, encompassing everything from pressing a restart button to repairing a machine. What then, are the 'unexpected' situations workers on the factory floor encounter?

Expecting the 'unexpected'
Casual workers must not attempt to fix any problems with the machines. If anything goes wrong with a machine, they have to call someone qualified in 'trouble-shooting.' This is absolutely stipulated. When a malfunction occurs, we are told, 'Keep out of the working

range of the machine, Do not touch any of the controls,' other than to, '1 turn off, 2 call, 3 wait.' We had this safety procedure drummed into us in our initial training. We were told that we casual employees were not permitted to deal with breakdowns, even if the problem could be fixed by just pressing a button.

Even regular employees, in their first three years in the company, and therefore not qualified in trouble-shooting, were not allowed to touch the machines. Those workers who had the qualification were able to restart stalled machines manually. On the cleaning round, every time a machine broke down, the section leader and the young team leader[7] would lose no time in dealing with the problem. Let us see what some of my diary entries tell us about 'trouble-shooting.'

31 July (Tuesday)

At 4 p.m., as soon as we had resumed work, the cleaning machine broke down. The section leader tried hard to get it going himself, but had no luck. Later, after about thirty minutes had elapsed, a specialist mechanic from the indirect assistance division turned up. He couldn't fix the machine either. Then, another thirty minutes later, a second mechanic joined him. All up, it was a good two hours before the machine was eventually running again. Apparently, a loose part had dropped down into the machine and brought it to a standstill.

22 August (Wednesday)

The cleaning machine broke down and work stopped for about ten minutes. Takenaka (15 years work experience) and Ogawa (10 years) were able to get it going again by themselves by pressing the reset button. When I asked them the cause of the problem they said they didn't know. It seems, by the time you get to be a section leader or a team leader you can at least restart stalled machines.

29 August (Wednesday)

The cleaning machine broke down again today. Takenaka took a quick look at it and got it going again straight away. I get the impression that this kind of problem is a daily occurrence and that there is a more or less fixed pattern for dealing with it.

3 September (Monday)

The cleaning machine broke down. It took a specialist mechanic over an hour to locate the problem and get the machine going again.

Major problems like this cannot be solved directly by workers in the manufacturing section. It seems the workers on site can only deal with those regular breakdowns that follow a fixed pattern.

As far as I could observe, workers in the manufacturing division did not locate the causes of breakdowns nor repair machines. Most of the workers on the assembly line are unable to do anything, as they do not have qualifications in trouble-shooting. Even the off-line workers[8] can only deal with very minor problems. These 'minor problems' are those that tend to follow a regular pattern and require no more action than pressing the restart button. For anything more complicated, a mechanic comes along from the production assistance division with the tools to open up the machine and locate the cause of the breakdown.

Dealing with the 'unexpected' on the assembly line is generally no more than this. As I mentioned earlier, the cleaning machine is fitted with a safety sensor that automatically stops the machine if you put your hand into it before the safety lamp comes on. When this happens, you have to call an off-line worker trained in safety procedure and get him to restart the machine for you. It is not as if casual workers could not do this themselves, but this procedure is laid down in the company's rules and must be followed.

On the inspection and packing operation, since the job itself is to detect faulty parts, they are frequently required to respond to problems. When a faulty part appears, they have to trace the stage in the manufacturing process where the fault occurred and shut down production as quickly as possible.

21 August (Tuesday)

After the mid-summer break it was discovered the parts on the chute had started to rust. Even though they had been put through a rust-proofing process before the vacation, most of the parts bore traces of rust. Apparently the extent of the rusting was very serious. They spent yesterday and today dealing with this problem. Every single part has had to be inspected separately to determine whether or not it can be used.

However, it was only the production engineers, some of the supervisors and the team leader who dealt with this problem. The general workers continued their work as usual. The fact is, only limited categories of employee deal with unexpected incidents of this kind.

Action taken following an incident

As we have seen, workers on the assembly line play very little part in dealing with unpredictable incidents. Even the off-line workers, for the most part, deal only with those minor stoppages that occur commonly in an ordinary day's work. But they do have to respond to the situation that arises from an incident. When a worker is unable to fill his production quota because of a machine malfunction, or because trouble in an earlier process has deprived him of the parts he needs, or the parts he has produced are wonky, he has to make up the shortfall later. This happens virtually every day.

To be frank, dealing with the effects of an incident, simply means increasing our overtime work. When something goes wrong we get home later. On the other hand, we can never knock off earlier than the stipulated finishing time, no matter how fast we work. Since management allocates workers on the premise that overtime work will be required, it is virtually impossible to achieve the minimum set targets within normal working hours. Even if you are required to stop work before the normal finishing time because, for example, a stoppage in a previous process is preventing parts from coming through, you have to spend the remaining time in the 4S's operation. The 4S's operation is a cleaning routine applied to the factory floor, encapsulated in the four Japanese words, *seiri*, *seiton*, *seiketsu*, and *seisō*, meaning 'neat,' 'tidy,' 'sanitary' and 'clean' respectively.

In my workplace the average overtime worked was about thirty minutes. This figure is less than for other positions. Apparently, where Kimata (a casual recruit who joined with me) worked, the machines were always breaking down and he frequently had to work more than two hours overtime. Kawakami, too, said that in his previous job he worked two hours overtime virtually every day.

When there was a sharp fall in the number of units produced because of trouble with the machines or some other reason, employees were sometimes required to work on their days off. For a while, when we were having trouble getting the rear end units, production of just that process was stopped. Later, to cover the backlog, several men had to turn up for work on a Saturday.

So, as you can see from all this, for most of the workers on the factory floor, responding to 'abnormalities' meant applying the concept of flexible working hours.

'Fine-tuning between manufacturing processes'

From what we have covered so far you probably have the impression that workers on the assembly line perform only standardized work. But if you observe work on the line carefully, you will notice that they also perform other tasks. These might best be referred to as fine adjustments between the manufacturing processes. Without these adjustments the flow of the assembly line would probably be slowed down considerably. Consequently, these actions play an important role in the smooth running of a factory.

In a convey-belt type assembly line, the machines dictate the flow of the line, so the workers do not have to do anything in particular to keep it going apart, perhaps, from helping out a worker higher upstream who has fallen behind the pace. But this is not the case in a line like ours, where not all the manufacturing processes are synchronized by a conveyor belt, yet, on the other hand, neither are they completely independent. To keep the line running smoothly, or to ensure that it does not stall, the workers need to make fine adjustments between manufacturing processes.

Fine adjustments required in the transportation process

The worker on the cleaning round takes the empty tray out of the cleaned-items chute, sends it along to the parts storage chute and then positions a new tray to be cleaned. He repeats this process over and over again. Described in these terms, it may seem as if transporting items around the cleaning machine is a very simple task. But this is not necessarily the case. You need pay very close attention to the order in which you take the empty trays out of the cleaned items chute.

Usually, a lot of empty trays, returned from the inspection and packing area, accumulate on the lower shelf of the cleaned parts chute and it is impossible for the worker on the cleaning round to take all the trays back at the same time. So, when taking the empty trays back to the parts storage chute, the cleaning-round worker has to make a choice as to which trays to take back and which tray of parts should go into the cleaning machine first. When I first started on this job, I just took the trays back in random order, but I soon realized that you need to keep in mind the progress of processes up and down the line when deciding on which trays to take back.

Inside the cleaning machine the trays are soaked in cleaning fluid at sixty to eighty degrees centigrade then exposed to hot air of between eighty and one hundred degrees. When the parts come out of the cleaning machine they are still hot enough to burn you if you happen to touch them directly. Consequently, they cannot be moved off immediately to inspection and packing, but are instead left to cool for a while on the cleaned-parts chute. If the parts are packed before they are sufficiently cooled, not only is there the risk of the packing workers being burned, but also water vapour condenses on the parts so by the time they arrive in America they are covered in rust. This means that the larger parts, which take longer to cool down, tend to be left to last. So, towards the end of the day as it gets closer to finishing time, only the larger parts are left and both the packing workers and the transport workers have to wait until they cool down. This can result in increased overtime work. To avoid this situation, those parts that take longer to cool, should be put through the cleaning machine earlier and this in turn determines the order of the trays brought back from inspection and packing.

Further, the workers on the cleaning round have to be aware of not only what is happening on the next process on the assembly line, but also know what is going on upstream. It is not as if new parts are being constantly carried to the parts-storage chute. And you have to be careful not to take empty trays to the parts-storage chute if no new parts are being delivered. Since the empty trays act as a *kanban*, if you return the trays when no parts are being put through the cleaning machine, or, conversely, if you move new trays into the machine when no empty trays are being returned, it causes havoc in the interim inventory of parts. The number of parts in the interim stockpile, for example, the number of trays (complete with parts) placed in the cleaned-parts chute, is fixed. There are five trays of drive pins (high capacity), seven trays of front ring gears (high capacity), five trays of front units (high capacity), twenty-five trays of C1s and so on. So, if an empty tray is placed on the parts-storage chute, even though no new parts have yet arrived, it has to be taken back to the cleaned-parts chute. In order to prevent this waste of time and energy, the worker on the cleaning round has to be constantly aware of the kinds of parts being delivered to the parts-storage chute.

In addition, if there is a stoppage in the flow of new parts because of a mechanical breakdown in an earlier process, he is called upon to make major adjustments, well beyond what we would normally call fine-tuning. When there is a long delay in the production of parts from the previous process, workers on the cleaning round sometimes go and collect the parts themselves. The transport worker from the previous process delivers new parts in a fifteen minute cycle, but sometimes work on the line is progressing at such a rate that we cannot afford to wait that long. This is when the worker on the cleaning round goes to pick up parts from the previous operation and these parts are put through the cleaning machine first. In this way, making adjustments over two or more stages in the production process, it is often possible to prevent stoppages on the line before they happen.

The situation I have been describing is what happens with medium capacity engine parts. Even more frequent fine-tuning is required with the transport of parts for high capacity engines and for assembled parts. Since the high capacity engines (excluding the assembled components) are produced in another factory, the timing of the return of the empty trays and the number of trays to be returned is strictly determined. The worker in charge of transport of parts for high capacity engines must place a specified number of empty boxes in the designated chute within a predetermined time frame (every thirty minutes) and stamp his logbook with a seal confirming that the operation has been completed successfully. But since the number of cleaning trays (i.e. *kanban*) is set at the last minute, sometimes the fixed number of empty trays does not come back from the inspection and packing unit within the specified time limit. If this looks as if it is likely to happen, the transport worker asks the inspection and packing team to give priority to the high capacity engine parts to produce the empty boxes required. He does this only as a last resort because it places an added burden on the inspection and packing workers by disrupting the fixed order in which they carry out their work. So the worker covering the transport of high capacity engine parts needs to carefully monitor what is happening around him up and down the production line.

In addition, the worker transporting parts for high capacity engines has to carry assembled units (differential and UD). Although there is no fixed time frame for the transport of the assembled units, it is difficult to judge the right timing of their delivery. If they arrive too late, it not only disrupts the following packing process, but it also slows down the previous operation. This is because you run out of space to put the differentials and empty boxes in which to pack the UDs. It is easy to forget about the assembled units if you are concentrating on the delivery of the high capacity parts. With the assembled units, the chute takes about fifteen minutes to fill up. If you are busy preparing empty boxes for the high capacity engine parts, you find this time passes very quickly. On the other hand, if you transport the assembled units before the chute is full, you need to make more trips, which obviously increases your workload. So, the worker carrying the assembled units has to be constantly aware of the timing of the transport of high capacity parts and the rate of progress of the sub-assembly process, in order to alternate the delivery of the parts accordingly.

Fine-tuning in the sub-assembly process
Workers on the sub-assembly operation are also required to make minor adjustments between manufacturing processes. However, in their particular case, it would be more accurate to say that the fine-tuning occurs in the relationship between the assembly worker and his or her assistant, rather than in the manufacturing process itself.

5 October (Friday)
Because the assembly worker's task is more demanding than that of the assembly assistant, the assistant needs to constantly consider the needs of his or her partner.

The speed of the assistant operation needs to be controlled to avoid putting undue pressure on the assembly worker. The assembly assistant, standing in front of the cleaning machine has to keep half an eye on the assembly worker and calculate the timing of the delivery of the next job. The way the job is received from the assembly worker is a bit tricky. I like to receive the job in my left hand (as the next operation is inspection, if you receive the job into your left hand you can begin checking immediately, holding the job in your left hand and checking with the right), but to do so makes things difficult for the assembly worker (because handing the job into the assembly assistant's left hand means you have to take it out of the caulking machine with your right hand then transfer it to your left hand before passing it over). So there is really no choice but to take it in your right hand first. There needs to be a good intuitive understanding between the workers for this process to run smoothly. As the two are not particularly close friends, it is not easy for them to discuss any concerns they might have, so this inevitably leads to accumulated stress.

17 October (Wednesday)
I'm getting quite used to the sub-assembly operation. I hate the way I'm constantly being given instructions, but I guess I just have to put up

with it. Getting a rhythm going with my partner is difficult. Whenever there is a problem with the machine or the supply of parts is held up, we have to take something we can work on from among the high capacity or medium capacity parts. The judgement as to which to take has to be made in an instant. Sometimes the components fit together easily and sometimes they don't. So there are minor variations in how long the exercise takes. The assembly work assistant has to pace his movements to coincide with those of the assembly worker. With the caulked jobs, sometimes the assembly worker hands the job to me (the assistant assembly worker) and sometimes I am the one who takes the job from the caulking machine. Sometimes, too, I take parts from the reserve pedestal. There is constant demand on us to make fine adjustments in our mode of work, which makes this job very taxing mentally.

This sort of fine-tuning by workers on the assembly line makes it possible for slight irregularities to be absorbed and for the flow of work to continue smoothly. But it is important to note that the fine-tuning required is not at all complicated or high level work. The degree of fine-tuning permitted is more or less fixed. What is required by the term 'minor adjustments in the work process,' is the physical capability to fill in any gaps in the assembly line and a keen awareness of the need to maintain the flow of the operation. These demands place a considerable burden on workers on the assembly line.

So far, we have been looking at examples of the realities of work on the factory floor. Day in day out, assembly line workers silently perform their monotonous, repetitive, physically demanding tasks. As if that were not enough, they are also required to deal with variation and irregularities and to make minor adjustments during the work process. These simply add to the burden on the workers as they perform their daily duties.

Kaizen activities and QC circles

In addition to their daily work, workers also go through improvement activities and join quality control circles. Below, I give some actual examples of participation in these activities.

As we shall be looking at *kaizen* activities in detail in chapter four, here we will confine ourselves to a brief description of the system and the patterns of participation.

Kaizen (improvement) activities

In the Toyota workplace the general workers, bottom-end management and project teams all participate in their own *kaizen* activities. The general employees suggest areas they would like to see improved through the 'safety proposal' or 'creative suggestion' system. Group leaders carry out *kaizen* activities as part of their daily routine and generally suggest larger scale improvements than the general workers. The project teams, made up of the management and factory foremen of each group, implement improvements aimed at increasing efficiency. Let us deal with each in turn.

Kaizen activities for general employees

Creative suggestion
The creative suggestion system celebrated its fifty-year anniversary in June 2001. All employees, including the casual workers, are expected to put forward at least one creative suggestion each month. This is done on a prepared form that requires the proposer to fill in, the present position and the nature of the problem, the suggested improvement, the expected effect (with concrete figures) and investment cost (the money and man-hours required to implement the improvement). For each proposal, rewards ranging from five hundred yen to two hundred thousand yen are offered according to the value of the contribution. Incidentally, my three proposals were each valued at five hundred yen.

A closer look at the pattern of participation in this proposal system, shows that the great majority of suggestions seem to be conjured up reluctantly just before the deadline.

Some of the general employees filled in their forms with the help of ideas they had got from management. Most of the casual employees only filled in their proposal forms in response to a reminder from management after the closing date. But for a very small number of employees, these proposals provide an opportunity for them to come to the attention of management. And conversely, from the management perspective, they provide evidence of worker enthusiasm.

Safety proposal
All employees, including casual workers, are required to submit a monthly 'safety proposal' submission in addition to the 'creative

suggestion.' This is, as the name suggests, a system in which workers can bring their complaints and difficulties regarding the work they perform to the attention of those above. You fill in the details of the incident on a prescribed form under the headings, '① When? ② Where? ③ Who? and ④ How?' It seemed, with this form too, that workers did not begin thinking about what to write until just before the closing date.

Other *kaizen* activities

The group to which I had been assigned was particularly enthusiastic about *kaizen* activities, partly because ours was a recently established assembly line and partly because we had been chosen as a workplace that places a special emphasis on improved performance. At our morning meetings our group leader would say, for example, 'even if it is going to cost us money, do not hesitate to keep coming up with suggestions for improving safety and increasing productivity' (23 August), and the team leader came around several times while we were working and told us to let him know if there was anything at all, no matter how minor, that could be improved.

Kaizen activities by supervisors on the factory floor

The group leader is usually away from the assembly line, attending meetings or catching up with paperwork in his prefab office. But from time to time, he turns up on site to discuss suggestions for improvement. For our group leader, *kaizen* activities were just another part of his daily routine.

But, seen from the perspective of the factory as a whole, our group leader could be regarded as exceptional. This was because the assembly line had just recently been established. I don't think group leaders in other workplaces were anywhere near as concerned about making improvements. This fact was also pointed out in an article in the union newspaper.

> The source of Toyota's strength lies in a strong workplace and it is the group leader who carries the central responsibility for building that strength on the factory floor. In the current climate, however, where group leaders are compelled to join the assembly line to make up for staff shortages, or are weighed down with excessive office work, they are not devoting enough time to their real work of improving the workplace and training their group members. So, discussions were held between workers and management to reassess the work of group

leaders. As a consequence, 450 workplaces have been designated 'model workplaces,' where the group leader plays a central role in actively promoting the building of a strong workplace (*Kumiaishi* (Union news) September 2001).

To judge from this special edition of the union newspaper, it seems that the majority of group leaders are so overburdened with daily production work that they have little time for *kaizen* activities.

Project team *kaizen* activities
The project team is a 'specialist improvement implementation group' made up of the managers and on-site foremen of each group. Their activities are aimed at the rationalization of the production process. During the time I was working there I had several encounters with the project team. They would come up and stand by where I was working to silently observe whether I was making the slightest 'unnecessary' movement. It is certainly not a very pleasant experience. There was often one of them timing the process with a stopwatch and another recording the worker's performance with a video camera. No doubt this was so they could analyse the worker's movement later. Our team leader told us that if the project team made any suggestions we had to change our work practices to accommodate them.

QC Circles

Overview of Quality Control Circles
QC Circles are held twice a month for about an hour after normal working hours. They are regarded as overtime work and we are paid for attending them. In essence, 'participation' is compulsory, even for casual employees.

This is how the system works. In each circle there is a circle leader and a theme leader. The former has the task of putting together the QC Circle as a whole and the latter is charged with ensuring that the discussion progresses smoothly. In principle, the QC Circle leader is a section leader (*hanchō*) and the theme leader changes with each new topic. In addition, there is a person who provides support from the side and a circle advisor. These roles are usually performed by the chief leader and a group leader respectively, although they are not actually present during the QC sessions.

In our group we had two circles, one organized around the sub-assembly process and the other around the inspection and packing line. I participated in the latter one. Our theme leader was the team leader, Nagata, with thirteen years experience working for the company.

Not only are the results of the QC Circles implemented at each individual workplace, but they are also announced at the General Quality Control Circle Conference. If we take our workplace as an example, first, the best Circle among the four groups from workplaces in our close vicinity advances to the Conference of the Machinery Section and the Circle that wins through there competes at the Machinery Division Conference. If you win there, you go on to represent the whole factory and compete against Circles from other factories. Finally, you can go on to appear at the General QC Circle Conference, at the level of the Toyota Company as a whole, or even go as far as the Toyota Group Conference.

QC format

All QC Circles follow the same special format. First, a theme is chosen from the five categories; 'quality,' 'maintenance,' 'cost,' 'safety' and 'other.' Then a particular aspect of that theme is set for discussion and the reasons for choosing the topic are revealed. Next, concrete goals are identified in order to solve the particular problem. By following this sort of procedure, abstract themes are boiled down to actual practical problems.

Once the topic has been established, the QC Circle moves on to analyse the present state of the problem. This is where the technical tools of trade such as histograms and characteristic factor diagrams come into play.[9]

As I mentioned before, the results obtained from QC Circles are presented at general conferences, so it is important for each Circle to show the procedure and results of their QC discussions in a way that is clear and easily understood. There is a column on the QC proforma in which you fill in details of the state of QC progress. Here, for example, you might write that at the onset of QC activities the rate of achievement of a particular goal was 30%, but that this rose to 50% after one month, 65% after two months, 80% after three months and finally to 95% after four months. You could illustrate this progress with a line graph. Further, concrete statistics are produced to show the rate of attendance and participation in each QC Circle, how often each participant spoke, the rate of achievement of final goals, the cost effectiveness of improvements and so on.

Finally, comments are sought from the QC Circle support officer and the Circle advisor. QC Circles follow this format working on the same theme over a four-month cycle.

An actual example of a QC Circle

I was fortunate enough to be able to witness the progress of a full QC cycle from beginning to end. In the following account I trace the progress, in order, one session at a time, of a QC Circle that convened a total of six times.[10]

9 August (Thursday) – 30 minutes overtime plus one hour QC

According to our Circle leader, Yamashita (section leader, 19 years work experience), the senior management of the company is devoting a lot of effort into quality control and has designated 'quality maintenance and control and early interception of faulty products' as company-wide priorities for the period July to December. As a consequence of this decision, 'quality' has automatically become the theme for all Circles.

As this was the first session of a new theme, our theme leader, Nagata, put forward a draft proposal. The topics and objectives of this Circle are, 'packing as the last line of defence – faulty products must not get through. It is imperative to stop any faulty products here, because failure to do so means they will be shipped to America in that state. We need to find techniques, simple techniques that anyone can learn, for intercepting faulty products and teach them to all employees. Train everybody to perfectly identify faulty products with their own eyes without relying on instruments to detect faults.'

Perhaps it was because this was the first meeting on a new theme, but the theme leader dominated the discussion with his explanations and there was hardly anything even vaguely approaching an opinion voiced by any of the other participants. During the meeting Yamashita gave me a brief overview of how QC circles work.

23 August (Thursday) – 30 minutes overtime plus over an hour QC

Continuing on from the last session, we reaffirmed the issues and objectives. To achieve our goal of 'acquisition of skills to ensure faulty products are not dispatched,' we considered each of the levels of skill acquisition required in the inspection and packing operation.

With the theme leader and Circle leader taking the central initiative we came up with these five skill levels,

0 points	Don't know, no experience.
1 point	Can detect wrong part or missing part.
2 points	Can distinguish medium capacity parts from high capacity parts.
3 points	Quality checking standard – rust/dent level.
4 points	Quality checking standard – rust/dent level + manufacturing fault + extrusions.
5 points	Zero faulty parts dispatched.

When we measured our present skill level against these criteria, we found that the average skill level of all the Circle members was 1.5 points. We will have everybody up to 5 points by the finishing date at the end of December. This gives us a very concrete outcome.

There is an explanation about the work procedure for those in the Circle who have not done inspection and packing work before. 'You take a part from the cleaning tray, hold it in your hand and spot check designated areas. If there are no problems, you either pack it into a cardboard box or put it into the rack provided. This sequence is performed in eight seconds. As this process is regarded as a "non-fixed-form process" rather than a "fixed-form process," it is not possible to detail all of the movements precisely. But even with the packing process there is a manual that sets out the "standard operation." This deals with the checking of product quality and must be followed.'

In addition, the theme leader had prepared a file with more detailed explanations. This included instructions on how and where to check and detailed diagrams of each of the parts showing where faults (extrusions, rust and dents) were likely to occur.

He spoke of the danger of over-reliance on the manual, since you might overlook scratches and rust on areas not specifically mentioned, and emphasized the need to look thoroughly over the whole product.

The theme leader and Circle leader virtually ran the whole QC meeting alone and, as in the last session, the other participants hardly said a word. It was only when they were asked questions that they murmured a half-hearted response. After an hour they all began to fidget and I got the feeling that they were just waiting impatiently for the time to pass.

7 September (Friday) – 30 minutes overtime and one hour QC

The theme leader, Nagata, came along with a cause and effect diagram (a fishbone chart) he had devised. We had been told that 'for homework' we should all go away and think about it, but nobody else came along with anything prepared. Today, while adding further detail to the chart, we analysed the factors that lead to faulty parts getting through.

We traced the cause of the dispatch of faulty parts to operator error brought about by a fall in the level of concentration.

The operators see more than two thousand parts a day. Naturally, this is very tiring on the eyes. There is a marked drop in concentration levels in the afternoon. To avoid this you need to give workers a change of scenery by rotation of jobs. The analysis of these issues proceeded, centred on the direction of the Circle leader and the theme leader.

Since there are some participants who have never done any inspection and packing work, it was decided that in future we should learn how to carry out an inspection holding a real job in our hands. Nagata said that he wanted everyone, not only the inspection and packing workers, to see this as an opportunity to learn the techniques required to prevent the dispatch of faulty products.

This time too, the session took the form of a discussion between the Circle leader and the theme leader. They are both trying hard to get everyone enthused about the project, but the majority of the participants are just looking down at the floor or sitting there with their eyes closed. What's more, it appears that the cost of the drinks from the vending machine for each QC session comes out of the Circle leader's pocket.

27 September (Thursday) – finished work on time, plus one hour QC

Surprisingly, today we had QC after the second shift. As a rule, the inspection and packing team has QC after the first shift, but because we have only had one session this month it was decided at the last minute to have another session after the second shift. QC after the second shift is tough. You don't get back to the dormitory until after 2 a.m.

As we had discussed at the end of the last meeting, this time we all learnt how to do the inspection work holding an actual job in our hands.

First, we confirmed we could tell the difference between medium capacity and high capacity engine parts. The medium capacity and high capacity versions of the same part are almost the same shape. It is very difficult to tell them apart at first glance. So it can happen that the packing and inspection team do not notice if a medium capacity part ends up in a high capacity box or vice versa. To make absolutely sure that an error of this kind does not occur, all of us went through each of the parts identifying, one by one, the differences between high capacity and medium capacity engine parts.

With some parts, the job has lines etched into the outer rim or tiny gears set into it and the only difference between the high capacity and medium capacity versions is in the number of lines or gear cogs. Working on the cleaning round, I just placed the parts into the chute according to the different numbers on the boxes. I knew nothing at all about these differences. It was only thanks to these practical demonstrations that workers like me, who had had no experience of the inspection and packing process, came to understand the differences between medium and high capacity engine parts.

After that, we all followed the example of our theme leader, Nagata, who took us through all the steps of the inspection process. Then we went on to do it ourselves and check each other's performance. Nagata began by showing us how to hold the job and the procedure for inspection. Then, he encouraged the other inspection and packing workers to discuss whether or not they carried out the process in the same way. Enoki, a regular employee in her second year with Toyota, did some things differently from Nagata. So, Maejima (12 years experience) after quizzing both of them regarding the reasoning behind their different methods, pointed out, 'There are probably very sound reasons why each of you does it the way you do, but isn't it possible that by comparing the methods we can come up with an even easier way?' For example, it seems that to confirm whether or not the washer is in place, Enoki looks at the size of the gap when she rotates the gear upwards, whereas Nagata does not do this. As a result of this discovery, Nagata declared that Enoki's method should be added to the standard checking procedure.

In this way, the QC circles provide an opportunity for each person's way of doing things to be shared around the team as a whole. Here, today, I felt for the first time that I have finally got a bit of an understanding of the inspection process. As a lot of our team missed today's session, because they were on a training course or something, it has been decided to go over the inspection method together again next time. A lot more people spoke up in today's session, probably because the Circle leader was away.

12 October (Friday) – 30 minutes overtime plus two hours QC

Today, after going over the results of our QC circles so far, we continued on from last time, checking each other's inspection and packing methods out on the factory floor.

Our theme leader, Nagata, summarized all we had done up to the end of the last session, then reminded us again. 'The parts coming off this line are shipped directly to the United States. So, it is absolutely imperative that no faulty parts get past the inspection and packing team. But the reality is that occasionally faulty parts do get through. How, then, can we prevent that from happening?' After highlighting the issue, he proposed the goal of 'all staff acquiring the techniques to intercept, without fail, every faulty part.' To achieve this goal, the workers must always reconfirm that they have checked all the steps in the inspection process. 'Standard quality checks' distinguish between easily mistaken 'rust' (bad) and 'tarnish' (acceptable).

If you can get a good grasp on all these points to be checked, then no faulty parts should get through.

But unfortunately that alone doesn't solve the problem completely. Imperfections such as rust and dents are frequently found on the spots detailed as inspection points, but this does not mean that they are not found elsewhere. There is a danger in specifying the points to be checked that, conversely, imperfections in places not listed for checking will be overlooked. This was the new problem we tackled today and it provided the culmination of the results of the QC sessions we have had so far.

So Nagata urged us to pay attention, not only to the checkpoints in the official 'quality check standard,' but also to other spots as well. But, if you considerably increase the number of places to be checked, it is impossible for all the inspection and packing workers to finish the task in eight seconds.

Whenever an imperfection is found during the checking process, the position and the cause of the fault are entered into a computer. Further, if a faulty part happens to be discovered after it is dispatched to the factory in West Virginia, we get a document sent back to us with a photograph of the affected area and a report on the cause of the problem. Consequently, the number of parts we have to check increases day by day. Isn't it true that in reality it is impossible to check so many spots? And if it is agreed that we should check all areas, isn't there a danger that our concentration will be scattered and we will end up hardly checking the item at all? These are the sorts of arguments that were put forward in opposition to Nagata's suggestions. Of course, Nagata himself does not check through every point one at a time. He says he can see at a glance whether a part is faulty or not.

According to Nagata, 'when faulty parts were produced, they would go back and investigate the cause. By stamping the box with the name of the person who packed it, they were able to raise the sense of individual responsibility among the workers. Increasing the "awareness" of the workplace as a whole is the most important factor in preventing the dispatch of faulty products.'

As a result of our discussions, we decided that, in future, whenever a faulty part was discovered, all of us would spend ten to fifteen minutes debating the cause of the problem to ensure that it would not happen again.

Certainly, to some extent, you can reduce errors that lead to the shipment of faulty products through the raising of awareness of quality. But simply shouting slogans about improving 'awareness,' does not mean that everyone can acquire the techniques for intercepting faulty parts. To get everyone to learn these skills, shouldn't we be focusing on practical objective criteria, like distinguishing parts that should be dispatched from those that shouldn't, rather than emphasising subjective aspects like 'awareness'? The objections and counter-arguments continued in this vein.

So, after listening to the criteria each of us put forward, Nagata came up with a reply along the lines of, 'anyway, find the faulty areas.' In contrast, Shiroki (8 years service) said that group leader Morita had told him, 'don't look for the bad parts, find the good ones!' Apparently, he does not spend time in painstakingly looking for faults, but adopts the attitude 'if there is nothing in particular wrong with it, send it off!' Then Kawakami (8 years service) responded that, in the past he picked up even the slightest scratch, but recently he is more relaxed about it and 'sends off virtually everything.'

Here too, there was a divergence of opinion, but we managed to settle on the conclusion that in deciding whether or not a part is faulty, rather than making a judgement based on that part alone, you should decide on the basis of whether or not other parts can be assembled onto it. Even if a part has an imperfection, it is OK as long as it can be assembled. If you don't keep this sort of practical criterion in mind, there is a danger that the inspection process becomes an end in itself.

In addition to the arguments outlined above against Nagata's proposal that we should increase awareness over the workplace as a whole, some voiced their dissatisfaction at being singled out for attention. Why, they said, should the inspection and packing team alone carry all the responsibility for intercepting faulty parts? Shouldn't those working on earlier processes also be responsible? And they were not prepared to accept any blame for anything that happened on the other shift. The response to these objections was, 'Now we were not concerned with what happened in earlier processes, but are considering the responsibilities of our own.' On the question of the other shift, the matter was settled more or less amicably around the 'grown-up view' that we should consider what happens on the other shift part of our own problem. Not everyone was convinced, however. Even Nagata himself just look peeved and remained silent when he was quizzed by the group leader of the opposite shift on whether he was properly covering all the specified areas for inspection.

As we were not able to pull the discussion together today, it was agreed that we should debate the techniques for intercepting faulty products again next Thursday, after confirming with the opposite shift how they handle inspection and packing.

Today, the long discussion drew the meeting out to two hours, but overall I felt it was a pretty boring QC session. Nagata and Maejima spoke enthusiastically, but the other participants did not seem to be particularly interested. Imagine two hours QC after the second shift, an hour and a half of it spent standing up on the factory floor! By the end of the session my body, which had earlier been covered in sweat, was freezing cold. There has been a debate over whether to link QC to the 'humanization of work.' But, before that, I would like to see them focus on the 'humanization of human beings.' 3 a.m. is a time when most normal people are asleep. For workers to function like real human beings, sleep is more important than the promotion of QC. As the bus is not likely to be running at this hour, I get one of my workmates to drive me home. I arrive back at the dormitory a little before 4 a.m.

19 October (Friday) – thirty minutes overtime plus one hour of QC

As the finishing date had been brought forward from the end of November to the end of October, we suddenly decided to end discussion of our current theme today. That meant that we had to reach some kind of a conclusion. But, as no real consensus of opinion emerged, in the end we had to leave it up to the 'subjective judgement' of each of the participants. The conclusion we came up with was, 'each individual must have a high "awareness" of quality as they work.' Personally, I would have liked to add that, as it is impossible to check everywhere perfectly, a priority checking order should be established, but I was so exhausted I just gazed silently at the floor. There is no way a conclusion like this could help a new recruit understand how to carry out an inspection. In reality, most of us who attended hardly participated at all, some even slept through the discussion. The casual workers never contributed to the discussion and mostly slept through all the sessions.

I also found myself dozing off. It is hard to take QC sessions after eight hours work. You have to use your brain when you are exhausted from physical labour. It might be all right for those who work off the assembly line, but for workers on the line, these QC sessions are an enormous burden. It would be a great help, at least, if they held them during normal working hours.

In addition to the above, there was some fragmentary discussion along the lines that we should keep rotation on a daily basis rather than every two hours, otherwise people don't take responsibility for their work. And there was some talk about whether or not we should hold a meeting every time a problem arises. The overall atmosphere of the session seemed to suggest that people were trying hard to find ways to pass the time until 5 p.m. when we were to have a volleyball tournament.

Finally, someone asked, 'How many skill points should we give ourselves now we are at the end of the QC cycle?' When our theme leader, Nagata, said, 'Lets make it five points for everybody?' somebody objected, 'That's a bit much, isn't it!' But as nobody else voiced strong opposition to the proposal, in the end we went along with Nagata. We also left it to Nagata to make the final wrap-up of the QC Circle. All of this just goes to show what a sham QC can be.

Rotation

It is not as if workers continue the same work indefinitely. Their duties change frequently. During the three plus months that I was there, most of the workers changed their positions on the line. Through this system of rotation, employees came to learn to perform a variety of jobs in our group (see Table 2.1).

The table shows only rotation between assembly, packing, transport, cleaning and shipment, but within these areas too the tasks performed change daily. On the sub-assembly process, for example, there are four types of machine. On the inspection and packing line there is frequent alternation of tasks between initial inspection, boxed items, rack items and cardboard box assembly. In this group, not only the regular employees, but also the casual workers participate in job rotation. Tabata experienced the four assembly tasks. Jōjima was moved several times from sub-assembly to inspection and packing to make up for staff shortages there. And my work position changed several times. First I was on the cleaning round, then I was on cleaning and assembled transport. Next, I

Table 2.1: Rotation

The table shows task rotation over time. Time columns across the top are: 1/8, 10/8, 20/8, 31/8 / 1/9, 10/9, 20/9, 30/9 / 1/10, 10/10, 20/10, 30/10 / 1/11, 10/11.

Name	Age	Position At 30/7	Rotation (positions over time)
Management			
Morita	38	Overall	Overall (to ~30/9)
Shiraishi	42	Assembly	Assembly → Overall (after 20/10)
Shimada	40	Assembly	Assembly (throughout)
Yamashita	37	Cleaning/transport	Transport (to ~30/9)
Regular employees			
Nishiyama	35	Transport	Transport → Assembly (after 30/9)
Ōki	41	Packing	Packing (to ~30/9)
Takenaka	35	Cleaning/transport	Transport (early) ... Transport (from ~30/9)
Nagata	32	Packing	Packing
Maejima	41	Shipment	Shipment
Ogawa	28	Assembly	Assembly
Shiroki	26	Packing	Packing
Kawakami	29	Packing	Packing
Tsuda	20	Packing	Packing → Cleaning (near end)
Murase	21 F	Assembly	Assembly
Enoki	19 F	Shipment	Packing → Assembly (after ~10/10)
Kuramoto	19	Assembly	Assembly
Fixed-term contract			
Tabata	22	Assembly	Assembly
Jōjima	32	Assembly	Assembly
Naganuma	18	Assembly	Assembly
Ihara	29	Cleaning	Cleaning → Transport → Assembley / Cleaning (end)
Kitamura	28	Joined 3/9	Cleaning → Packing
Yada	23	Joined 17/9	Packing
Nonaka	23	Joined 17/9	Packing → Cleaning → Transport
Hayashi	31	Joined 5/11	Packing
Okada	28	Joined 5/11	Packing

Note: This table shows a rough allocation of tasks. Actually, work positions change more frequently. For example, when regular workers are on annual leave, other workers fill in for the period they are away, often just a day or two. The areas not marked with black lines indicate periods before joining or after leaving the company, transfer or 'support' to another group or the end of a period of support from another factory. From Kitamura to Okada the date of joining the company is given in the column for the position at 30/7.

moved to assembly transport and assembly assistant and finally, I moved back to the cleaning round.

What we need to clarify here is whether or not rotation was carried out in a properly planned manner. Let us look more closely at my actual experience of rotation.

30 July (Monday) – 31 August (Friday) cleaning round.

3 September (Monday) – 19 September (Wednesday) first period, cleaning round and assembly transport. Partner: Kitamura.

19 September (Wednesday) (Second period) – 3 October (Wednesday) cleaning round and assembly transport. Partner: Nonaka.

4 October (Thursday) alone on cleaning round.

5 October (Friday) first and third periods, cleaning round and assembly transport. Partner: Shiroki. Second and fourth periods, assembly.

8 October (Monday) – 15 October (Monday) first and third periods, cleaning round and assembly transport. Partner: One of either Shiroki, Kawakami, Tsuda or Nonaka. Second and fourth periods, alone on cleaning round.

16 October (Tuesday) – 24 October (Wednesday) first and third periods, cleaning round and assembly transport. Partner: Nonaka. Second and fourth periods, assembly.

18 October (Thursday) as above, except in the second work period I was moved for a while into assembly, then back into cleaning then onto assembly again.

25 October (Thursday) – 7 November (Wednesday) cleaning round. Partner: Nonaka.

This is clearly unplanned rotation lacking any educational consideration. Regardless of what management says[11] and what is written in the textbooks, this is not 'equitable' and 'regular' rotation.[12] I was not the only one. All the workers on the inspection and packing line had been assigned to assembly duties numerous times at irregular intervals. The supervisors and team leader only consider their quota for the day and simply assign the various tasks *ad hoc* as the need arises. On the factory floor there is just not time for the long-term perspective needed for personnel education. The same is true for what is usually referred to as 'support.'

Takenaka (15 years experience) came from another group on 30 July to give 'support,' then, on 3 September, he moved on to another group (not the one to which he originally belonged) and on 1 October he came back to our group again. Apparently this is how he was recruited to 'support.' One day when he was working, the chief leader approached him and said, 'Hey, Takenaka. Sorry mate, but you're gonna have to move again. You're the only one I can ask.' Of course, there is no way you can refuse. For him it is almost as if he has no 'home base' at all. He himself feels he has been passed along like a hot potato. Ōki, who is in his seventeenth year with the company, came from Plant M on 'support,' but returned there after just two months with us. Apparently, about once every four years, he goes to offer 'support' at another factory. Half joking, he said, 'Maybe there won't be a job for me there when I go back.'

Sometimes even casual workers are moved in from other factories. Hayashi, a casual worker assigned to our group on 5 November had previously worked at Plant T. Not only might your work position be changed at irregular intervals, but you might be required to do work that had no connection at all with your original job. In my case I changed from the cleaning round and assembly transport to assembly assistant. Takenaka had been working here on the cleaning round and on transport, but he was moved to assembly duty. Similarly, Ōki, who worked in the Materials Section of the Production Management Department (where they supply the equipment for the Direct Production Division), was transferred here to work in inspection and packing.

Workers on the factory floor, being moved around suddenly like this from one job to another, must not only endure the physical stress of having to learn a new job, but also the psychological pain of losing their own personal location.

17 October (Tuesday)

I find moving from the cleaning round to sub-assembly very painful. As the work is completely different, I have to start learning the new job from scratch. I don't think I would find it such a problem moving from the cleaning round into inspection and packing, because I've learnt a bit about it through the QC circles. The other day I said as much to the team leader, but he wasn't prepared to accept my suggestion. It is not only the content of the job that is different. There is also a far greater variety of abilities required. Assembly requires speed and concentration, whereas for the cleaning round you need strength and the ability to make adjustments between processes. So, changing from one to the other every couple of hours throws your body out of kilter. And although the cleaning round and sub-assembly are in the same group, the atmosphere of the two workplaces is completely different. Those 'above' are fond of saying glibly; 'you got the hang of the new job straight away!' But it takes a good deal of time to be accepted into the culture of the sub-assembly unit. It is a great strain for the person concerned, both physically and mentally, to be frequently shifted from one workplace to another. For a while now, I have been feeling considerable stress because I never know what I might be asked to do when I turn up for work. I feel downhearted from before I start work and by the time I hit the sack at night I'm feeling positively depressed.

Of course, some people may feel differently about changing their workplace, but at least I can say that this desperate juggling of tasks that goes under the name of rotation is not the regular, planned rotation we read about in the textbooks.

3 The 'Skill' of Shop-floor Workers

'Skill' is one of the topics that have attracted most attention from researchers into the Japanese automobile manufacturing industry. If we take a very broad overview of the research to date, we can say that from the beginnings of research in this field in the 1960s, up until the end of the 1970s, the emphasis had been on deskilling under increased automation. Since the 1980s, on the other hand, the focus has been more on the aspect of raising skill levels.[1] The mainstream of the debate holds that while routine work does not require particularly high degrees of skill, superior skill levels are built up over time as workers gradually forge their careers in the company, through the processes of job rotation, QC circles and in dealing with non-routine work (i.e., change and abnormalities).[2] More recently, there have been those who claim that competency, perhaps best described as 'mass production type skill,' is acquired in the process of performing core duties, i.e. routine work.[3]

Consequently, in this chapter I shall explore the two aspects of, skill acquired through 'career' formation, and skill formed in the performance of standardized work.[4] In addition, I would like to touch very briefly on skill acquired through fine-tuning between the manufacturing processes.

Skill formed through daily work

Skill to lessen the workload

In the past, assembly line labour was regarded as unskilled work. The commonly held view, gained from the image of conveyor belt production and held by the general public and researchers alike, was that these basic repetitive tasks required no skill at all.

In recent years, however, some researchers have claimed that what they call 'mass production type skills' are required even for 'standardized work.' They say 'over time, with the repetition of the regimented tasks that are a necessary condition of mass production labour, the work itself undergoes change. Responding to these changes and fine-tuning the production process is seen as quite naturally being part of a worker's job. That is to say, given that each single task may change, it follows that work conditions change and, consequently, it is necessary for human beings to respond individually and consciously to these changes. This is where we find "mass production competence".' (Tsuji, 1999: 117). First, let me clarify this kind of skill.

Conceptually, you can divide labour into qualitative and quantitative aspects. Skill is required to respond to the former and for the latter you need endurance. As I made clear in the previous chapter, you need to be able to endure the burden of a considerable workload to perform standardized tasks. Consequently, the capacity formed through this kind of work is not skill but endurance. Of course, that is not to say that there is absolutely no need to consider quality in the performance of standardized tasks.

Assembly line workers are required to maintain a high level of quality while working at a fast pace. But it is important to note here that the capacity to produce high quality products of this kind is quite different from the skill artisans needed to practice their craft in former days. Management has broken down the work to be performed into as many small, standardized tasks as possible. The production of high quality parts is no exception. It is simply a matter of having appropriate designated checking points on the line. To take the sub-assembly process as an example, only three spots are checked before the job is placed in a box. In the transport process there is just a check to see if the right cleaned-parts tray has been put into the chute correctly and with inspection/packing only those points specified in the 'quality check standard' are verified. As a result, the capacity to produce high quality parts in this context is not a creative skill, but a purely automatic processing technique. It is not the capacity to produce better products, but a way to intercept bad ones. So the attributes required are, dexterity to handle designated tasks rapidly, concentration to spot any malfunction and nervous tension to ensure no faulty parts get through. In short, we might say the ability needed is the one to cope with the ever-increasing intensity of the work to be performed.

In this fashion, while it is true that the requirement on the factory floor is to produce quality parts, we can also say that the work itself is not a skill corresponding to quality but rather a matter of endurance to produce quantity. Fundamentally, what is required in the performance of standardized work is not skill formation, but becoming accustomed to the strenuous workload. I would like to make this point abundantly clear from the outset.

Can we say then that skill formation has no part at all to play in standardized work?

When you actually experience work on the lines you come to realise that this is not necessarily so. Here I shall follow up this point, becoming accustomed to the workload, in the light of my own actual experience.

The process of embodiment

If you consciously analyse what happens from the time you have grasped a general mental understanding of a procedure, to the point where your body has become physically acclimatized to it, you come to understand that the task encapsulated in the expression 'embodiment' includes a deal of 'skill formation.'

When I first started in the factory I would consciously confirm in my mind each of the movements I made as I worked. In particular, when there was a range of different parts being produced, I found that it was easy to make mistakes unless you always keep in mind the variation among the parts. However, when you are paying very close attention to something as you work, your mind tends to become confused and it is extremely difficult to respond rapidly to a complicated range of variations. This contributes to the burden I discussed in the previous chapter. So, at the beginning, I felt as if my body was not able to keep up with my mind and that these two parts of me were functioning independently and out of synchronization. After about a month I came to feel that my mind and body had fused to the point where the body was able to react instantly to the directions from the brain. After I had spent a little more time getting used to the work, I was able to perform my duties without even being consciously aware of the variation in the parts. It reached the point where I did not need to pay any attention to what my hands were doing and I even had time to think about other things as I worked. At this stage the actions processed in the brain become 'embodied' and it responds subconsciously to the variation in the parts.

Let us now consider how this embodiment applies to the sub-assembly process. When I first started work in this area I consciously concentrated my attention on the differences between the parts I was handling. I would be constantly confirming the alternation of parts, repeating to myself in my head, 'medium capacity parts before high capacity parts.' The assembly assistant separates the assembled medium capacity parts and high capacity parts and puts them in separate boxes.

You might think that the variation in the parts would not be much of a concern in such as simple process. But to carry out the work as quickly and accurately as possible, you need to be constantly aware of these differences. If you let your mind wander for a second you can forget which type of part you are holding. In this case you have to consciously check and that means a loss of time every time you look down. You can easily fall behind schedule through a small slip like this. I carried out this task constantly reminding myself 'medium capacity part followed by high capacity part,' but the conscious effort to remember tensed up my body and made it impossible for me to work any faster. There was no way I could complete the process in the allocated *takt* time. So, in my case, I was moved out of the assistant assembly job into another position on the line.

In the cleaning round, however, I was able to move on to the next stage. The most taxing aspect of this job is the requirement to distinguish twenty different parts and place them correctly into the chute. It is particularly important not to confuse medium capacity and high capacity engine parts. For some time after I started this work, I concentrated intensely, determined not to make any mistakes, but the reality is that it is impossible to maintain such a high level of concentration continuously for eight hours on end. You become exhausted and your mind is such a blur that you cannot even remember what you were doing just seconds before. After returning the empty trays to the parts-storage chute, I move to place the same kind of tray onto the trolley, but realise I've forgotten how many and what kind of tray I have returned. I take a rough guess at how many new trays I should send on for cleaning and then discover that the number of boxes does not match. For a while I frequently made little mistakes like this.

But the mistakes decreased markedly after about a month. I had probably become more conscious about product quality, but there was also another reason behind this change. The quality of my work had improved. While I had previously had to consciously concentrate to avoid making mistakes, I found that gradually I came to be able to detect any mistakes intuitively. For example, if I happened to put a tray into the chute the wrong way around, at that very instant I would suddenly get a feeling that something was wrong. I had developed the skill of unconsciously monitoring for errors and the number of mistakes dropped as a result.

The other casual workers who started at the same time as I did, told me that they had also gradually achieved a level of fusion of body and mind that enabled them to work more efficiently. In all their cases too, this process took something over a month. Young Naganuma (18 years old), who was in the same group as me, said after two months that he could do his job in his sleep (5 October). Kakegawa (25) said it took him more than a month before he could complete his task in the allocated *takt* time. Yamano (35) said the same thing. Apparently Yamano's job is even more complicated than the sub-assembly process on our line. He has to make split-second decisions more often because of the greater variety of parts he is required to assemble. He takes the jobs as they come along in order on the conveyor belt and assembles, either, six, four or two parts onto them. To make matters worse, there are also some jobs that do not require any additional parts at all. The information about which part to attach to which job is conveyed on a *kanban* that comes along on the conveyor belt with the job. Yamano says that if you think too hard about each part as you do the assembly work, you gradually reach the stage where you cannot tell one part from another and you end up in a panic.

Moreover, since, unlike ours, his is a conveyor-belt assembly line, if you cannot finish your assembly task within the *takt* time allowed you bring the whole line to a halt. In Yamano's words, 'You are under constant pressure not to be a burden to your workmates. So no matter what, you have to get your speed up to par. But even so, it still took me almost two months before I could do the job without thinking' (14 September). Then he went on to explain, 'Once the movement of my hands had become almost a conditioned reflex, I found I would either think about nothing at all, or think about food. So sometimes I would have no recollection at all of a whole work session. Lately, I can't even remember what I assembled just moments before. That's just how unconscious my movements have become. Now, I find myself suddenly brought back to reality when someone else's mistake stops the assembly line' (29 September).

Yamano tells me he finds it irritating when other worker's mistakes bring the line to a halt, because it breaks up the rhythm of the work and any lost production simply means more overtime work. He also thinks that part of the problem might be that the stoppage is a rude awakening from his daydreams. 'Until I got used to the work I would be concentrating so hard that the time passed very quickly, but once I got the hang of it time seemed drag. I'd think a long time had passed, but when I looked at the clock it had hardly moved since I last glanced at it. I'd be overwhelmed by fatigue. To take my mind off the time I would consciously try to think of other things. So to be suddenly jerked out of my flights of fantasy meant that I had to start all over again enduring the long, boring labour' (*ibid*).

Individual work method

In the previous chapter I wrote that line workers do not deal with 'abnormalities,' but close observation reveals that this is not always entirely true. Line workers do, in their own way, deal with abnormalities.

The sub-assembly process workers attach parts onto the job that flows along the line to them. They repeat the same movement over and over again. But even though the type of part may be the same, not every job is absolutely identical and the part they attach to it is not exactly the same. Sometimes the job may have been manufactured with a slight imperfection, or the part to be assembled onto it may have rough edges. Invariably, irregular, 'unexpected' parts of this kind crop up. Workers just beginning in this job cannot deal with these cases within the prescribed *takt* time so the line is interrupted and time is lost. However, as they get used to the job, they learn the techniques required to cope with these irregularities within the *takt* time. They handle 'abnormalities' on the job without interrupting the flow of the production line.

Let me give you an example. When I was working as an assembly assistant I had to carry out the extremely simple procedure of picking up three small gears in one hand and placing them on a stand. Sometimes the three gears would get stuck together and it was quite difficult to separate them. These were not faulty parts, but there had been some slight irregularity in the manufacturing process. Nevertheless, when this occurred it was impossible to handle the gears with one hand. I had to pull them apart with both hands before putting them onto the cleaning plate. Of course, it took longer to use two hands and this increased the time of the cycle. As I mentioned above, our line was not of the conveyor-belt type, so the work did not stop, but any delay meant the assembly worker was kept waiting. As I gradually became more accustomed to the work, however, I found that even if the gears were stuck together I could separate them with one hand.

Workers on the assembly line come to be able to cope with changes and avoid stoppages in production by training their bodies in this way. Only the worker concerned is aware of the irregularity. Those working nearby have no idea that anything is amiss. So, in this context, strictly speaking, coping with the 'unexpected' means taking action to prevent irregularities from coming to the surface. Either way, it is true to say that assembly line workers do respond to abnormalities within the repetitive tasks they perform.

In addition, whether they are dealing with abnormalities or not, workers on the assembly line devise their own individual ways of working. It is virtually impossible to endure the extraordinary pace required for eight hours if you follow the 'standard work' guidelines. So workers do whatever they can to lighten their burden by devising their own original work method.

Let us consider an example from the inspection and packing section. Actually, it is impossible to check thoroughly each of the spots specified within the allocated *takt* time of eight seconds. Even so, the number of points to be checked seems to increase daily. Given that the time allocated remains unchanged, adding more tasks increases the intensity of the work. Workers desperately try to do whatever they can to lighten their load. This struggle results in the creation of individual work strategies for checking. It is difficult to put these new methods into words, but if we take an analogy, it might be like winding the clock backwards on working methods from our present digital technology to the earlier analogue system. For example, by developing the ability to detect any irregularities by taking in the whole object in a single glance, rather than checking each of the spots individually.

In this way, workers on the assembly line were able to perform their work faster by recombining processes management had subdivided into minimal components.

In the early stages, workers try to increase their production speed by mastering the standardized work practices as quickly as possible, but in the end they perform even faster and with greater accuracy by incorporating their own methods. No matter where they are on the assembly line, workers inevitably devise their own individual ways of doing their work.

In the previous chapter, I mentioned that standardized labour demands the ability to endure a strenuous workload. But if we carefully monitor their process of acclimatization we can see how assembly line workers too acquire a kind of 'skill' in their adaptation to the workload.[5] Thus we can say that this finding supports the research of Tsuji and others. But if we look more closely we see that on a number of points it differs from previous research.

Firstly, there is the question of the level of skill. Tsuji explains this kind of skill as follows.

> This kind of fine-tuning cannot be realized without a human mental process. People engaged in the work learn through experience that machines do not function rationally. Human beings strive to detect any change in the work process before it happens by staying alert and mobilizing the combined forces of all five senses. If we use the term 'intellectual skill' for the mental labour workers perform in order to ensure that, 'next time will be the same as this,' then clearly there is a considerable proportion of 'intellectual skill' in routine work (Tsuji, 1999: 117).

But, in my case, the opposite was true, in that I acquired skill by excluding the intellect altogether. I 'physically' devised my own work method to cut down on the tiny amounts of time lost in making judgments about change or being confused by abnormalities. So this type of skill is a physically acquired capability, not an intellectual skill as Tsuji claims.

Secondly, there is a difference in the way skill is evaluated. Take the following quote from Tsuji.

> Certainly, any adjustments made are minute, but when you are dealing with a level of accuracy that demands tolerances of one micron, neglecting to make an appropriate response means you end up accumulating a mountain of faulty products (*ibid*).

Tsuji's argument is an extension of Fukuyama's concept of 'skill,' but I really wonder whether workers like Fukuyama make up the majority of employees in automobile factories. Fukuyama had, in his own words, 'moved on, from mass production work of preliminary drilling and pre-processing of axle rings in a small local workshop, to a major automobile manufacturer, where I was engaged until my retirement in the mass manufacture of cog wheels for gears' (Fukuyama, 1998: 121). He has been closely involved with grinding process work and holds a first-class certified skilled worker's license for a numerically controlled lathe. I do not deny that there are some workers like Fukuyama on the factory floor, but I don't think the majority of workers are expected to meet 'one micron' accuracy. The work itself, if you exclude the speed element, is a basic task that could be performed by anyone. But even the simplest task becomes difficult if it has to be performed at extraordinarily high speed. In our workplace the question of quality has nothing whatever to do with how accurately something is made. It is nothing more than a matter of the speed of production. So you certainly cannot say that the level of 'skill' required to meet that requirement is of a particularly high order.

This fact is reflected in the age structure of workers. Almost all the employees on the assembly line are under thirty. Let us look at the sub-assembly process for example. The workers are eighteen, nineteen, twenty-two and thirty-two. On the opposite shift, too (assembly assistant included) they are; nineteen, twenty-one, twenty-two, twenty-three, twenty-five and twenty-six.

You would expect to see older, more experienced workers on the line if there really were a high level of skill required. In our workplace, the need was not for accumulated expertise, but for those qualities in which younger workers – the younger the better – excel. That is to say, we needed strength, speed, concentration and endurance.[6] I think it is difficult to claim that assembly line workers need the kind of high-level skills that are acquired over a long time through accumulated experience.[7]

My third point concerns the evaluation of the worker's 'skill' in controlling the labour process. Previous research has pointed out that this skill can lead to, not only a consciousness of the company or corporation, but also to a professional craftsman consciousness.

> Re-evaluations of this kind tend to indicate the need, when considering worker consciousness, to move the emphasis away from consciousness of the corporation or company alone, to a separate professional consciousness or job consciousness, which may at times cause tensions, or be in conflict, with the company (Tsuji, 1998: 119).

I shall confine myself to a few brief remarks here, as I shall be dealing with this point in detail in the next chapter. Assembly line workers also have something of a sense of professionalism and a commitment to their work. But their commitment is not the kind that may cause tension or conflict with management. On the contrary, it tends to take the form of a sense of responsibility for their work, which is very much in harmony with the principles of management. In fact, the acquisition of this 'skill' makes it easier for the worker to be drawn willy-nilly deeper into management thinking. The workers themselves devise their own individual working methods (what we have been calling 'skill' formation) to lighten their burden a little and escape the pressure of unreasonably rapid production, but in so doing, they are complying with intensification of work.

Seen in this way, assembly line workers certainly do acquire abilities that we may call 'skill' through performing their normal standardized work. But this is quite a different kind of 'skill' from that alluded to in previous research. I repeat. The ability to stand up to the workload is practically the only capacity demanded of assembly-line workers. They have to develop 'skill' to lighten this load. Originally, the term 'skill' was applied to the capacity to produce quality and not to that required to produce quantity. In this respect, it is indeed very doubtful whether we can properly use the term 'skill' for the kind of abilities assembly-line workers acquire.[8] Rather, shouldn't we be focusing our attention on the fact that the extraordinary assembly-line speed required, is forcing workers to develop this kind of 'skill' whether they like it or not?

Skill required in fine-tuning between manufacturing processes

As I mentioned in the last chapter, workers not only carry out the work to which they have been assigned, but also make minor adjustments between manufacturing processes. Fundamentally, the capacity required to carry out this task is also the ability to withstand the workload, but certain kinds of 'skill' are also required. One of these is the capacity to comprehend the flow of parts. Another is the ability to communicate. We might also describe this as the ability to regulate human relationships. But neither of these abilities could be called high-level skills. With the former, it is simply a matter of learning the flow of parts then just letting your feet and nerves do the rest. There is no particular need to have a detailed knowledge of the manufacturing process or the workings of the machine. Moreover, most workers make no attempt to do anything if the line comes to a halt. In reality, they just wait for directions from the team leader or a supervisor. For the latter, the communication skill they need does not really go beyond what we use in our everyday lives. Of course, it all depends on the point of comparison, but, for example, they do not need the special kinds of 'communication skills' or negotiating ability required for dealing with customers. Fine-tuning between work processes is really more just a matter of being alert and considerate. At best, we could say that this 'skill' is not entirely absent from the factory floor.

Skill acquired in career building

Workers on the assembly line undertake, not only their fixed work, but also unscheduled work (dealing with change or abnormalities), *kaizen* activities and QC circles. They also experience a variety of jobs through the system of rotation. Through this work they acquire a high level of skill, comprising 'intellectual skills' (Koike, 1982 etc.), 'organizational skills' (Yumoto, 1989–90), 'social skills' (Tsuji, 1989) – the ability to systematically grasp the manufacturing process as a whole, the ability to improve the process and the ability to organise workers.

Workers on the line gradually develop these skills as they carve out their careers[9] with the company. Since the 1980s the argument stressing the importance of skill has been almost universally accepted. Let us consider, then, the acquisition of skill in the process of career building.[10]

There is no need for me to reiterate here in detail how skill is developed in dealing with what previous research has labelled 'change' and the 'unexpected.' As I explained in the last chapter, dealing with change and abnormalities falls within the range of normal standardized work for virtually all assembly-line workers. We have already identified the kinds of skills developed in this way. What then of the skill formed in off-line activities and in job rotation?

After work, or on their days off, workers have to think up two proposals, a creative suggestion and a safety proposal. The reality in our factory was that many of the workers reluctantly threw together their proposals just before, or even after, the closing date, after being prompted to do so by those above. It was, you might say, work cobbled together at the last minute. You cannot possibly imagine these proposals contributing anything to skill formation.

QC Circles can, on occasion, provide an opportunity for skill formation. I myself learned a lot through QC circles. In my case, since my goal was to observe the workplace, I rubbed the sleep out of my eyes and participated positively in the sessions. Most of the other workers, however, considered participation in QC Circles a burden only tolerated because it brought them a little overtime pay.

Perhaps the situation could be tolerated if the QC sessions were held in normal working hours. But from the point of view of one who has had to sit there shivering at three o'clock in the morning participating in a QC Circle, there is a very empty ring to the claim that this is contributing to skill formation.

If introduced properly, both the proposal system and QC Circles could indeed tie in with skill formation, but in our workplace it is very difficult to say that they provided us with any such opportunity.[11]

That leaves only job rotation to provide opportunities for skill formation. Job rotation is part of our everyday routine in this workplace, but it has no educational motivation and is not aimed at increasing workers' skills. In our group it is all we can do to meet our daily quotas, let alone take on the additional burden of planned job rotation for training purposes. In other groups, too, circumstances demand that even the group leaders join in on the production line. They just do not have the time to worry about staff training, which should naturally be their prime responsibility. So, it is also very hard to think of job rotation contributing to skill formation in this workplace.

As far as I have been able to judge from my actual experience working on the factory floor, I cannot agree with the claims of previous research that high levels of skill are attained. But it is no doubt possible that workers develop certain types of 'skill' gradually as they advance in their careers. Perhaps, with experience accumulated on the factory floor, they come to learn, little by little, those skills that management requires of them.[12]

In that case, firstly, what is the probability of upward progression for general factory employees? And secondly, what precisely is the connection and degree of continuity between the abilities formed by general workers and the skills that are required higher up the ladder? In the following section I would like to consider the 'skill' assembly-line workers may perhaps acquire in the course of career progression by clarifying the connections and continuities, both qualitatively and quantitatively.

Possibilities for promotion

What is the likelihood of promotion for general workers? A glance at our group's organizational chart reveals that, as at 5 November, we have one group leader, three section leaders and eighteen general workers. This gives some idea how difficult it is to move up into a managerial position.

Moreover, if you look more closely, it becomes clear that not all managers are involved in supervising work on the factory floor. Essentially, only a limited number of leaders control the on-site work. Let us turn our attention to the team leaders to demonstrate that this is indeed the case.[13]

In our workplace it was basically the team leader who ran the show. Our team leader, Nagata, had joined the company straight after graduating from high school in Saga prefecture. He is now thirty-two years old and in his fourteenth year of service. While the majority of workers on our line had been assigned to start in July, he had been here since May participating in the set-up of the line. I heard from Nagata himself that when our group leader, Morita, moved to another group on 1 October, he entrusted the running of our line to Nagata.

The real authority for the every-day running of our line was in the hands of the team leader rather than with higher bottom-end management. The two young section leaders spent a lot of their time on the line and their daily work was not all that different from ours. Those above treat the bottom-end management and the team leader differently. It was not only the group leader, but also the chief leader and the section head who treated Nagata as one of the next generation of leaders. Whenever anything went wrong he was the one they consulted, not the section leaders. Nagata himself does not seem to feel that he has any special authority, just a little more responsibility than the rest of us. But we general workers see him as an elite company man. He had been chosen as the theme leader for our QC Circle and he had been involved in large-scale *kaizen* activities. It is not as if these opportunities are made equally available to all workers. Nagata is not management, but a limited number of workers like him are given the authority to control the day to day running of the line. Thus we can see a big difference in the management structure between the real leaders who wield the actual authority and the bottom-end managers.

I came to understand that, while all of them appeared to be progressing upward in the same way, there were differences from one managerial role to another. That is to say, gaining real authority is more important in skill formation, than acquiring formal titles. In this regard, one certainly cannot say that the possibilities for ordinary workers to advance to managerial positions are high. The odds are even lower if we are talking about the possibility of holding actual authority on the shop floor.

You could not say, judging from the present situation, that there is much upward career mobility for most workers. Even if you make it to section leader, the skills you have are no more than a simple summation of the experiences gained below. Of course, it is not inconceivable that workers competing for the few posts available raise the skill levels as a whole, but in our workplace there was little evidence for that interpretation. With the exception of a very small number of individuals, like our team leader, Nagata, I got the feeling that workers lacked the motivation to go that far.[14] To date, most researchers have overlooked the fact that there is considerable variation in the authority of managers. They have also grossly overvalued the possibility of upward progression. I wonder, perhaps, if this is not why they also overestimate the level of skill learnt through experience working on the factory floor.

Continuity of skill

Perhaps you are wondering whether our team leader, Nagata, has actually worked in all the jobs in our workplace. He has not. Quite the contrary, he has experienced hardly any of them. He has not even done inspection/packing or the cleaning round, let alone the sub-assembly operation. I just recall that he asked me a question about the cleaning round just before I left the company.

25 September (Tuesday)
    Today Nagata learnt about the shipment process from Maejima (12 years experience) and also tried his hand at the diff. The idea was to give him a basic mastery of these processes as our group leader, Morita, and our section leader, Yamashita, will be leaving at the end of this month.

Nagata is allowed to work for short periods on a number of different tasks to gain an understanding of the line as a whole. He is in charge of the daily running of the line and improvement of the workplace as a whole, in spite of the fact that he himself has had hardly any experience performing the tasks concerned.[15]

Clearly then, it is authority, not experience gained through work on the line, that is needed to shape the capacities management requires. The ones who have the opportunity to build and apply these skills are those who have been given the authority to do so, not those who have accumulated experience working on the production line. It is not as if the capacity to become a manager or a factory foreman is automatically created through long experience on the line. The managers undergo quite separate, intensive education, including 'off-the-job training.'[16] It is clear from this that there is a considerable gap between the abilities *required* of managers and team leaders and the abilities *formed* through work on the factory floor.

However, of course, I do not want to entirely deny a link between accumulated work experience and skill formation. Merely in mastering a number of different processes, even if it is rather like playing musical chairs, undoubtedly you achieve a certain degree of skill. But skill formation is not the main purpose of this work practice[17] and the skills thus acquired are certainly not of a high level.

Further, those arguments that only emphasise the relationship between accumulated work experience and skill formation, ultimately result in justification of the harsh assembly-line labour. Even if we accept, for the case of argument, that experience on the line leads to the formation of the kinds of skills required in a supervisor, there is no reason why workers should have to suffer over ten years of hard labour on the line to develop those. If the only aim were to build those capabilities there would be less onerous and quicker ways of doing so. The fact that we have team leaders illustrates the validity of this assertion. Any appraisal of skill formation in the workplace, should, I feel, be based on a re-examination within the context of the shop floor and not on slavish adherence to earlier analytical frames.

Summary: The evaluation of skill

In this chapter we have been looking at two kinds of skill – that formed through daily work and that acquired in the course of building one's career – interwoven with my own experiences working in the factory. To sum up, assembly line workers do not conform to the frequently cited stereotype of unskilled labourers. Even after the demise of traditional skilled craftsmen, skill did not disappear completely from the factory floor. Assembly-line workers also needed, to a certain extent to have skills – the ability to grasp the manufacturing process as a whole, the ability to improve that process and the ability to organise workers. This aspect of factory labour was given little attention in the research of the 1960s and

1970s. But the situation has been largely redressed since the 1980s. If anything, I feel that perhaps since the 1980s there had been an overemphasis on the concept of skill without sufficient attention being paid to its limitations. In this chapter I have tried to analyse this point in the light of my own experience.

4 Worker 'Autonomy'

In any workplace the reality is that there is never complete control over every move workers make. A degree of worker autonomy is exercised. It has been continually claimed that Toyota workers are given a particularly high level of autonomy through the system of QC Circles, *kaizen* activities and on-site management. Moreover, it is said that opportunities to exercise worker autonomy have increased in recent years with the policy of easing back on automation.

Previous research on autonomy can be seen to fall into two broadly differing assessments. On the one hand there is the positive evaluation that this is a humane system sympathetic to the needs of workers.[1] On the other hand we see the negative view that worker autonomy is nothing more than a way to win over workers into accepting management logic through 'participation.'[2]

However, I do not wish to imply that all previous research espouses only one of these views. Individual researchers develop their arguments in recognition of the fact that both of these aspects exist in the 'Toyota Production System.' This can be seen in the assessments that, despite the insistence that they themselves promote rationalization of production, Toyota workers find that through participation their work becomes easier, they are more committed, they gain mental satisfaction and in some cases even have their own concerns addressed.[3] Certainly, I get the feeling that there is more substance in recent research compared with the former studies that emphasise only one of these two aspects.

However, these studies invariably do not go beyond pointing out the logical possibility of the existence of these two sides of the question. It would be difficult to say that they adequately explain how these two aspects of autonomy actually co-exist on the factory floor. What needs to be clarified is, so to speak, whether the negative or positive aspects have the upper hand and in what form the two poles combine. How can we avoid arbitrary interpretations and properly understand this relationship?

I believe the way to do it is to focus our attention on control over workloads, the point where the two aspects meet. Do workers exercise autonomy to control their workloads, or are they obliged to contribute to work intensification by participating in the evolution of the system? Or are they merely participating in rationalization of a type that does not bring about change in workloads? I think we can reduce the range of interpretations by considering the process and conclusions in the light of what actually happens in the workplace.

In this chapter, I shall clarify the realities of worker autonomy as it is exercised through daily work, *kaizen* activities and on-site management. In addition, I shall seek to explain the workings of autonomy and control and the relationship between the two.

Worker autonomy on the factory floor

The cause of fluctuations in product quotas

Raising the speed of production

As I explained in the previous chapter, when assembly-line employees first start work they follow the standard work procedures, but gradually incorporate their own individual methods. As the speed on the line is fixed, workers try to give themselves a little breathing space by lifting their work-rate by introducing their own methods.

The principal reason why workers on the line try to lift their work speed is to create a time buffer to reduce the physical stress they have to bear. But that is not the only reason. They are also under mental pressure from their workmates and superiors. Newly recruited employees are not accepted as fully-fledged workers until they can perform their tasks within the specified *takt* time. While they are learning the ropes other workers tend to give them the cold shoulder. In my case too, when I had just started as an assistant on the sub-assembly process I continually felt that my co-workers were rejecting me. So in my own way I desperately tried to devise my own way to lift my speed so that my fellow workers would not think I was a no-hoper or a burden to them. Later, when I had more or less got the knack of the job I continued for other reasons to work on polishing my technique.

In the factory there are often two or more workers doing the same job and inevitably a sense of competition develops. The individual techniques workers develop to help them work faster are often driven by a desire not to be beaten by a workmate. I am not the only one affected by this sense of competition. Everybody on this shop floor has it. The competitive impulse is fanned to a particularly high temperature in tasks like the sub-assembly process where workers are sitting side by side in a row. I often heard my workmates on sub-assembly commenting that so-and-so was just a beginner if he was still doing it in such and such a way, or so-and-so has finally learnt this or that technique.

There is also competition between workers on different shifts. Take the case of my contemporary, young Naganuma. He was in competition with Murayama on the opposite shift over who could assemble the greater number of jobs. I often saw him gleefully reporting to Murayama on the change-over between shifts that he had created a new record.

In the same way, Yada who was working in inspection and packing harboured a strong sense of rivalry *vis à vis* his colleagues. Apparently, he particularly disliked being beaten by the regular employees and he would compete with them, especially Kawakami (8 years' service) on speed of operation. I knew very well how he felt. When it came to the regular employees, most of us casual workers either had a sense of inferiority or antipathy towards them. I dare say Kawakami also rose to the challenge. When the two of them were working together the speed was even faster than usual. Unless there was some major problem, when they were sitting alongside one another they always finished on time. This demonstrates how the relationships between workers on the factory floor can be a factor in raising the speed of production.

It was the same story on the cleaning round. Gradually the work took on the feel of a game with me raising the speed of product delivery to urge on the section leader from behind. What's more, and I often felt it strange myself, even though no-one was pushing me to do so, I found I was unconsciously driving myself to greater effort. Perhaps at the back of my mind there was the feeling that since the quota was set I would have to make up any shortfall with extra overtime work. I found that if I concentrated hard on the job the time seemed to pass more quickly and I was less conscious of how tired I was. So, even when you are working alone, you strive to get through your work faster.

Ignoring the function of the *kanban*
So, as we have seen, workers can gain a little time for themselves, trifling though it may be, by raising the speed of production to produce a build-up of finished products. For Yamano, working on the

assembly process on a conveyor belt, this means working flat out to gain just a second or two and Kimata on machining strives to make up two or three seconds so he can relax and draw breath. By creating time for themselves in this way they are able to exert a modicum of control over the rhythm of the work. Besides, it is probably true to say that it is easier for workers on tasks like the cleaning round, where you are not directly controlled by a machine, to exercise 'autonomy' by creating variations in the volume of items processed.

But regardless of the task to which they are assigned, workers cannot reduce the absolute volume of their output. If a worker on the cleaning round were to place a cleaning tray straight into the cleaned-items chute without first putting it though the cleaning process, this would probably be picked up by the person in inspection and packing. This makes it virtually impossible for the worker on the cleaning round to reduce the absolute volume required. But it is possible to cut corners without reducing the quantity produced. On the cleaning round, by carrying a lot of trays at one time it is possible to cut down the number of trips you have to make and reduce the burden on your legs. It is difficult to do this when you have just started in the job as management is watching you constantly and the slightest pause in the flow brings a prompt reprimand.

When I was working with the section leader, when even one of the trays that don't go through the cleaning machine (the medium and high capacity front units and the rear units) was returned to the cleaned item chute I had to go and get it and replace it with a new tray. With those trays that go through the cleaning machine, I had to clean four trays at a time, so I had to wait for four trays to accumulate before I could return them to the spare-parts storage chute. That meant, for those trays that did not go into the cleaning machine, that I had to make a complete circuit for just one tray. But later when I was working in tandem with another worker we were able to let a certain number of these empty trays build up before carrying them across all together.

After some time I was also able to add another technique to my armoury. Even though the parts might not yet have arrived in the spare-parts storage chute, when an empty tray has been brought back from the following process you have to put it back into the cleaned-items chute. If you don't do that it throws the number of parts held in interim storage out of sync. When I was working with the section leader I faithfully followed this rule. But, when I was working with another worker we would not return the empty trays to the chute one at a time, but pile them up beside the parts storage chute. Then, as soon as a new part came along, we would send the pile of trays along on the parts storage chute and put the new part through the cleaning process. By doing this we were able to avoid the trouble of doing the same thing twice and at the same time to go about our transport work without worrying about the progress of the previous process, i.e. whether or not the new parts had arrived.

In the end I was completely ignoring the operation manual procedure. I transported the trays in a haphazard fashion and then, just before the end of the day's operation, I would make up any shortfall. As there is a fixed number of parts placed in the cleaned items chute as interim storage, I would make sure the correct number of parts was there just before I finished work. By handling the operation this way I was able to work without the nervous strain of worrying about the situation of the supply of parts from the previous process and by cutting down on the number of trips I needed to make I greatly reduced the distance I had to walk in a day.

21 August (Wednesday)
I've hurt a tendon in my left leg. But I can't take any time off for such a minor injury. I worked trying to put as little strain as possible on the left leg. Consequently, I managed to keep the distance I walked down to 14,000 paces compared with my normal load of around 18,000. There was no change in the number of parts transported, but a considerable reduction in the distance covered.

If you are working with an understanding partner you can also gain time by going to the toilet. I had a number of regular partners who would cooperate in this way. Apparently they used to have a smoke in the toilet. You couldn't do it with assembly tasks, but with certain jobs it was not impossible to gain some 'autonomy' through developing a cooperative relationship with your workmates on the same job.

Participation in the setting-up and evolution of a production line

Not only the specialists from the Production Technology Department, but also workers from the factory floor participate in the setting up of a production line. Moreover, once the line has been established it continues to evolve in the hands of the on-site workers. It has been said that the source of Toyota's competitive superiority lies in this 'bottom-up' approach in the workplace. Let us now consider how this really works.

'Participation' in the setting up of a production line

As I have mentioned before, our line was set up in January 2001. At that time the only member of our group who participated in the set-up was the group leader Morita. In May the section leaders Shiraishi and Yamashita and the team leader Nagata joined him. The other employees only started working in July when the line had begun operating in earnest.

I did not know exactly how they had participated in the setting up of the line because it was already up and running by the time I joined the company. So when I asked Nagata about it, he explained that Morita had been involved in the overall setting up of the line and that he, Nagata, and two workers from the opposite shift had been engaged in honing the detail of the inspection and packing line.

Once at our morning meeting I heard a story that went more or less as follows. It seems that the day before, when group leader Morita had been inspecting one of our subcontractors, he noticed in that particular factory they did not have a separate inspection unit as we do, but that each individual worker had the responsibility to check the quality of the product. And based on what he had seen there he indicated that in future we might change the configuration of our line. Somehow it seemed that when our line was set up, it had been Morita himself who had proposed an independent inspection unit. As far as I could tell from his reputation on the factory floor, Morita was extremely brilliant and stood head and shoulders above the other group leaders, but it seems there were also other on-site suprevisors who, like Morita, had been involved in the overall setting up of the line.

Without having anyone instruct him to do so, Nagata, the team leader, voluntarily created a standard procedures manual for the inspection and packing line.

Links to the 'evolution' of the production line

The merit of *kaizen* activities comes to the fore after the line has been established. Let us look at the improvement plan for the cleaning round as an example of what I mean. I understand from Nagata that a comprehensive proposal for improvements on the cleaning round is currently, as of September 2001, before the division council. Apparently there is a debate going on over whether the extremely heavy labour load of the cleaning round should be reduced by automating the transport of parts from the cleaning machine to the cleaned-items chute. The question was asked whether it is economically feasible to introduce improvements of this kind. To which the reply was that a certain level of economic investment could be justified on the grounds that the line had just been established and that this workplace had been designated as one giving high priority to improvement. The improvement proposal had been the brainchild of our group leader, Morita. We do not know yet whether this proposal will be implemented, but, nevertheless, the line is constantly evolving through *kaizen* activities of this kind. Let us now take a detailed look at the small-scale improvements suggested for the cleaning round.

I learnt from our section leader that improvements had been made to the parts-storage chute just before I was assigned to the workplace. To make it easier for the transport worker from the previous process to deliver new trays, the parts-storage chute was inclined slightly inwards, i.e. towards the following process. But with this configuration the transport worker would sometimes overestimate the strength required and place the tray so that it was overhanging the end of the chute.

To correct this, a stopper was placed at the end of the chute (seen from my side, the end from which the trays were removed). The problem with this was that the stopper made it more difficult for the trays to be taken off the chute. When a number of the heavy trays of parts built up on the chute, the front tray would become tightly wedged between the stopper and the next tray. So they tried adding a further improvement. By using a slippery steel material for the stopper they were able to prevent the overshooting problem and at the same time make it easier to remove trays from the chute.

A succession of small improvements like this continued to be made even after I joined the group. Here they are in order of introduction.

20 August (Monday)

Three giant refrigerator units have been installed in the packing area. With these we can rapidly cool the parts that have been heated in the cleaning process. Up until now, the inspection and packing workers have had to wait twenty or thirty minutes before handling parts from the cleaned-parts chute. From now on they will not have such a long wait before they can start working on the parts.

24 August (Friday)

Minor changes have been made to the cleaned-parts chute and the packing chute. The positions of the drive-pin (medium capacity) chute and the front-ring (medium capacity) chute have been reversed. Formerly, inspection and packing workers would sometimes make the mistake of placing the box they had just packed onto the chute next to them, so that boxes with medium capacity drive-pins in them ended up in the medium capacity front-ring chute.

In spite of the fact that we have packing boxes with and without lids, both these parts are packed into boxes with lids. So once the items are packed you can't tell whether or not you've put a box into the wrong chute. If you had parts in boxes without lids alongside different parts in boxes with lids, even if a box were placed in the wrong chute, someone would notice it before it reached the final shipping stage. So the chutes were swapped over as I mentioned above. In addition, the positions on the cleaned-items chute were changed to accommodate the changes in the packing chute. These minor innovations were part of the overall strategy aimed at entirely eliminating shipment of faulty or incomplete products.

28 August (Tuesday)

They have made a stand next to the parts-storage chute where I can pile up cleaning trays for the high capacity engine parts and another in front of the cleaned-parts chute for those parts (rear and front units) that don't go through the cleaning process. It seems this idea came from our group leader, Morita and Nagata, the team leader. The effect of having these stands is largely just a matter of keeping the workplace neat and tidy. It would be difficult to find a manufacturing plant that is laid out as precisely and in such an orderly fashion as our workplace is.

3 September (Monday)

A stand has been installed for the preliminary inspection of the rear units and front units. Before, we had to squat down to check the parts and this placed a considerable load on the legs and lower back. The addition of this stand now means that the preliminary inspection worker can place the cleaning tray containing the parts on the stand and remain standing as he checks the parts.

24 September (Monday)

Today a brake had been added to the assembly parts transport trolley. Until now if you wanted to keep the trolley still while you were loading it, you had to steady it with your hand.

16 October (Tuesday)

Our team leader Nagata, tells me they are considering improvements to the cleaning round trolley. The top section of the cleaned-parts chute (where the trays of parts are placed when they come out of the cleaning machine), is further divided into two shelves. The trays have to be lifted from the trolley up onto the top shelf of the chute and this places a considerable strain on the worker. So, apparently they are thinking of overcoming the problem by making it possible to raise or lower the height of the trolley. However, there have been some objections to this proposal from workers on the opposite shift. They say that the addition of the device needed to achieve this would make the trolley too heavy. What's more, budgetary considerations make the overall improvement of the cleaning round virtually impossible. I suspect that the plan for a complete overhaul of the cleaning round has been rejected so they have changed their thinking in favour of low cost improvements to the trolley.

29 October (Monday)

There were two points of improvement today. The first concerns the removal of dust. By way of experiment we first tried spreading a vinyl plastic dustsheet under the divider (steel mesh) of the top half of the high capacity driven gear cleaned-parts chute. When you put a cleaning tray down on the top of the upper chute the vibration sends dust down onto the tray on the shelf below. Since dust and grit can lead to the production of faulty products, you must not allow dust to fall on the lower tray. To prevent this happening a roll of plastic was spread over the trays on the lower shelf. To date we have been using polystyrene foam sheets for this purpose, but this has proved to be inadequate. For a while no dust or grit falls through, but gradually the dust builds up on top of the polystyrene and little by little works its way through to the lower shelf. So, we replaced the fixed polystyrene sheets with plastic that could be rolled up so the dust could be removed at any time. This provides a glimpse of just how thoroughly committed they were to quality control.

The other improvement was with the transport trolley. The new trolley we have been hearing about for some time has finally appeared.

It seems they were made on order by Plant A. The finished product is not a trolley that can be raised or lowered at will, but simply one in which the height of the fixed platform has been raised. Certainly, this has reduced the distance between the top of the trolley and the top shelf of the chute, but now, conversely, the distance between the cleaning pallet and the trolley has increased, making it exceedingly difficult to lift the trays coming out of the cleaning machine onto the trolley. Further, since the lower shelf in the upper half of the chute is now lower than the top of the trolley, it is difficult to place the trays onto the shelf. In addition, to make it easier to slide the cleaning trays on and off the trolley, the platform has been surfaced with dimpled steel plate, but this has proved counter-productive as the trays tend to catch on the raised bumps.

The upshot of all of this was that the new trolley was returned to the storeroom and hardly ever used.

1 November (Thursday)

Today, once again a new trolley was delivered. The height of the platform had been returned to the height of the original 'un-improved' version. The dimples on the surface were smaller than they had been on the earlier prototype so the cleaning trays slid on and off easily. This meant that less effort was required to transfer the trays from the trolley to the chute. Improvements are achieved through this process of trial and error.

At this point I would like to move on to consider how management dealt with my own 'creative suggestion' and my 'safety proposal.'

20 September (Thursday)

This week I submitted my creative suggestion and my safety proposal to my supervisor. Not that there was anything in particular I wanted to improve, but since submitting proposals is compulsory I had to rack my brains to come up with something.

For my creative suggestion I wrote about the rail on the parts-storage chute. To reduce friction and make the trays containing new parts slide easily, the floor of the chute is formed by a sequence of parallel steel rollers rather than a single sheet of steel plate. Several times in the past when I had placed trays of high-capacity front units and rings from the previous process into the chute, the edge of the tray had caught in the space between the rods and the contents had spilled out onto the floor. Parts that fall on the floor go straight into the rubbish bin. So my proposal was to reduce the size of the gap by putting an additional steel roller between each pair of rollers.

For my safety proposal I wrote about the curtain over the entrance/ exit. The inspection and packing area is enclosed in clear plastic sheeting. Only the entrance-cum-exit is covered by a curtain made of strips of vinyl. The worker on the cleaning round has to weave his way through the gaps in this curtain when entering or leaving the area. There had been times when the curtain had brushed against the trays in transit, knocking the parts onto the floor. So I proposed that the curtain be modified in some way to prevent this from happening.

Today I got a response to these proposals from our group leader. In regard to my first suggestion he said that they were currently considering large-scale improvements to the chute, but in the meantime they would go ahead and install the additional rods as recommended. Already this afternoon, people have been over from the company that makes the chutes to check out the details of what is required. With the curtain, he explained, there were already three proposals under consideration. The first was to use a thinner, lighter curtain. The second was to have a larger number of narrower strips. The idea was that this would soften the impact so that even if the curtain brushed against the parts they would not fall on the floor. The third proposal was to have a sensor to automatically open the curtain when the transport worked approached.

11 October (Thursday)

Today I put in my creative suggestion and safety proposal. The former concerns transport for the sub-assembly process. To transport the differentials to the chute on the inspection and packing line you have to move the trolley along the rail in front of the chute from the left-hand edge then bring it up alongside the chute (figure 4.1, Before *kaizen*). But with the high-capacity engine parts there is no reason to go all the way to the left-hand end of the rail to place the parts into the chute. You can reduce the distance the transport worker has to travel by bringing the trolley in from the right. So I proposed that it would make sense to have the right-hand end of the rail open out to allow trolleys to enter from the right (Figure 4.1, After *kaizen*). I got an immediate reaction to this proposal. The rail was improved along the lines of my suggestion.

For my safety proposal I wrote that I would like something to cover my arms with. Sometimes, in placing the cleaning trays on the trolley or into the chute I get burns on my arms as they brush up against the

Figure 4.1: An example of kaizen

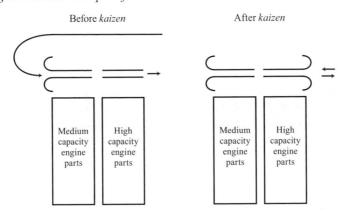

Before *kaizen*   After *kaizen*

I stress, as I have mentioned several times already, that ours was a new line just recently brought into operation and was regarded as a model production line. For this reason they were particularly keen to implement improvements.

In view of these rather special circumstances management was quick to react and most of the improvement proposals the general workers put forward were immediately adopted.

Autonomous workplace management

In some shape or another, variation and abnormalities are daily occurrences on the factory floor. People take annual leave, there is slowing of production, parts fail to come through from the previous process and so on. These occurrences are dealt with at the group level and generally do not require intervention from more senior management. I have no idea what our division head or the deputy division head look like, let alone the factory manager. I very occasionally saw our section head. The chief leader, I suppose, I saw about once a day, but even that was just as we exchanged greetings before work. Only when there was a particularly unusual variation in our routine, such as a spate of faulty products or an inspection by a VIP, would the section head and the chief leader set foot on the section floor. Despite the name, Production Engineering Division, the senior head was not aware of the details of actual conditions on the production line. Once a section head from the Production Engineering Division came to look at our workplace. I was amazed at the very elementary questions he was asking about the cleaning round. Each individual worksite, i.e. each process along the line, deals with change and abnormalities on a daily basis.

Flexibility in the workplace – the role of team leaders
The central figures on the factory floor are the bottom-end managers or supervisors, i.e. the group leader and the section leader. But they are not the only ones who run the show. On-site management could not happen without the team leaders. As I mentioned earlier, the term team leader is used to refer to young workers with initiative who show leadership in the workplace. It is not a formal position. They act between the supervisors and the general workers to ensure that on-site management runs smoothly. Whereas the group leader's role is to bring together the workplace as a whole, the team leader is involved with the detailed on-site management of individual work processes.

Nagata plays that role on the inspection and packing line. The group leader has put complete trust in him to take responsibility for the running of the line. There is a similar team leader on the opposite shift. From what I've heard from Segawa who joined with me, a young worker of twenty-one or twenty-two runs the whole show.

The team leader's most important 'job,' if you can call it that, is in the assignment of workers and the allocation of tasks. If someone is away on annual leave, another worker has to step in and fill his (or her) place. As a general rule, off-line workers step in to cover just the short periods line workers are on leave, but in reality it is usually a little more complicated than that.

Let us assume that two people are on leave from the inspection and packing line. One of them can be replaced by an off-line worker. But for the other, he asks for help from the sub-assembly process. So, an off-line worker and a worker from sub-assembly step into the inspection and packing line. In a case like this it is not simply a matter of making up the numbers, the team leader has to allocate positions and assign the tasks giving due consideration to how fast the newcomers work and how well they will cooperate with their fellow workers. Even when they are performing the same task, one worker who can perform it with time to spare might be given an extra job to do, while another whose work is slow might be paired with a more skilled operator. The group leader cannot be expected to keep track of all these details, so it falls to the task of the team leader to perform these duties.

Further, when something 'unexpected' happens the problem needs to be dealt with by those on the spot. Whenever there is a breakdown in a machine upstream or there are large quantities of faulty products coming out, the team leader has to make adjustments in the number and rate of products produced. Sudden emergencies of this kind are addressed through redeployment of personnel or increased overtime work, not by taking on additional staff.

When there is a delay in parts coming through from earlier processes, it is the team leader who goes to investigate the hold-up. If the problem looks as if it can be fixed within the day, he does what he can to reduce the amount of overtime by going upstream to fetch the needed parts himself. When he has to increase output in a certain area, he concentrates more people into that process and raises the speed of production. For example, when on the sub-assembly process there was a shortfall in the number of rear-end units produced, he increased the rate of production by allocating two workers to the task. Moreover he often also has to make minor adjustments to the daily deployment of personnel when, for example, one person might suffice for periods one and three, but two be necessary for periods two and four. Also, it is the team leaders, along with management, who carry the walkie-talkies for in-house radio communication. Whenever a problem occurs, they use these to keep in close touch with their counterparts up and down the line.

Whether or not there will be overtime work, and, if so, how long it will be, is also decided by the team leader. Since it is not a conveyor-belt system, the speed of the inspection and packing line varies considerably from one worker to another. Consequently, the team leader comes along about thirty minutes before the end of the regular working day, after monitoring the progress of each of the workers, to tell us if we need to work overtime. If it looks as if we are to reach our quota before the end of the day, we are instructed to carry out the 4S's procedure (*seiri, seiton, seiketsu, seisō*), i.e. making our workstation neat, tidy, hygienic and clean.

In addition, the team leader has to observe how workers are handling their tasks and fitting into the positions assigned to them and occasionally move them on to other areas if he feels they are not performing well. Young Nonaka, on a fixed-term contract like me, was first assigned to the inspection and cleaning process, but was then moved on to the cleaning round, then into sub-assembly and finally back into the cleaning round again. Our team leader Nagata told me he was moving him around to see where he was 'best suited.'

When Naganuma got a rash on his hands from the chemicals on a part he was assembling, he had himself transferred for a period to another sub-assembly process. In my case too, when I first started, the team leader told me several times that I should ask him if there was anything at all I didn't understand. Minor troubles on the shop floor are often solved in this way through the intervention of the team leader.

Mutual help in the workplace

The running of the assembly line is not solely dependent on the guidance of the team leader. It also relies on the spirit of mutual help between the workers themselves.

When I was first assigned to my position and my body had not yet adapted to the work, I was slow and soon fell behind. Takenaka (15 years experience), who was working on another task, noticed my predicament and came running over to help. When he saw that my work was beginning to run more smoothly he went back to his own position. This sort of thing occurred frequently.

Takenaka was my designated supervisor, but there were other workers at the same level as me who also gave me help. On the cleaning round it gets particularly busy just before knock-off time. You have to make fine adjustments such as letting workers upstream know if there are shortfalls in any particular part and giving priority to those parts that are taking longer to come down the line when feeding parts into the cleaning machine. Conversely, on the inspection and packing line the volume of work eases off as you approach finishing time. This is because the work winds down progressively as the day's quota for each part is met. Close to finishing time, they are either waiting for parts to cool down after the cleaning process, or waiting for the backlog of parts to come down the line to them. When this happened there were some workers in inspection and packing who would, of their own accord, come and help me with the cleaning-round transport.

By just before the end of my time at the factory, it had come to the point where workers from the inspection and packing line would regularly take it in turns to go and help make up any shortfall in production in the sub-assembly process. I should have gone to help too, but as I had only a short time left to go I didn't feel inclined to do so. It's not easy to learn a new task. So when my turn came around a couple of times I got Shiroki (8 years experience) to go instead. It would be difficult to run the operation without a degree of this sort of mutual help among workers.

Regulation of workload

In the previous section we saw how worker autonomy is actually played out in the workplace. Autonomy is exercised in a variety of spheres from daily work, through *kaizen* activities to workplace management. Let us now consider whether there is any connection between autonomy and the regulation of workloads.

Autonomy and the intensification of work

Autonomy promoting rationalization

There are two types of autonomy exercised in the course of normal daily work. One type is aimed at raising the speed of production. The other is the autonomy to ignore the function of the *kanban*. The former is exercised by workers, faced with the frantic speed of the production line, in an attempt to establish their own pace and buy a little time, no matter how infinitesimal, for themselves. But exercise of this kind of autonomy has the opposite effect to that intended and actually results in the worker losing time. If managers see that a worker has been able to create a little spare time, they will simply allocate part of somebody else's job to that worker. Take the sub-assembly process for example. This is an extremely simple task that involves picking up a gear in one hand. If you progressively go on assigning one part of that worker's job after another to a number of workers, then the original worker's job will eventually be completely redistributed among others. In this way one worker can be taken out of the assembly line altogether.[4] Things can be considerably rougher in actual practice on the assembly line. In our workplace, it was not just a matter of calmly giving more work to those who had won a little time to themselves, but an oppressive measure that involved putting a greater burden on those workers and encouraging them to use their 'autonomy' to deal with the situation. Work intensification comes first.

What's more, it is not as if this increased workload is all absorbed through the exercise of autonomy alone. Rationally, you can alleviate the intensive magnitude of your work by changing the way you do it. In other words you can compensate for the increased workload by improving your work. So, while this does result in improved productivity it does not amount to work intensification.[5] However, in order to raise the speed of production, workers introduce their own methods, but in doing so they also increase the speed of their movements. In practice, in the workplace the two are inseparable. It is not possible to raise productivity without changing the intensity of work. Logic to the contrary cannot stand up to the test of reality. In this way, then, while in the short term workloads can be alleviated a little through the exercise of autonomy, in the long run autonomy goes on to become a means for continually intensifying the work.

You could say that autonomy had a certain role to play in regulating workloads if the time workers saved by increasing their speed of production were their own. In the current situation, however, any time workers save is appropriated by management. Although workers are simply raising their speed in an attempt to exercise some control over their workloads, the more successful they are in this task the more they find themselves drawn into the system of workplace rationalization.[6]

What's more, management on site is fully aware of how autonomy is related to rationalization. So, by intentionally giving workers a modicum of free discretion, managers encourage them to become involved 'voluntarily' in rationalization.

In our orientation training we casual workers were told, 'You must do the work as you have been shown, closely following the standard work guidelines.' But this was just putting on a face for the outside world. Or, to be more to the point, you could say that this was also a way of avoiding responsibility for any accidents or injuries that might occur through workers using their own individual working methods. Just after they were assigned to their tasks, Yamano and Kimata, who joined the company at the same time as I did, were told directly by their immediate boss that they should find their own methods to increase their production speed.

On the other hand, then, what can we say about the type of autonomy exercised by ignoring the *kanban*? This does not lead to improvements in productivity. Quite the contrary, it leads to inefficiencies in the production system.

The management side explains this point as follows.

On a production line the greater the fluctuations in product flow the greater the waste. This is because the essential elements of production, such as infrastructure, personnel, stock inventory and so on must be provided at the level required for peak production. If an operator down the line has to work with discrepancies in the timing and volume of product flow then those same discrepancies spread back up the line to affect processes upstream. We must strive to completely eliminate any fluctuations in the final assembly line in order to prevent discrepancies in product flow from occurring in all other lines, including those of Toyota's outside affiliates. The final process in every Toyota Motor factory is not to consolidate to produce the same product. We use *heijunka* (production levelling) to operate on the premise that every vehicle we make is different (Ōno, 1978: 224).

Consequently, in Toyota, raising speed to produce a surplus of products, or ignoring the function of the *kanban* to produce an oversupply of just one part, fundamentally means a lowering in the efficiency of production. But in the former case, as we have just seen, management can turn a worker's surplus production into an improvement in productivity, so that, in essence, it does contribute to efficiency of production. In contrast, with the latter situation, there can be no argument that this is an unproductive practice. For example, if we take the actual example I gave of the transport operation, cutting down on the number of trips to save the wear and tear on the legs creates large fluctuations in production, puts greater demands on the interim stock inventory and adds unnecessarily to the 'waste' on the line as a whole.

So, in this way, the autonomy workers exercise in their daily routine can either improve productivity or be detrimental to production efficiency. I must add, however, that as soon as management discovers a case of the use of unproductive autonomy, they move immediately to correct the situation. I've seen it happen many times on the factory floor. As I shall be dealing with this in detail in the next chapter, let me give you just one example here.

Workers on the inspection and packing line have to carry out their work following signals from an indicator lamp. For example, they might have to inspect and pack a high-capacity engine drive-pin followed by a high-capacity front ring gear. But this variation in the products they handle places a considerable burden on the operator. It is easier for them to find a rhythm if they have a sequence of the same part to check and pack. So, the casual worker Yada would sometimes build up a pile of the same product and process them all together. But the team leader would invariably discover him doing this and give him a severe reprimand for his trouble.

Perhaps because our line had just been established and it was, moreover, a special case in not being set up as a conveyor-belt type, it was comparatively easy at first to use this kind of autonomy, but as the line gradually became more systematized it became very difficult to exercise the kind of autonomy management disapproved of.

Autonomy with workers as a buffer

In the previous section, in dealing with autonomy in normal daily work, I discussed only cases of autonomy in the performance of standardized work, but workers also display considerable autonomy in carrying out fine-tuning between processes. In order to clarify whether this use of autonomy plays any role in controlling workloads, let us first confirm why it is necessary for workers to do any fine-tuning at all.

According to past research, Toyota has worked to lift its productive efficiency by avoiding '*muda* ' (waste). In particular, it has focused its efforts on eliminating the unnecessary accumulation of parts in its interim stock inventory. Unnecessary stock means unnecessary raw materials and unnecessary plant infrastructure, all of which leads eventually to unnecessary personnel. So, to break the chain of waste, they had to start at the source of the problem and eliminate accumulation of surplus stock. However, if you are working with just the bare minimum of items in stock the line can easily be brought to a standstill through lack of parts or empty boxes. So, if the assembly line stops, this 'weakness' has to be corrected on site. By reducing waste to a minimum, 'weaknesses' are exposed and corrected and as a consequence there is a continual reinforcing of production. This is how the workplace goes through a constant process of evolution. That, at least, is the picture painted by most commentators.[7]

Certainly, in the actual workplace there are indeed instances where weaknesses are exposed through this kind of process. But weaknesses are *not* always corrected through *kaizen* activities on site. The fact is that on-line workers often just varnish over the problem somehow with a temporary solution. For example, to avoid bringing the line to a standstill a worker might use his or her autonomy to go back up the line to fetch spare parts, or have extra empty boxes made up beforehand. Without these kinds of adjustments the line comes to a stop and workers downstream are inconvenienced. Any lost time has to be made up in overtime work. These minor adjustments between processes would hardly be necessary at all, if there were just a little more stock on hand and if the speed of the line were slightly slower. In fact, workers find they are forced to take on the added burden of this kind of fine-tuning.

Moreover, there is no consideration given to the time involved in these adjustments between processes when planning daily production quotas. When 'weaknesses' appear on the line, workers have to somehow scratch together the time to deal with them. So you have to carry out any adjustments as quickly as possible and return to your position as soon as you are finished. If you don't act quickly you cause problems, not only for your fellow workers further down the line, but for yourself too. I repeat, any time lost has to be made up in overtime. From the point of view of the on-line worker, the 'work' they should be doing is just the regular standardized work. Fine-tuning is extra work to be avoided as far as possible. It is not spare time that workers can apply to regulate their workloads. Perhaps the leeway to exercise this kind of autonomy does relieve line workers of some of the pressure of a line stoppage, but it also means they have to respond to unreasonable demands. It does not necessarily follow, then, that this leeway makes their jobs any easier.[8]

The line is inflexible in the face of external change. So, to respond sympathetically to outside changes, management has equipped the line with the flexibility of the human body and required workers to play the role of a buffer between processes. This places workers under great strain. Far from regulating their loads, the autonomy to carry out fine-tuning itself increases the burden on workers.

Work intensification through 'Participation'

Kaizen activities to alleviate work intensification

Next, let us now consider the relationship between off-line activities and regulatory control. It should be clear from the actual examples I have given that none of the proposals put forward contradict management philosophy. When we casual workers got together, we would often say, half jokingly, that the best improvement they could make would be to reduce the speed of the production line. Of course, no worker would ever make such a suggestion and even if they did it would be ignored.

The same can be said of QC Circles. You would never find a worker prepared to say anything like that at a meeting attended by the section leader. Of course, only proposals that fall in line with management thinking are adopted, but even before that, only proposals following the company line are ever put forward.

That does not mean to say, however, that *kaizen* activities necessarily work against the interests of the worker. They do at times result in improved levels of safety, easier working procedures and creation of some leeway in time. If workers could put that leeway to their own use, then perhaps you could say *kaizen* activities gave workers a certain degree of regulatory control. But as I have explained before, any time saved as a result of these activities does not belong to the worker, but to management. This is because the managers' response is to use any time saved through *kaizen* activities to reduce staff, i.e. 'manpower saving' (*shōjinka*).

Moreover, that is not to say that all rationalization is necessarily carried out in this gentle manner. As I have already pointed out, there are times when management first increases the load and then applies improvements to absorb the excess.

To take one example, as there were not enough workers in the sub-assembly unit to handle the demand for increased output of parts, it was decided to move people from the inspection and packing line to the sub-assembly unit. At the time, it was the cleaning round that came under their scrutiny. As it happened, on 4 October Nonaka (fixed-term contract, joined 17 September), with whom I had been paired, had knocked off early because of his asthma. Seeing this as an opportunity, management ordered that I should continue alone doing the job 1.5 workers had been doing. It turned out that Nonaka was unable to work for the following week, so little by little it became an established fact that the cleaning round work was to be done by one person. Thus, despite the fact that absolutely no improvements had been implemented the workforce on the cleaning round had been reduced by one-third.

The effect of this decision was obvious. I now had to do the cleaning-round work by myself and a worker on inspection and packing had to cover the transport of parts for the sub-assembly unit. Clearly, this was an intensification of our work. Although we were all dissatisfied with this outcome, we couldn't very well refuse to go on working. So all of us on-site workers got together to pool our brains to come up with a way to alleviate this intensification of our duties.

Figure 4.2: Before kaizen

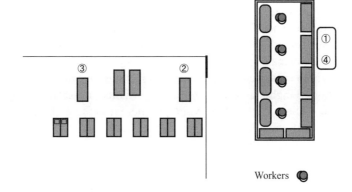

Workers

Figure 4.3: After kaizen

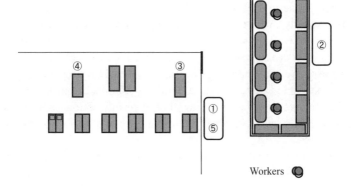

Workers

Until then the rear units had been transported along the course shown in figure 4.2. First, you would go up next to the assembly machine and load a tray of parts onto the trolley that you had positioned alongside the machine (①). Then you would push the trolley over to the medium capacity parts chute and load the tray of medium capacity parts into the chute. Then you would stack onto the trolley the empty trays that had been returned from the inspection and packing line (②). In the same way, you would push the trolley to the high-capacity engine parts chute and place the tray of high capacity parts into the chute and stack the empty high capacity parts trays onto the trolley (③). You then brought the trolley up alongside the rear-end assembly machine and returned the empty trays into the chute (④). Then you returned to your position.

To ease your workload you like to keep the distance you have to walk as short as possible. So we introduced the improvements set out in figure 4.3. As we have now stationed the trolley between the inspection and packing line and the sub-assembly unit, we go there to get the trolley (①). Then we push the trolley up alongside the rear-end assembly machine where we return the empty boxes to the chute (②). As in the case before the introduction of improvements, we load both trays of high-capacity parts and trays of medium-capacity parts onto the trolley. We take these and put them into the high-capacity and medium-capacity chutes respectively and load back onto the trolley the empty boxes from the inspection and packing line (③) (④). Then we take the trolley with its stack of empty trays and park it between inspection/packing and sub-assembly (⑤). Then we return to our position on the line.

The only difference to the situation before and after improvement was that instead of returning the trolley to the spot beside the assembly machine, we left it parked between inspection/packing and sub-assembly. As a result of this change we were able to cut down a little on the walking distance. Before making the improvement, the worker concerned would have to walk back to his or her position (on the inspection/packing line) empty-handed after leaving the trolley stationed alongside the assembly machine. But by leaving the trolley stacked with empty trays between inspection/packing and sub-assembly, we were able to eliminate some of this unproductive walking.

I don't think this change had a major effect, but by building up a number of minor improvements in this way we sought to alleviate, even by the slightest margin, the impact of the increased workload. Even my own proposal, which I mentioned above, was intended to lesson the burden of labour by slightly reducing the distance walked in transporting the differentials. Another way of looking at it is that conditions in the working environment are constantly so severe that workers cannot meet their quotas unless they keep on making trifling improvements of this kind. Workers 'participate' in *kaizen* activities in the hope that they may be able to achieve some slight reduction in the workloads they bear.

Kaizen activities that stimulate intensification of labour

If *kaizen* activities could compensate entirely for increased workloads, they would contribute to raising productivity without causing job intensification. It is possible to explain the effect of *kaizen* activities in this way. However, the theory does not match the practice on the shop floor. This becomes immediately evident if we consider how the labour load changed after staff reductions on the cleaning round.

The most obvious change, after the staff reductions and improvements on the cleaning round, was in the number of paces devoted to transport. Up until the end of August, I never walked more than twenty thousand steps a day. But from the end of October into November I walked over twenty thousand paces everyday and on some days over thirty thousand. Although there had been an increase in the number of items produced, there had been a reduction in the number of staff on the job. This increase in the number of steps required in the transportation process clearly brings home the reality of job intensification.

A worker from inspection and packing took over the transportation for the sub-assembly process. Despite increased volume of production, this worker had to take on a responsibility beyond the task to which they had been assigned. This is obviously a case of job intensification. There was no way simply changing the position of the trolley was going to absorb all the increase in workload. We carried on working with this allocation of staff for a while, but, as we expected, this caused an overload in the inspection and packing area, so the assistant assembly worker was put onto trolley transport duty. It was just about this time of reallocation of duties that I had been assigned to the assistant assembly worker's position. I found this task alone kept me extremely busy and I never had any time to spare at all. It was these circumstances that led to my being injured, fortunately not seriously.

24 October (Wednesday)

In the second period I was working as assistant on UD assembly. In the middle of my work, since I had relatively more spare time, I had to go and attend to the differential trolley when it had filled up with parts. While I am away doing this, the assembly worker has to continue working alone. He finds this annoying. So, in my haste to get back to my position as quickly as possible, I knocked my leg up against the bar where we park the trolley. I could see my shin swelling up as I watched and my sock was dyed red with blood. Still, I couldn't very well stop work because of this. I continued doing the assistant assembly work dragging my injured leg behind me. Somehow I managed to get through the rest of the day, but by the time I got back to the dormitory my shin was throbbing.

25 October (Thursday)

At the morning meeting I reported yesterday's injury. The section leader's initial reaction was to treat the matter lightly and suggest that all it needed was a dab of the antiseptic kept in the workplace first-aid kit. He told me to keep an eye on the injury but resume work on the cleaning round. The group leader was not present at the meeting, but as soon as he got word of my injury there was a rapid turn around in events. He asked me how the accident had happened. When he discovered that the accident had happened yesterday and not today he became flustered. This was probably because of something to do with the workers' compensation regulations. He seemed relieved to learn that I had not sought medical treatment outside. He marched me off to the site of the accident and made me explain precisely what had occurred. Again, after that, I had to go back to the spot with the chief leader and explain, yet again, all the circumstances leading up to the accident. Then, accompanied by the chief leader, I went to the factory's health and safety room. There too, the doctor, an industrial accident specialist, asked me to explain in detail the cause of the injury and gave me a simple examination to check whether I had suffered any damage to the bone. He also gave me a sermon on the requirement to report any accident immediately to the group leader. As soon as an accident occured, he went on to say, 'For all we know, you might have got injured outside the factory.' When I got back from the health and safety room, I had to go off again to report to the head of section. He also reprimanded me for not reporting the accident immediately and for running on the factory floor. On top of all that, someone came along from the Health and Safety section to interview me about the accident. Half the day was lost through all this fuss.

Later, on 26 October, I was taken back to the health and safety room. Then, on 31 October, they came along again from the Health and Safety section to confirm that the wound had healed.

There was a great hue and cry over the incident, but the question should have been why had this injury occurred in the first place. There is no doubt that my own carelessness had contributed to the accident, but it seems that other workers had often knocked their legs against the same bar in the trolley bay. Even the group leader has a scar on his shin as evidence of the fact. But if workers were not under such pressure, if they had a little more time, there would be no reason for incidents like this to arise. You might say that the workload, insufficiently alleviated despite the *kaizen* activities, manifested itself in the form of my injury.

This is simply one example of how *kaizen* activities fail to compensate for work intensification. Work intensification accompanying the 'evolution' of the production system has spread to cover the entire factory. For a short time after I was assigned to my workplace, we had a little leeway in staff numbers. Every day one or two people would be on leave. At the time, the group leader had explained that it would be hard to take paid leave after November when the work gets busier, so anyone who wants to take annual leave should take it now. In fact, when we got into November it became extremely difficult to run the operation with two people away. It certainly was not the kind of atmosphere in which you could ask to take leave.

Management also acknowledged the fact that labour was becoming intensified in the wake of the evolution of the production system. When the line had just been set up, the section leader of the sub-assembly process, Shiraishi, warned us not to go at it too hard from the beginning. This was consideration on the part of management to give us forewarning of the fact that work on the line would gradually become more intense.

Autonomous workplace operation to achieve management targets

What then is the situation regarding autonomous workplace operation? In any workplace there is bound to be an element of uncertainty. No matter how meticulously management plans its operation, things do not always go as expected. If managers were to attempt to standardise every movement its workers made, the workplace would not be able to respond to unexpected incidents and would quickly become dysfunctional. Yet, on the other hand, it is impossible to oversee everything workers do day in day out. The monitoring cost is just too high. Currently, in Japan you would hardly ever see direct control in its purest form. Management recognises the need for a degree of free discretion and lets its workers deal with unpredicted events.[9]

This applies to the Toyota workplace. There are various strategies to deal with indeterminacy. These may differ from one workplace to another, or sometimes even vary between different shifts working on the same task. Take the sub-assembly unit for example. In our group the work was performed on a rotation basis that included the casual workers. On the opposite shift, however, in principle casual employees continued performing the one task to which they had been assigned. Even in dealing with the problem of staff on annual leave, each workplace responded differently.

Let us consider, then, how much regulatory power workers have in the running of an 'autonomous' workplace.

To give the conclusion first, workers on the factory floor have no say in production plans. Their only concern is how to achieve the production targets those above have set for them. The workplace utilises autonomous operation to meet its production quotas. It does not use it to regulate the volume of production.

It is certainly true, however, that one aspect of autonomous workplace operation is that it does take the pressure of management off the individual worker. You could say that the autonomous workplace acts as a buffer between those above and the general worker. Consequently, I cannot say with absolute certainty that there are no workers for whom autonomous workplace operation results in regulation of workloads. Nevertheless, if we are to base our assessment of autonomous operation from the actual conditions of the factory floor, this aspect cannot be overestimated.

The target product numbers are planned to include overtime and are set to almost the full capacity of the group. That is why all the resources of the line are mobilized to meet these quotas. So, if the team leader notices that a worker has even a little time to spare, he gives him more work to do. Workplace 'freedom' is, frankly speaking, the freedom to thrust an additional burden on anyone by any means at your disposal. It is the freedom to manipulate the flexibility of overtime work and to get workers to do any job you want. In short, it is the freedom to bring to fruition the plans of management. The workers, however, are just ordinary people who feel fatigue and antagonism. That is why, the more on-site supervisors and team leaders espouse management logic, the less inclined they are to ignore the conditions of workers. This is the reality.

They, the on-site supervisors, do not give consideration to workers' conditions out of sympathy for the issues they raise. They do so because they are forced to by the severity of the quotas they have to achieve. Without consideration for workers' conditions they simply could not do their job. Probably the most obvious example of this is how carefully they select the workers and have them alternate each work period between the sub-assembly unit and the inspection and packing line.

Seen like this, we can tell that autonomous workplace operation is not evidence of control by the workers, but rather evidence of the penetration of capitalist logic.[10]

Summary: autonomy and control

In this chapter we have examined the relationship between the exercise of autonomy and the use of regulatory power. Workers have attained a certain degree of autonomy, which they exercise in the course of their work. At first glance, this autonomy seems to have some bearing on the regulation of workloads. But, contrary to this superficial impression, in the longer run, the exercise of autonomy leads to an intensification of work.

First, workers are presented with the challenging environment of reduced in-process inventory, increased speed of production[11] and a reduction in personnel. Responding to these pressures, on-site workers strive to absorb the intensification of work by devising, within the discretion available to them, their own working methods and by implementing improvements. In this way, it can be said, in the short term, assembly line workers are able to exercise a degree of control over their workloads. But, as the work intensifies, they find that their improved working methods cannot compensate for the increased load. In addition, as workers raise the speed of their movements to cope with demands for increased production, there is a gradual build-up in the number of products they are expected to produce. In this way the density of work goes on increasing with the 'evolution' of the production system.

It is the same story with the fine-tuning between processes that workers carry out on the factory floor. This too, turns out to be, not a source of control of the labour process, but the cause of increased workloads. While the leeway through which workers achieve minor adjustments between processes may somewhat relieve the psychological pressure, the adjustments themselves simply increase the workload.[12]

It is said that factory workers' autonomous activities have in essence both positive and negative aspects for the workers concerned. In this connection, 'industrial democracy' is often cited on the one hand and 'capitalist logic' on the other. But, regardless of the aspect you emphasise, I think reducing the argument to its essentials hides a number of important realities. There are firm logical principles operating on the factory floor below what is visible on the surface.

The more autonomy a worker exercises the greater the certainty that his workload will increase. What I am seeking to emphasise here is not so much the *conclusion*, i.e. that autonomous activities result in the intensification of work, but the ingenious mechanism by which this result is achieved. Management encourages workers to participate and to exercise autonomy to alleviate their workloads, to hide the reality that their workloads are increasing. So, not all workers are necessarily aware of the fact that 'improvement' means intensification of work. Some even feel that improvements are making their work easier. Certainly, as these activities bring some relief, both physically and mentally, from increased workloads in the short term, it is easy to see how this interpretation can surface. In reality, however, there is a continual increase in workload beyond that which can be absorbed through the implementation of improvements.

So, what should be considered are not the *kaizen* activities *per se*, but the relationship between labour and management[13] in their implementation and the uncertainty of the workload. The biggest problem is that the increase in workloads is being allowed to continue unchecked. To date, workplace autonomy has been largely seen from the aspect of human relations theory as a means of psychologically winning over the workers. But I think perhaps now we should rather be focusing on the point that it is intensification of labour in disguise.

5 Supervision on the Factory Floor

In the previous chapter we focused on the labour process and considered how workers work autonomously in line with the objectives of management. Here the question arises as to why workers do not, or cannot, abuse the free discretion they are given.

Two points of view emerge from the previous research on this issue. One is the view that the Toyota Production System controls the worker. As I mentioned before, management intentionally creates 'weaknesses' on the assembly line and has factory workers correct them. That is to say that management, instead of unilaterally supervising its workers, wins them over to the company line by fulfilling their demands.[1] The other argument is that workers are controlled through personnel and labour management that includes human relationship activities, efficiency control, merit ratings and management ideology. In short, the worker is cleverly drawn into the administrative web that covers, and extends beyond, the workplace.[2] What the two viewpoints have in common is an image of control that combines coercive and voluntary aspects.[3]

In this chapter I focus on processes of control as they actually operate in the workplace.

Power exercised through plant infrastructure

Power exercised through machinery and tools

Although managers do not show up on the shop floor to control workers directly, they can do so indirectly by using machines. The conveyor-belt assembly line is a prime example. It forces workers to respond whether they have been instructed to or not. Of course, this is not confined only to Toyota. It is general throughout the automobile industry and in manufacturing industries across the board. But in our workplace, which is not based on a conveyor-belt type set-up, there is a more intricate mechanism for controlling workers.

On the cleaning round, the trays that hold the components (i.e. *kanban*) play an important role in the control of the worker.

Originally, the *kanban* was simply a piece of equipment used to help in the management of production. But, in so much as it is there to be seen by anyone standing nearby, the *kanban* becomes a means to exert indirect control over the worker concerned. You can tell at a glance how many trays have piled up at the cleaned-items chute, so you can get a good idea of how the work is progressing and how diligently the worker is applying himself to his task. A big pile of trays by the chute means the worker has been lazy. On the other hand, if there are hardly any trays there at all, this is a good indication that the worker has been diligent and is doing a proper job. By the time you notice that a manager has come on one of his occasional rounds to check on progress on the factory floor, it is already too late to start tidying up the backlog of trays. So, despite the fact that he does not have a supervisor standing over him, the worker on the cleaning round just cannot afford to slacken off. Moreover, the chute is set up in a position where it is clearly visible. So the worker is always conscious of the eyes of unseen managers. The worker on the cleaning round performs his work under the gaze conveyed through the medium of a *kanban*.[4]

In the sub-assembly process a machine controls the operator's movements. The sub-assembly machine is fitted with a device called the '*pokayoke*,' which automatically stops the machine if there is an operator error or a faulty product. This device prevents bad products from flowing on to the next manufacturing process, but at the same time it also meticulously controls the operator's movements.

What's more, not only does the assembly machine physically control workers, it also controls them psychologically. In so far as the task allows workers no physical or mental leeway, every time the machine stops, one or other of the operators, who work in pairs, lets out an exasperated 'not again!' In addition, a buzzer goes off and a light starts flashing to bring the mishap to the attention of those working in the area. Workers operating in this environment strive to work as accurately and quickly as they can, determined not to cause any problems for their partner or embarrassment to themselves. Every time the machine stops they feel everyone around is blaming them for their ineptitude. By fitting the machine with a *pokayoke* (fail-safe) device, light and buzzer, management ensures that the gaze of power extends into the furthest corners of the factory. Even without the direct control of management, workers on the assembly-line work frantically, continually conscious of this scrutiny.

However, in recent years in Toyota the trend has been away from over-reliance on the fitting of automatic devices of this kind. Management argues that when too many devices are fitted to machines, workers rely on them rather than maintain high levels of consciousness regarding the work they perform. And without this conscious understanding, workers cannot respond on site to the slightest machine malfunction.

That is why on our assembly line, as far as possible, they avoid the installation of automatic devices like the *pokayoke* device. Management is very actively promoting this new policy that it calls 'visibilization' (*mieruka*).

Power exercised through the working environment: 'Visibilization'

'Visibilization' does not only mean cutting back on excessive automation of machines and plant. It is concerned with making it clear at a single glance just how work on the factory floor is progressing and extends to cover the simplification of work procedures and the orderly arrangement of the working area. Evidence of the application of this principle can be seen everywhere in the workplace. The prefabricated sheds, erected on the floor of the factory as an office and rest area, have large sheets of glass all round. There is a much greater expanse of glass than in the usual opaque prefabricated structures you often see on building sites. From his prefabricated glass office the group leader has a clear view of what is happening on the shop floor. On the cleaning round, as it happens, there is a blind spot our group leader can't see, but the whole operation is clearly visible from the office of the neighbouring group leader. He has a panoramic view of the inspection and packing line, and the sub-assembly process. The inspection and packing area is covered with transparent vinyl sheeting so every movement the workers inside make is clearly visible from outside. Even within the same factory there are still some production lines in a state of clutter and disarray, but our line is so clean and orderly that you would hardly think you were in a manufacturing plant. Even the trays are stacked with great care. They are piled up neatly in a specified location, not a single one out of place. This applies not only to the industrial work areas, but also to the prefabricated offices and toilets. All are kept scrupulously clean. Waste is discarded into separate bins for cotton work gloves (*gunte*), paper and vinyl, rubber, aluminium cans, steel cans, and cigarette butts. You don't see graffiti in the toilets.

What then is the effect of this *mieruka* ('visibilization') on work on the shop floor? Frankly speaking, having the work area open to view means that the eyes of power reach into the furthest corners of the factory and, conversely, from the workers' point of view it leaves little room for them to control the labour process without being seen by management. The worker's informal domain is placed under surveillance from those above and is changed in the process into a formal domain. In this way, increased transparency for management results in increased scrutinization for the workers and robs them of the opportunity to use their 'autonomy' to make any changes that do not lead to improvement in productivity. Of course, that is not to say that no activity of this kind goes on at all. But the idea behind 'visibilization' is to reduce this to a bare minimum.

In a workplace run along these lines, it is not only a matter of supervisors unilaterally observing the workers. As the whole area is divided with glass partitions, the supervisors themselves are exposed to the observation of their superiors. Neither can they escape the gaze of the general workers in the factory. Of course the workers don't supervise the managers, but it can undermine the bosses' authority if workers see them smoking or aimlessly chatting away in their glass offices. So, even the managers cannot help but be conscious not only of the gaze of their superiors, as you would expect, but also of the eyes of the workers in general. Visibilization affects both observer and observed alike.

Workers find themselves in a situation in which someone is always watching them. But they do not know by whom or from where they are being observed. It is just a waste of nervous energy to be constantly looking around the factory to see if it is safe to cut corners in your work. It is easier just to keep working as you have been told. In this way, although managers might not be directly supervising the workers, by making them feel *conscious* that someone, somewhere may be watching them, they can get the workers to toe the company line.[5]

Power exercised through workplace management

Management does not only exercise indirect control of workers through machines and equipment. Of course, there is also direct control. Communication between the members of the group, delegation of authority and apportioning of responsibility are indispensable to the running of any organization. In the following

I hope to clearly demonstrate the realities of direct control over workers with actual examples of workplace management.

Apportioning of authority and responsibility

Authority bestowed through paternalism

The autonomy assembly line workers acquire is a privilege, not a right. As long as they are obedient and follow the management line, workers are given a certain degree of free discretion. But this discretion is such that it can be withdrawn immediately if they show the slightest attitude of defiance. There are also occasional cases of blatant suppression.

As I mentioned before, there was a period of about two weeks when I worked with the section leader. For the whole of that time I was placed under his direct supervision. If I stopped moving for a second he would often rebuke me with a sarcastic comment like, 'you're lucky to have so much free time' or 'there are still some left over there, you know.'

Young Naganuma, who joined with me, told me how angry he was when, just after he had been assigned to his workplace, the section leader said, 'If you're not prepared to work you can just go home!' (30 July). But as time passes the section leader moves away from the new recruits. Probably during this initial period he is able to judge whether or not a worker can be trusted to work on his own. After that, I did the cleaning-round work almost entirely on my own and came to acquire a certain degree of autonomy. It even reached the stage, when Kitamura, a new casual worker, was assigned to the cleaning round in September that I was given the job of training him. Generally, a foreman or a team leader instructs new recruits, but, apart from one early visit when the group leader came along to see how I was teaching, I had full responsibility for training Kitamura. During this time I was able to do my job pretty much at my own pace. But circumstances changed suddenly when more new casual workers joined us.

On 17 September two new workers were assigned to our group. On their first day both of them were sent off to the inspection and packing area, but one of them was reassigned to another task almost immediately. The group leader had stepped in immediately when the new recruit had let through some faulty or incomplete products and had incorrectly stamped the seal of certification on a dozen or more boxes. From the second work period of his second day he was transferred from inspection and packing to the cleaning round. Then, according to the principles of chain-reaction personnel management, Kitamura, who had until then been my partner on the cleaning round, was shunted off to inspection and packing. The group leader said nothing to the men concerned about the reasons for their reassignment. I suppose he just made the excuse that it was to meet the contingencies of the workplace. I myself did not learn the circumstances behind the move until the team leader, Nagata, told me later.

It seems that management was not satisfied with the way the new recruit was performing on the cleaning round either. They complained about every single thing he did. He always responded in a defiant manner. The bosses seemed to be at a loss over how to deal with him. They told him that they might have to move him across to another group to replace a worker who had developed blisters on his feet. But this plan came to nothing. It was not long before he changed his position again, this time from the cleaning round to the sub-assembly process. He was to spend work periods one and three on the cleaning round and periods two and four on sub-assembly. But it seems that there too he had been assessed as 'useless.' So within a day he was back full-time on the cleaning round.

Before, when I had been working with Kitamura, we had no strictly fixed division of labour. Basically, I was on high capacity parts and sub-assembly transport and Kitamura was on the transport of medium capacity parts, but when one of us was busy the other would help out. After I began working with the new recruit as my partner, however, the boss insisted that we have a clear division of duties. So I was in charge of the high capacity parts and the sub-assembly parts, plus the rear and front units (both medium capacity parts) and he was given charge of the transport of the remaining medium capacity parts. In addition, the carrying of the empty trays, which had previously been done on a flexible *ad hoc* basis, to which the boss had half given his tacit approval, now that I was working with the newcomer, had to be done strictly by the book. So the restrictions not only affected him, but me too. This meant of course that I could only send on for cleaning the same number of trays as I had returned and even the number of trays that could be carried at one time was fixed at either four or eight trays. Even after that, he continued to be directly monitored and instructed by the supervisors. Because of all this, the considerable autonomy I had gained was lost in the return to fixed working methods and I now had virtually no opportunity to exercise any discretion.

While it is true that managers afford compliant workers a degree of discretion, they do all they can to remove that privilege from those who display the slightest attitude of defiance. They monitor the performance of the former, gradually increasing the permitted amount of discretion, but with the latter group they enforce absolute observation of the standard working procedures. Workers who understand this are constantly aware of the latent threat of power and, although they appear to be freely going about their daily tasks, they are actually paying careful attention as they work so as not to go beyond management's range of tolerance.

An analytical framework from management theory can bring to light the power relationships underlying the above situation. Workers negotiate with management even before they go through the factory gates. Management agrees to pay them wages and they agree to provide their labour. A contract is signed. But it is not possible to specify in advance all the details of the work to be performed. So, inevitably, any contract is an *incomplete contract*. At this stage, the worker is compelled to sign a contract to provide the commodity of 'labour power,' i.e. the ability to produce labour. Unlike commodities in general, where it is usual to clarify in the negotiating stage the performance of a product or the content of a service, with the commodity of labour power, it is not until after it has been tried in the workplace that its content becomes apparent. Seen from the viewpoint of the worker, this situation is fraught with risk. He, or she, does not know what degree of exploitation to expect.

However, it is not only the worker who bears a risk in these negotiations. Management is exposed to the risk that perhaps the contracted worker can only offer a level of labour lower than the value of the wages the contract provided. As I mentioned in the previous chapter, in any workplace there is an element of uncertainty. It is possible that at times workers can exploit this uncertainty to avoid work. This is the problem of the so-called 'moral hazard.' The contract is 'in that sense, a major source of uncertainty for the principal[6] (i.e. for management – Ihara)' (Itami, 1986: 71).

So management seeks to limit workers' control over their work to ensure that they work to produce profit for the company. This is the essence of management control. There are three methods through which this is achieved, influence, direct intervention and selection.

'The exercise of influence means trying to give workers in the process of making up their minds the impression that they are getting something management desires. With direct intervention management intervenes in workers' decision-making and issues directions to be followed. And selection is when management decides which process to entrust to which worker' (*Ibid.* 34–5). In contrast to influence, which is an indirect method of control, intervention and selection are direct control activities that can at times result in the deprivation of authority itself.

The actual examples we have seen so far could be classified as direct intervention. In exchange for the little free discretion they gain, workers here have to take on additional burdens, such as fine-tuning between processes, which do not fall within the range of their minimum 'duty.' If a worker abuses that freedom, management steps in immediately and completely revokes any discretion. A worker can avoid having to take on these additional tasks, but only at the price of losing autonomy and being labelled 'useless.'

This kind of direct intervention is a blatant use of power. And the stronger this power is, the more likely it is that a worker, who has gained a degree of 'free discretion,' will work 'voluntarily' following the management line, even in situations where there is no direct intervention.

Unlimited responsibility

Let us now consider just how much responsibility workers are required to bear and how management ensures that this responsibility is being met. The minimum responsibility of assembly line workers is simply to maintain production within the allocated *takt* time. An assembly line worker should be required to assume a *limited range* of responsibilities. However, in Toyota, an extremely *high level* of quality is required for every single part and it is no easy task to meet that demand. Line workers shoulder an extremely heavy responsibility in this regard.

Just how heavy that responsibility is can be seen at a glance in the following statistics. Take, for instance, Yamano, a casual contract worker who joined with me. In his group the yearly production target (up to the end of December) is to keep faulty products down to below 2.8 for every hundred thousand units produced. For all practical purposes this is tantamount to saying do not produce any faulty products. As at 1 November 2001, twenty-one faulty products have been produced. Apparently the matter was brought up in a group meeting and they were again cautioned to the effect that on no account were they to let through any more bad products. At this Yamano, no longer able to restrain his anger, said, 'If you're insisting on such high quality, let me have a little more time. Otherwise I'll have to stop the line and don't blame me if there's a drop in the operation rate.' A high level of quality is demanded in every process, but they are particularly fussy on the inspection and packing line that absolutely no faulty or incomplete items get through because any part that passes through here is shipped directly to America.

But no matter how often and how loudly the supervisors call for quality control that is not the only reason workers strive to meet this heavy responsibility. They accept this excessive burden of responsibility because the eyes of management take in the entire factory floor. Now, for example, let us look more closely at work on the inspection and packing line.

18 September (Tuesday)

Whenever a faulty part happens to get through to America, a detailed report with a photograph of the offending part is sent to the office of the section responsible. Each of the prefabricated offices is equipped with computers and it is through these that information about faulty products is conveyed. The site foreman immediately puts in place measures to prevent a reoccurrence. From the data provided it is possible to deduce which individual was responsible for sending on the faulty part.

22 October (Monday)

According to young Yada in inspection and packing, very occasionally, a cleaning tray that has not been through the cleaning process is placed into the cleaned item chute and conveyed to inspection and packing. This is probably caused by carelessness on the part of one of us in the cleaning round. This happened again today. Apparently he thought it had not been cleaned because the high capacity front ring gear seemed greasier than usual. But even though he thought it was a bit strange he continued the packing process. It was not until he had finished packing four or five boxes that he thought he had better get the team leader to check and, sure enough, it turned out they had not been cleaned. I thought Yada must surely have been praised for bringing this to his boss's attention, but, quite the contrary, apparently he had been ticked off for not mentioning it earlier. After that, his work was placed under the direct supervision of the group leader. A little while later, he said the group leader accused him of having at some time in the past carelessly mixed some medium capacity drive pinions into a tray of high capacity parts. Understandably, Yada was not happy with that accusation. The row between them went even further.

In fact, after that, they deliberately put medium capacity drive pinions into a tray of high capacity parts to test Yada's checking ability. Fortunately, Yada noticed the wrong parts so nothing came of the incident, but he was outraged that they should have so little faith in him. Then, when the same kind of 'check' was made again after lunch, Yada was unable to control his anger and lashed out at the team leader. Apparently, the team leader apologised immediately, but that did not prevent the atmosphere in the workplace from hitting rock bottom.

30 October (Tuesday)

To raise workers' consciousness of quality, from now on we are to consider the next process downstream from us as our 'customer.' And when a faulty product goes on to the next stage we are to consider that as a 'complaint from a customer.' This was to make the point that all workers should put as much care into their work as they would in handing over a piece of merchandise they had sold to a treasured customer.

31 October (Wednesday)

At the morning meeting it was announced that in future assembled parts are to carry the name of the person who inspected them. It seems this measure is to clarify individual responsibility.

2 November (Friday)

From now on, detailed information about any faulty part detected is to be entered into the computer.

This move is to prevent reoccurrence of the problem and at the same time to monitor the costs arising from production of faulty items. In addition it was decided that when any problem regarding quality arrises a report must be made to the quality audit office. They are clamping down even more thoroughly on quality control.

Not only does management hive off responsibility for quality onto each individual worker, it also places this burden on the team as a whole in the form of collective responsibility. Every worker is under heavy pressure not to cause any trouble for the team.

10 October (Wednesday)

Today my work ran smoothly and it was looking as if I was going to get home on time. However, thirty minutes before knock-off time a problem occurred in the shipment area. Apparently a faulty product was found in C2. The centre of the component was slightly out of alignment, but the degree of the fault was so small that it would not normally be picked up in the inspection process. Yada did not think it would be a problem, but nevertheless took the precaution of reporting it to his team leader. The upshot of this was that the incident turned into a major commotion. We had to open all the boxes that had been packed and recheck the parts. As a result of this exercise it was discovered that most of the C2 parts were faulty. So I ended up with an hour's overtime after all. Even those of us not directly involved with the rechecking had to stay back until the fuss died down. The atmosphere was such that nobody dared to say they were going home.

No-one at all criticised Yada over the incident, but for some time after he acted very apologetically to everyone.

As there had been a spate of faulty products coming off the inspection and packing line, it was decided to convene a 'voluntary' quality control meeting.

30 October (Tuesday) – 30 minutes overtime plus a one and a half hour meeting

We had a quality control meeting after work. In the past we had had an incident when medium capacity front units had got mixed into a tray of high capacity parts. So we had a meeting of just the inspection and packing staff to ensure that this mistake does not happen again. (In addition, we had planned to discuss faulty rear gears, unstamped boxes and incorrect substitution of medium capacity and high capacity drive pinions, but we ran out of time).

First, we all put forward our suggestions regarding the possible cause of the problem. The candidates considered were; the assembly worker putting items into the wrong tray, an oversight on the part of the pre-inspection worker, and, an error in the packing process. Next we talked about methods of prevention. Someone suggested that an indicator lamp might be used to prevent assembled parts being put into the wrong tray. In response came the comment that that might be difficult as our line was one that avoided the use of *pokayoke* and other electronic devices. Anyway, it was agreed that we should at least ask if an indicator lamp could be used on the sub-assembly process.

> In regard to the problems in pre-inspection, inspection and packing, it was decided that the number of pins should be confirmed prior to inspection. In future, it seems, we shall call a meeting like this every time faulty products appear.

There was fierce criticism of the operators on the inspection and packing line for letting through the faulty items, not only from the supervisors, but also in the form of pressure from fellow workers. So they did all they could in the mere eight seconds they had for the task, to make absolutely sure that they did not overlook a fault anywhere on the products they inspected. From the outset there had never been completely clear criteria to distinguish between good and bad products. But that did not prevent them from being severely censured whenever a faulty product got through.

The workers inspected the parts in accordance with the 'quality check standard.' In fact not all points are checked for each item, but even if all items are checked against the standard, this does not mean that no faulty items at all would get past the inspectors. No matter how many places you check, you are inevitably left with a vague area of judgement at the borderline between good and bad products. What's more, differences in judgement arise from one operator to another. So, who then makes this judgement? Ultimately, it is the operator on the next process. If the worker downstream judges that a part is faulty it is faulty. So, if a bad product gets through, it is, after all, the workers in charge of inspection and packing, the last in the line, who have to foot the blame.

When an inspection machine is used to check parts, this limits the responsibility workers have to carry. But in workplaces like ours, where workers do the checking, all the responsibility for quality control falls on the operator in charge. This is particularly so in Toyota, which demands extremely high levels of quality. Coupled with the vagueness of the assessment criteria, this results in virtually unlimited responsibility falling on the workers concerned. On top of the physical effort of scrupulously checking for faults, workers in inspection and packing have to accept the heavy psychological responsibility of judging whether a product is faulty or not. Those working nearby consider inspection and packing to be the easiest task on the line, but, in fact, the casual observer cannot imagine the heavy physical and mental pressures they are under.[7]

Seen in this light, it is clear that there is an imbalance between authority and responsibility in this workplace. That is to say, the level of responsibility workers are required to bear is too heavy in comparison with the authority they are given. While any authority workers may have is bestowed upon them as 'a favour,' they are compelled to accept responsibility for anything that happens on the factory floor. In addition, they are at times even made to take responsibility for things that are, despite their greatest efforts, simply beyond their control. The fact that workers can be compelled to accept such imbalance is ample testimony to the strength of the power management wields.[8]

Control through communication

The role of rotation in the moulding of consent

For management the aim of rotation is to make workers multi-skilled so that they can fill in for workers on leave. As we saw in chapter two, rotation in this workplace is not planned and it is doubtful whether it can be linked to multi-skilling at all. But even so, management is able to fill gaps in the workforce by having workers learn a number of different jobs. When you actually see it at work on the factory floor, however, you realise that rotation also plays another different role.

The supervisors and team leaders never raise the slightest objection to upper management's plans for increased production. Their only concern is how to achieve the increased production targets. And they actively exploit rotation as a means of meeting the goals they have been set. The workers also use rotation to share information among themselves and the supervisors and team leaders also join in to find out as much as they can about what is going on in the workplace. They soon pick up information about who has time to spare and where they can pull someone off the line. So this workplace information works to the benefit of management rather than the workers.

Mangers collect information about the workplace not only from rotation, but also through a variety of means including QC Circles and from the 'zero accident notebooks' (*zerosai nōto*). So they are perfectly aware of what constitutes a *suitable* work distribution. They allocate tasks to workers according to the workers' capacity to handle them. Then they make a point of coming back and checking when they think workers should be used to the work, to gradually increase the workload, or, if they judge this to be out of the question, to move a worker on to a different job. Kakegawa, who joined with me, finally managed after over a month of trying, to complete his assignment within the specified *takt* time. But no sooner had he done that than they increased his production target and he fell behind the *takt* time again. So they immediately pulled him off the line (5 September).

Careful 'consideration' and subtle 'adjustment' is indispensable in the process of getting workers to perform to the upper limits of their capacity. Even the most docile worker can rebel if he is forced to do a job that is clearly beyond him. But if a worker feels he might be able to meet the increased production target if he really put his mind to it, he might complain, but he will end up complying with the order.

It is not just a matter of managers unilaterally imposing greater workloads. The workers themselves are subtly won over to acquiesce with the management line. Rotation is cleverly used as a means of achieving this.

Rotation severs the special individual relationship a worker has with the job he regularly performs. The feeling of ownership of the task, the idea that 'this is my work' is weakened. To establish an identity for themselves on the factory floor, workers develop a strong sense of belonging to their own group. There is a strong consciousness of the fact that 'this is our group.' Some do so more enthusiastically than others, but all workers come to feel through this sense of working together that the will of the group must be given absolute priority. In fact, as it happens, the will of management comes to replace the will of the group (the workers as a whole). Unconsciously the workers acquire the practical thought patterns of management. So when management calls for increased production, these 'practical' workers, though they might grumble 'not again,' soon swap dissatisfaction for resignation and turn their minds to the implementation of the new reality imposed upon them. Quite unconsciously, they begin to think of where it might be possible to reduce staff or where production might be suitably increased. Through the daily rotation a kind of vague consensus is formed among the workers concerning their place on the line. So, if a 'victim' goes on complaining too long, his or her workmates will argue, 'we're all in the same boat,' or warn the complainant 'not to be so selfish.' Of course, I do not think the majority of workers are actually enthusiastic about taking on increased workloads. But it is difficult for them to show any opposition. This is because rotation ensures that the pain is shared around, so you get the feeling, 'I'm not the only one being sacrificed here.' In this way, management is able to increase workloads with the formal acquiescence of the workers.

There are times, however, when the workers do not meekly accept management's orders. Sometimes a worker, particularly a worker in charge of a particular process will express strong dissatisfaction at demands for increased production. If this happens management resorts to even more cunning means to gain the agreement of its workers.

On the factory floor there is no clearly fixed number of personnel. That is to say, there are no guidelines to say how much work should be allocated to each worker. I suppose the managers apply some kind of standard, but the method they use is never conveyed to the workers. In an extreme case, I suppose you could say that if anyone at all can manage to handle a particular task, then that is a fair work allocation. Let us assume the situation where a manager explains that, because our line had just recently been established, two workers are engaged on a particular task that was originally performed by one. Employees would have no grounds for complaint if the manager were suddenly to announce that from today he wants to revert to having just one worker on the job. Workers have self-respect and a sense of competition. They are vulnerable to comparisons with other workers. Once, in response to staff reductions on the cleaning round I complained to my boss, 'Why are you decreasing the number of workers without even introducing any improvements? Can't you see that's increasing my workload?' He simply replied, 'Others can handle it, so you should be able to do it too.' By making comparisons between workers like this, they also use the rotation process as a means to get workers to take on heavier loads. So rather than a production line, 'where anyone can work,' we have a line 'where there is someone who can do the job.'

Of course, there is nothing about rotation that is intrinsically contrary to workers' interests. I suppose there are some workers who feel rotation is giving them a change of scenery. Occasionally, a manager's arbitrary reallocation of tasks can result in a greater level of worker control.[9] Perhaps it is also a step towards creating a line 'where anyone can work.' But in my workplace rotation worked to the benefit of management, not the workers. Rotation functions as a means for managers to win agreement from their workers and provides them with the opportunity to collect information from every corner of the factory floor.

Control through language: the role of the QC circles

By maintaining close communication with the workers, management not only sopped up information from the factory floor, but also at the same time inculcated workers with the language and world-view of management.

I have been through the experience myself, so I know. New recruits into a company, particularly the white-collar workers, in most cases during their orientation training sessions, are thoroughly drilled on how to talk and behave as a responsible member of society (*shakaijin*). Not only the trainers from the personnel department, but also senior workmates and their bosses in the office are involved in this process of 'correction.' And once the 'corrected' individual has learnt, after a fashion, to talk and behave like a responsible member of society, he or she takes on the task of 'correcting' those who come behind. In this way, order is maintained in the workplace.

That's not to say that language and behaviour were all that strictly controlled in our workplace. Neither was there a particularly strong sense of hierarchical relationships. We had some workers who would not hesitate to speak frankly using the same informal language to anybody regardless of their rank. But we did have a special language, Toyota terminology, which played an important role in the administration of workers.

We casual workers had Toyota terminology explained to us during our initial orientation upon entering the company. We acquired a superficial understanding of Toyota speak, from 'Toyota Production System (TPS),' through '*zaiko*' (stock), '*rain sutoppu*' (line stoppage), '*pokayoke*' (fail-safe device), '*gohin*' (faulty product), and '*keppin*' (imperfect product) to '*heijunka*' (production levelling), '*genkateigen*' (cost reduction), '*jasuto-in-taimu*' (just-in-time), '*jidōka*' (autonomation) and '*kōsū*' (man-hours). But I imagine very few of the casual workers manage to take all this in after just the orientation training.

The regular employees use this 'Toyota speak' at QC circles and so forth and also in their everyday conversation, but at first we casual workers had trouble understanding what they were saying. On our days off, when we new casual recruits got together, the phrase, 'I ain't got a clue what those guys are saying' often came out in conversation. It is not as if our bosses insist on the use of Toyota terminology and not understanding it is in no sense an impediment to your work. The casual workers carry on performing their duties for some considerable time without knowing the Toyota jargon.

But language plays an important role in the construction of identity. The casual employees feel that they are not recognised as fully-fledged factory workers until they have acquired 'Toyota speak.' They are fully aware of the fact that the factory revolves around 'those guys' who speak the Toyota lingo. They cannot get rid of their sense of alienation as long as they remain ignorant of Toyota terminology. So, probably without realizing themselves what is happening, they voluntarily go on to acquire this language. Sometimes, at the beginning they resist in a display of bravado to mask their sense of inferiority, but they gradually come to enjoy the feeling that they are mastering the jargon of their workmates. In this way, in Toyota too, the acquisition of the *right* language maintains order in the workplace. And the Toyota technical terminology does more than simply maintain order. It plays a more active role in the control of workers.

Toyota terminology is a kind of technical jargon. But it is in no sense a neutral language. It is the language that gives expression to the rational framework of the 'Toyota Production System' and carries within it the philosophy of Toyota management. That is why, in the process of acquiring Toyota jargon, workers gradually and unconsciously become imbued with management's way of thinking and come to act in accordance with its principles.

Workers would doubtless show some resistance to the words, '*kaizen* (improvements) leading to intensification of labour.' But if they hear '*kaizen* to eliminate waste' or '*kaizen* to make work easier,' they are more likely to embark on the improvement with minimal resistance. The phrase 'workmates helping one another' gives the impression that perhaps workers can cooperate to lighten their mutual workloads. Whereas, what it actually means is that workers have to take on the added burden of fine-tuning between processes. Toyota terminology is not a language that management has forced onto the workers. It is a technical, workplace jargon, which, on the surface at least, appears to be neutral, so there is no reason why workers should refuse to learn it. Without taking the form of overt administration or control on the factory floor, management thinking permeates the workplace through the medium of Toyota jargon.

From the controlled to the controller
Workers are controlled through their shared experience of management philosophy and world-view. But it does not end there. Unconsciously, they also gradually go on to control other workers.

Takenaka, with fifteen years service in the company, performed the task of training workers on the cleaning round, but when he was busy I trained a casual worker. I did not feel responsible for him as the training of new recruits was not my 'job.' I would not have cautioned the new recruit working alongside me if he had happened to take a rest during his work. But my partner, young Nonaka, made no attempt to take a breather even when there was a lull in the work. When I asked him why he did not take a break he said, 'I worried about the way you kept looking at me, Ihara.' His work and mine were clearly defined and quite separate. If he were to take things easy it would have no effect at all on my work. Nevertheless, I had, in fact, been checking Nonaka's work.

I had no idea that I was controlling him, but I was no doubt unconsciously monitoring what he was doing. At least that is what *he felt*. So, without being aware of it themselves, workers come to develop this managerial gaze and other workers become conscious of the fact that they are being watched.[10]

On the factory floor it is not just a matter of the managers having unilateral control over the workers. Somebody is always keeping an eye on someone else. Everybody *feels* someone is watching them. Every single worker is subject, one way or another, to the managerial gaze.

Summary: the context of the factory floor

In this chapter we have been looking at the process of control in the workplace. Workers do not automatically act in accordance with the logic of the 'Toyota Production System' from the moment they set foot in the factory. Nor are they completely manipulated by the management of the personnel department. It is not the case that the production system regulates everything a worker does, nor is it true to say that every worker is spurred on by a sense of competition with other workers. If we turn our eyes to the actual state of control on the factory floor, we discover that power is exercised through machinery and plant and that workers are controlled through communication.[11] Through the 'visibilization' of the working environment and human relationships, the gaze of power permeates to the furthest corners of the factory. And it is because they are conscious of this gaze that workers 'voluntarily' act in accordance with the will of management.

Moreover, the authority of the free discretion workers are given is nothing more than a favour that can be withdrawn immediately at any hint of deviant behaviour. On the other hand, workers are required to shoulder extremely heavy responsibilities and in the running of operations on the factory floor that responsibility is unlimited. Indeed, it is power that makes it possible to enforce this imbalance between authority and responsibility and it is power that makes workers labour in concert with management thinking, even when they are not under direct supervision.

Further, not only are the general workers *controlled* through communication with their bosses on the shop floor, they themselves end up *controlling* other workers. Young workers, in particular, are likely to be seen as candidates to be controlled. In this way the eyes of power, through the medium of the workers, penetrates deep into the recesses of the factory, making the whole area a zone of mutual surveillance.

It should be noted here that workers are not necessarily overtly managed and controlled, nor are they obviously oppressed. There may indeed be some workers who feel they are leading happy working lives free of control or management. Or, at worst, they may just feel a little inhibited about saying what they think in the stifling atmosphere of the bosses' prefabricated offices. People outside the factory, and even the workers themselves, are often unaware of this binary power-relationship between management and labour. This is because, although there is an invisible net of eyes spread across the factory to control and direct the workers and the workers feel 'something' constraining them, they do not feel that 'someone' is controlling them.

From the point of view of the workers, I think perhaps this kind of workplace might be reassessed as follows. Management does not give detailed, explicit direction to workers on a daily basis. Instead, the workers behave in accordance with the 'code of the factory floor' (i.e. behavioural norms). As workers recognise this code as a set of 'workplace rules' rather than as orders from above, anyone who deviates from the code attracts scorn, not only from the factory supervisors, but from their workmates as well. In short, the code functions as a strong constraint on the workers.

Workers who have just recently entered the company cannot read this code. Consequently, they can only perform tasks under direction and need to have their mistakes pointed out to them. At this stage these workers are not fully accepted by their workmates and are labelled 'useless' or 'stupid.' But they gradually become aware of the code and do all they can to abide by it. A case in point is the way I myself voluntarily took on the job of fine-tuning between processes that had not been part of my standard workload when I was first assigned to the cleaning round.

Furthermore, this code does not apply only to your own position on the line. It covers the entire factory complex.

In our workplace, we can take a rest before work or during our break periods in a prefabricated structure provided for this purpose. The prefab. is hardly abuzz with conversation. Most of the workers just sit there in silence with heads lowered. There is a refrigerator in the room where some workers leave their drinks, but most workers have no particular reason for resting in the prefab. The reason they do so is partly because there is nowhere else to go, but more than that, it is to covertly demonstrate their compliance with management and harmony with their fellow workers.

At first, the casual workers took their rest breaks outside the prefab, but gradually, as they became aware of the code, one by one they started to make use of this facility. When I asked them why, Kitamura answered in a self-deprecating way that he had been 'sucked in' and Naganuma said aggressively, 'I want to get what I can out of those guys.' Yada seemed to be thinking of co-operation when he answered, 'I want to get to know the regular staff.' They all gave different reasons, but what they had in common was that they had perceived the code and had begun to behave according to its principles. To continue to fall out of line and maintain an attitude of resistance to the code indefinitely, is bound to invite antagonism from the entire group. In addition, once someone has been labelled a 'non-conformist,' everything about them, from their behaviour to the way they dress, becomes a butt for criticism and eventually they end up becoming completely ostracized. Most workers fear that possibility, so to prevent it happening to them, they faithfully act in line with the code.

6 Labour Management and the Everyday Lives of Workers

There has been considerable research on Toyota's control of labour. Researchers have pointed out that Toyota controls every aspect of its worker's lives from the factory floor to their homes. But most of this research concentrates on the system itself and you could hardly say that it has fully grasped the significance of its actual implementation. There has been even less work on how it effects the worker's world.[1] Consequently, in this chapter, I intend to focus on the actual implementation of the system and the effect it had on the daily lives of those being controlled.

Selection

Appointment of personnel

There was a reshuffle of personnel during the period of my contract. On 1 October our group leader and one of our section leaders were directed to move to another group and one of the remaining section leaders was promoted to group leader. (Officially deputy group leader. He was to become group leader on 1 April 2002). The remaining section leader was left where he was and two general workers were promoted to the position of section leader. Apparently, Morita, the group leader who was transferred, had so impressed those above that he had been moved to a post where he had overall control of the entire assembly line. This was an extremely exceptional appointment, given that he was still in his thirties.[2]

It is not at all easy for a general worker to rise to the ranks of group leader, let alone chief leader (*kōchō*) or section head (*kachō*). Of a total workforce of approximately two thousand five hundred, there is one factory manager (*kōjōchō*), five division heads (*buchō* – engineering division, production engineering division, casting and forging division, machinery division 1, machinery division 2) and thirty-three section heads (fourteen in the two machinery divisions alone).

There are indeed some ambitious workers who seek promotion. Sometimes, in just a short chat with these people, you can sense the drive to move up in the world and the spirit of competition.

9 August (Thursday)

Kawakami (8 years' service) spoke in our QC circle today. Apparently, sometime before, he had discovered a major defect that may have had dire repercussions for the company. Consequently, he proposed a plan to intercept imperfect products and prevent them from going on to the next process. When the section leader, assuming Kawakami had been appropriately rewarded, asked him how much he had received for his suggestion, Kawakami said, 'I just got five hundred yen.' We all gave a bitter smile in sympathy, but the section leader said, 'Don't be disappointed. I'm sure those on high have taken note of your name.'

2 November (Friday)

Some of the workmates I'd been close to threw a farewell party for me. This was when the topic of conversation turned to the team leader. One of the central figures on the sub-assembly operation commented, 'Why on earth has he partitioned off the whole workplace? I just can't work it out!' Apparently there is strong dissatisfaction with the fact that Nagata, the team leader of the inspection and packing line, has partitioned off the whole group (made up of both the inspection/packing and sub-assembly teams).

Workers vie with one another for the limited number of positions and are concerned about impressing their superiors. But the question as to whether the screening process gives rise to competition among workers or whether competition leads to workers being more closely integrated into the enterprise[3] is, in reality, slightly more complicated than this. While I have no way of knowing the true feelings of each individual worker, it seems to me that, with a few exceptions, most workers go about their tasks modestly wishing to be seen on a par with their peers, rather than through a strong desire to stand out from the crowd. Even though they may have a sense of competition, the majority of workers avoid openly revealing their aspirations for promotion. The exceptions are the elite likely to be designated team leaders and those casual workers who are hoping for an extension of their contract or an appointment to the regular staff. As I have already touched upon the team leaders, here I shall focus on the battle for survival among the casual workers.

Casual employees cannot automatically extend their contracts simply because they want to, let alone get onto the permanent staff. To stay on beyond the period of their contracts casual workers must pass an exacting assessment carried out by management. Casual workers are employed on contracts ranging from a minimum of three months to a maximum of six months.[4] As a general rule, casual workers leave the company when the term of their contract is up, but sometimes it is possible to extend the contract. We were given a detailed explanation about this during our induction training.

A personnel department document puts it like this.

Extension of contract is only possible if;

1. At the time of expiry of the contract period, the employee concerned so desires and the company's need* for the position remains.

* The company's needs include the circumstances of production and the suitability, capabilities etc of the employee concerned.

2. Extensions may be for a period between three and five months. (On no account should the total contract period, including any extensions, be in excess of one year. Note: As at September 2006, it is possible to work up to a total of two years and eleven months*).

* However, if the initial contract period is less than six months, the extension is for a single period of up to six months.

Put simply, the principal condition for an extension of contract is to be liked by management. As the starting point is a letter of recommendation from your immediate boss, it follows that it is virtually impossible to get an extension of contract unless you are on good terms with your supervisor. So you are expected to work diligently, not take time off or arrive late for work and get on well with your colleagues. But even if you fulfil all these conditions it does not necessarily mean that your contract will be extended. The second condition is that at the time of expiry of your contract the demand for production remains strong and that the company still needs to employ a casual worker. No matter how excellent casual workers may be, their contracts will not be extended if there is a downturn in demand.

At our initial orientation training we also heard about the procedure for becoming a regular employee of the company. There is an examination to become a provisional member of staff for casual employees with at least six months' service with the company and a recommendation from a supervisor. The examination comprises both an interview and a written test (on general knowledge). There are many candidates and the competition is fierce. Even those who succeed in becoming provisional members of staff do not immediately become full members of the company. During their period of probation (in principle three months), they are obliged to take a further interview examination. Only after passing this do they become regular employees of the company. However, depending on fluctuations in economic conditions, the entire system of conversion to regular employee status can be cancelled. The education officer told us the average age of those who become regular employees is about twenty-three. He said that between ten and fifteen percent of candidates succeed in the examination, but we should not be discouraged by the low success rate as we would all have a chance if we were prepared to work hard.

Anything to do with conversion to regular staff soon spread among the casual employees. You would often hear rumours along the lines that only five percent of candidates had passed the last exam. Such was the level of interest among casual employees, particularly the younger ones, in becoming regular members of staff.

Incidentally, I was approached about extending my contract. I suppose they were impressed with the fact that I had never been absent without leave or late for work. Apparently, even before his first month was up, the group leader had told the casual worker, who had been paired with me, that he would have no chance of getting an extension. People like him, who, for the wrong reasons, have come to the notice of the bosses, have virtually no hope of extending their contracts. In addition, two casual workers who joined before me will be taking the exam for conversion to regular status in mid-November 2001. They may well pass, as they are both good workers and are liked by their superiors. Tabata, in particular, has a very good chance, as he is still young. He is very co-operative and enjoys the trust of his colleagues. He also takes his monthly creative proposal very seriously, typing it out on the computer and including graphs and tables, not just dashing off anything to get it out of the way. I think the bosses must have appreciated the effort he put in, because I understand he had once even received a six thousand yen award. I once said to him, 'You should be fine, because your boss recognizes the contribution you're making.' But he answered modestly, 'I don't think I'll make it. You need the support of someone higher up, say, head of section or above.' Of course, not all casual workers want to extend their contracts or be converted to the status of regular employees. It is true to say, however, that all of the fixed term employees around me, even though they were half-resigned to the reality of the low success rate, were very conscious of the regular staff conversion policy.

Core and periphery

We have seen how competition goes on in the higher and lower strata of the workplace pyramid structure. Most workers, however, go about their working lives hardly giving a thought to competition.

Actual conditions on the factory floor are a far cry from the image of integration with the administrative elites through competition and selection. Why then, we may ask, do most workers avoid being drawn into the spiral of competition? I think one reason is that management divides workers into the categories of 'core' and 'peripheral' and applies different rules to the two groups. So you don't often see the phenomenon where workers are competing for a limited number of positions. Of course, management does not openly discriminate in favour of a particular group of workers. If you were to ask them they would say they treat all workers absolutely equally. The reality, however, is that workers are treated differently and the workers themselves are very sensitive to these subtle differences. Here, let us consider the differences in the way management treats regular staff as against casual employees, or high-school graduate recruits in contrast to those employed from previous work experience, or male employees versus female employees. In so doing, I would also like to examine how the workers concerned respond to these differences.

Regular employees and casual workers

There is no overt indication that management is drawing a distinction between regular staff and casual employees. On the contrary, they strive to treat the two groups equally. The young regular employees work on the production line and the casual workers also participate in QC circles and *kaizen* activities. Observing from the sidelines, the only difference you would detect would be in the design of the caps they are wearing. All workers must wear a cap while they are on duty. There are subtle differences in the design of the cap, depending on whether the wearer is a casual employee, a provisional member of staff, a regular member of staff, a section leader, a group leader or the chief leader.

It is not only in the allocation of hats, however, where the two groups are treated differently. No matter how hard managers may try to show that they are treating regular employees and casual workers equally, they cannot hide the fact that they see casual workers as a human resource that can be sacked at any time.

As I have mentioned several times before, in Toyota, frequent changes are made to the number of workers on the line in response to fluctuations in the number of vehicles produced. When production is increased, the number of tasks to which a worker is assigned is decreased and more operators are taken on. The reverse is true when there is a decrease in production. When the demand for labour is high, they employ more casual workers and when the demand falls, they run the line around regular employees. Management sees the casual workers as a buffer to guarantee the flexibility this approach demands. Moreover, it is not only the managers, but also the leadership of the union who hold this view.

Union activities in the workplace do not go much beyond the odd meeting in the lunchtime rest period. There were only two such occasions in the time I was working there. The union newsletter I received at one of these meetings contained a sentence to the effect that a branch representative had asked, 'Given the present high rate of employment of supplementary labour, what does the union leadership feel about this policy?' The answer given by the deputy chairman was that, 'Toyota will do all it can to maintain its level of employment and making use of casual contract labour is one strategy to achieve this goal. In the medium to long term, it is estimated that the number of vehicles the company produces in Japan will fluctuate between three million and three and a half million. If we assume that at some point production were to drop to three million, the company would then have to peg back the level of the casual workforce to guarantee the jobs of union members. Working on the premise that in any factory it is necessary to have a certain number of casual workers, we are negotiating with management for professional development through multi-skilling training and the adoption of processes for integrating inexperienced workers and so on. But, at the same time, we ourselves should grapple with the task of strengthening the operation on the factory floor.'

Even the union leadership considers that there should be an 'effective use' of casual labour to protect the employment of the regular workers. This view of casual workers held by management and the upper echelons of the union also exerts an influence in the workplace.

The regular employees view the casual workers as 'outsiders.' In return the casual workers regard the regular employees as 'those guys.' Whenever faulty products slipped through the line or anything went missing from the dormitory or there was a car accident, the whisper would soon go around, 'not the casuals again!' Every time there was any incident, the casual workers got a bitter reminder of their different status. It was as if there was a great wall in the workplace dividing the two groups.

High school graduates and experienced appointees
There were similar walls even within the ranks of the regular employees. One of them was between the high school recruits and the regular experienced appointments. When I was assigned to my place, there were eleven new high school graduate recruits and five appointed from jobs outside the company. I don't know if the bosses were deliberately treating the five outside appointees with indifference, but they certainly did not seem to be given a particularly warm reception.

This was particularly apparent in the way they were moved around. I have already given the example of Ōki (an outside appointee with sixteen years service with the company) and Takenaka (an outside appointee with fifteen years service). They would never have been passed around like hot potatoes if they had been regarded as core personnel. The same could be said of Maejima (twelve years experience) who, conversely, had never changed his work position. He had been left out of the rotation process altogether. Clearly, he had not been given a central role. Perhaps it is because they have been influenced by this kind of treatment, but from just talking privately with these people, I get the feeling that their attitude towards the company is quite different from those recruited directly from high school.

When one of the supervisors, a mid-career recruit, heard how much I was earning, he said that he reckoned I had taken the wrong path. His assessment of Toyota was that it was an 'outrageous' employer. Despite the fact that he was in a supervisory position, he was completely browned off with the company.

Even Takenaka affirmed, 'Toyota is not a humane employer. It's a company that gets everything it can out of its workers.' He spoke with the conviction of experience, having been frequently sent off to 'support' other groups. Apparently Kawakami (mid-career recruit, eight years with the company) had once been reprimanded by his team leader with a remark along the lines of, 'Don't you want to move any higher up, then?' It was not as if Kawakami was at all lazy, but if anything, he lacked the team leader's ambition for promotion. Ōki would say, 'My motto is to just get the job done somehow, then get away home as quickly as possible!' He didn't lose any time hanging around in the prefab. after work. I suppose even the high school recruits have their gripes against the company, but they seem to be more closely involved than those employed from other companies outside.

In Toyota there are different staff social clubs catering for employees recruited in different ways. The high school graduate appointees, for example, belong to the *Hōseikai* and the outside recruits join the *Hōryūkai*. I recall that once in the lunch break they collected membership fees for each of the groups separately (23 October). This seems to be a trifling point, but little things like this no doubt contribute to the consciousness of difference between the two groups.[5]

It is not only the disparity in the treatment meted out by management that is the cause of this sense of difference. One of the outside appointees gave me his assessment of the high school graduate recruits one day when we were having lunch together. 'They come into this company straight from high school. You could say they go through a process of "uncontaminated cultivation." So they don't know what it is like in other companies or that there are various different types of people out there. They're not aware of any "abnormalities" in this company or that there are different ways to treat people.' I suppose, by way of contrast, that those employees recruited from outside, automatically tend to make comparisons simply because they have experienced factory work with other companies.[6]

Male workers and female workers
In our group we had two female workers, Murase (high school recruit, 2 years experience) and Enoki (high school recruit, 1 year experience). From what they were saying it seems that, including the opposite shift, there are about ten women working in this factory, that is, No. 3 Factory of Plant K. They deduced this from the number of female names on the lockers that are allocated to each staff member.

When I inquired about the rate of intake of women into Plant K, I discovered that four years ago it was two or three. Three years ago there were eight women taken on in a total of eighty new staff and eight again last year, though last year ninety new staff were employed. There was only one woman among the two hundred and ninety-two casual employees who joined the company when I did. It is only recently (the women said four years ago) that this plant has started employing women and you still rarely see a woman on the factory floor.[7]

Can we assume then that women workers work in exactly the same way as the men? To start with the conclusion, women are not assigned to all of the tasks of this group. On the sub-assembly process, women only work on the rear ends. As I explained before, it is only with the rear units that you have one common part for both the medium and high capacity engines. All the other parts come in different versions for medium and high capacity engines. The smaller the number of parts there are, the lighter is the load on the operator. On the inspection and packing line they were in charge of inspection and packing of boxed parts and in the assembling of cardboard boxes. Making the boxes simply entailed pushing the folded cardboard cartons into shape. This was regarded as the lightest workload in our group. But, as I have mentioned several times before, the inspection and packing operation is a very demanding task that needs to be performed at an extremely fast speed. Women workers also do this job. But Enoki, who was in charge of inspection and packing, found it extremely difficult to finish the task within the designated *takt* time. This was because from the outset the specified standard operation time was not set at a level suitable for 'a line that anyone can work on.'

The standard operation time sometimes came up for discussion at quality control meetings (30 October). Nagata the team leader said that he had timed how long it took to inspect and pack the rear rings. He claimed that it took a male worker two minutes to inspect and pack a carton of parts, whereas Enoki was taking three minutes. So apparently he decided to make the *takt* time for the operation the average of the times of the male and female operators. Obviously, calculating the standard operation time like this more or less ensured that she would never be able to complete the task on time.[8]

Despite the concept of a workplace where 'anyone can work,' the situation in this factory is such that it is not possible for women to work in the same way as the male workers. In recent years Toyota has sought to extend its appeal to women workers. But from what I have seen in our factory, all this means is that it is not so much a case of women working, or being able to work, anywhere at all, but more a matter of it not being impossible for women to work on certain tasks. Even so, the present situation may well be an improvement over what happened in the past. Nevertheless, I feel that the image is still way ahead of the reality.[9] Of course, this is not to say that no consideration at all has been given to women. For instance, only female employees are provided with a key to the purpose-built women's toilets. Although it smacked a little of mere formality, we were educated about sexual harassment in our induction training. But, as things stand at present, women are not regarded as an equivalent 'fighting force' to the men and there is no way they can become 'core' workers.

Once I asked the female workers why they had chosen to join such a harsh company (12 September). Here is a summary of our conversation.

> Ihara: 'Why Toyota? Did you go to a technical high school or something?'
>
> Enoki: 'No. I went to an advanced vocational school specializing in sewing. I was just singled out by my teacher.'
>
> Murase: 'I went to an ordinary high school.'
>
> Ihara: 'Didn't you want to go into a clerical job?'
>
> Enoki: 'They weren't employing office staff.'
>
> Ihara: 'Didn't you think of a clerical job with a company other than Toyota?'
>
> Enoki: 'They'd already decided on someone else.'
>
> Murase: 'Toyota suits me.'
>
> Ihara: 'How come?'
>
> Murase: 'This is my hometown. I can take one hundred percent of my menstrual period leave.'
>
> Enoki: 'But I didn't think it would be this tough.'

Murase, the one who said the company suited her, frequently took time off. She did not appear to be very well integrated into the workplace either. There were some male workers who would say to her half jokingly that it was a dumb idea to be taking so many holidays. Because they had no female workers on the opposite shift, you could really notice the difference when there was a call for increased production. When time pressure on the shop floor became tight, an atmosphere of resentment over the presence of the women began to develop. But some female workers can handle this pressure very cleverly. Murase wasn't particularly adept at using her *feminine wiles*, but Enoki was always very charming in her dealings with everybody and she seemed to be able to cope pretty well with any pressure from the male workers. She had succeeded in carving out a niche for herself as a member of a minority group.

From the above it will be clear that even the regular workers are divided into two groups, 'the core' that plays a central role in the factory and those situated on 'the periphery.' Though differences in ability and commitment cannot be dismissed as contributing factors, neither can it be said that these distinctions are the result of fair competition. Certainly, not as long as staff are treated differently according to the pattern of their recruitment into the company.[10]

Under these circumstances workers are very sensitive to these distinctions between themselves and others. They divide their fellow workers into those they regard as mates and those they do not. This division of habitat is not desirable from management's point of view. There tends to be a lowering of morale and less commitment from those workers located on the periphery. Occasionally it can lead to hostility between workers and jeopardize the smooth running of the workplace. This is the kind of situation that management, which naturally wants to extract the greatest possible contribution from every worker, wishes most to avoid. Despite the fact that they have divided the workers into core and peripheral employees, the last thing they want is for the workers to see themselves in those terms. So, even while they are selecting and sorting out the workers, they are also seeking to integrate them into the company structure.

Integration

Incentives: wages

Wages constitute a strong incentive for both core and peripheral workers. When I asked several workers why they continue to endure this punishing work, their instant response was that they do so because the wages are high. The question of bonuses was also raised at the workplace meetings of the union. Apparently this year (2001 fiscal year) workers received bonuses equivalent to over five months salary. This is a great attraction for regular workers.

On the other hand, for casual workers there is an end-of-term payment. This performs the very important function of getting the casual workers situated on the periphery to complete their work. Let us now examine the wage system for casual workers.

The basic daily wage differs according to the number of terms served (one term is a continuous period of six months or more). For workers like me working for the first time with the company, the basic daily wage is ¥9,000. Workers in their second term earn ¥9,500 and in their third term the daily rate rises to ¥9,800. The wages, which are paid monthly, include just this basic daily rate (standard wage) plus overtime earnings (allowance for additional time worked) plus various allowances (late night work allowance, out-of-hours allowance etc). A glance at my detailed-breakdown-of-wages slips reveals that, after deducting my social insurance payment, tax and the cost of lunches, even in the highest month, my salary was below ¥180,000. You certainly could not call that a high wage! But at the end of your period of work you are rewarded with the final gratitude bonus (*irōkin*) and the end-of-term payment (*hōshōkin*). These play an important role in integrating casual workers into the company.

The final gratitude-bonus is an allowance payed to casual workers on expiry of the term of their contracts. It is not payed to employees who leave before their contacts have expired. The amount paid varies according to the length of the contract period. For workers on three-month contracts it is ¥500 per day, increasing to ¥700 for four-month contracts, ¥1,000 for five months and ¥1,500 for six months. The final gratitude bonus, then, is this amount multiplied by the number of days worked, i.e. roughly ¥30,000 for three months, ¥56,000 for four months, ¥100,000 for five months and ¥180,000 for six months. This end-of-term bonus is the incentive that drives casual employees to work out the full period of their contracts.

In addition, there is a separate amount paid as reward money at the conclusion of the contract. This payment of ¥1,000 per day is only paid to those casual workers who have worked the full period without any record of absenteeism, arriving late or finishing work early. You have to be careful, as an infringement in any of these areas results in not only loss of the bonus for the day concerned, but for that entire month. This means that just arriving late for work one day can result in the loss of ¥20,000 in reward money. This system is very tough on casual workers. Missing one day means losing around ¥30,000 – that day's wages plus the whole month's reward payment.

Several times I wanted to take the day off, but each time the thought of losing thirty thousand yen flashed into my mind and persuaded me to turn up for work. Even missing a day for a legitimate reason such as illness, results in the loss of that month's final reward bonus. For that reason, workers cannot afford to take time off for light colds and other minor ailments.

8 August (Wednesday)

My workmate Kimata, who has been complaining recently that he has not been feeling well, collapsed at work. He came to my room to see me as soon as I got back home from the factory. He said, 'I felt terrible all day yesterday, but I was trying to get through my quota somehow or other. Then, after lunch, I broke out in a cold sweat and I started to feel faint. The next thing I knew, I was lying on the bed in the first-aid room. It's really strange, but I hardly remember a thing that happened around that time. They took my temperature and found I was running a fever of 39.7. I went straight to the nearest hospital where they put me on a drip and gave me a suppository to bring down my temperature. Today, I spent all day in bed. I'm going back to work in the factory tomorrow.' Segawa, a casual worker on the opposite shift, also took three days off work at the beginning of August with a temperature over thirty-nine degrees.

12 September (Thursday)

This morning I had a temperature, but I whipped my body to go off to the factory. At work I felt uncontrollably weary. I couldn't summon the strength to lift anything heavy. At one point I could feel the cleaning tray slipping out of my arms. I came to my senses just in time to prevent an accident. During my lunch break I tried taking some cold medicine just as a sop and surprisingly it worked. Not that it cured my cold, but it sent my mind into a high. I suspect the medicine contained some kind of stimulant. No wonder some athletes are put on doping charges for taking cough medicines. I worked through the afternoon with a blocked nose and shortness of breath.

I became hooked on the medicine and continued taking it for a while to get me through my work. The wages system they have here binds workers, forcing them to push their bodies to the limit so they can keep working without taking time off. Regular staff get annual leave as a matter of course, but the casual workers are under constant pressure not to miss a single day off work.[11]

In addition, only those casual workers who have completed the full term of their contract are paid travel expenses to return home. Those who leave before the end of their term get nothing at all. Many of the casual employees, attracted by the salary ranging from ¥312,000 to ¥337,000 mentioned in the promotional pamphlet, travel considerable distances to come and work at Toyota. This figure is the monthly average of all wages and allowances including the end-of-term payment and the final gratitude-bonus. This is not to say that the pamphlet is lying, but the fact is, to the uninitiated, it does give the impression that you get over three hundred thousand yen in your hand every month. It is only after they have actually started working that casual workers *find out* about the wage structure. They work on in silence, counting on the end-of-term payment, the gratitude bonus and unemployment insurance (paid to workers on continued service of six months or more).

Events

The management puts on a variety of events to create a feeling of identity with the company. Even in the short period I was working there, we had a number of events in the factory and in the dormitory.

28 July (Saturday)
We're having a *Bon-odori* festival (dancing associated with the *Bon* Buddhist All-Souls festival) in the dormitory parking lot. They've been calling us to participate over the dormitory internal broadcast system.
It appears people form the local community will also be coming and there will be stalls serving fried noodles and frankfurts.

30 September (Saturday)
I discovered that today we will be having an event in the factory called the K-Fiesta. One of the highlights of the festival is the *ekiden* (long-distance relay) race. Our workplace group is putting up two groups of runners. Those chosen to run have been training on the track in the factory after work. Casual workers, one from our group and two from the opposite shift, will also be participating in the event.

13 October (Saturday)
They are putting on a barbecue for the employees in the dormitory. All you can eat and it's free.

19 October (Friday)

We are having a volleyball tournament as part of the company's medical fitness program. The event is being held as the company's contribution to health-and-hygiene month. Everyone is participating except those employees who commute from Dormitory A. Apparently a boxed lunch is included. I've opted out, making a few plausible excuses. Volleyball after work and a QC circle meeting is just too much! Yamano tells me that yesterday his 23rd machine section all participated in the giant rope skipping contest.

Toyota workers follow a different pattern of living from workers in general. There is a change of shifts every other week and the factory does not stop for public holidays. Workers here follow the 'Toyota calendar.' The various events too, naturally are slotted into the company schedule. This may also be convenient for the workers.

You would imagine that the workers look forward to these events. Speaking at least for the people around me, not just the casual workers, but regular employees as well, I can say that they participate in these events because they consider them an extension of their work. So, it did not seem to me as if the workers were being integrated into the company through these events.

But because they are held so frequently and participation is so strongly encouraged, you begin to consciously take company events into account when planning your own private schedule. If you are free you are tempted to go along just to have a look. I was surprised to discover that even I gradually became more conscious of these events. In this way, the presence of the company becomes incorporated into your private life. Furthermore, the change in your thinking does not stop there. As your consciousness of being a member of the company strengthens, your connections with the local community become progressively weaker. You suddenly realise that most of your attention is focused on the company and you hardly give a passing glance to the world outside. I do not feel that I am working for the benefit of Toyota and I am not especially proud of the fact that I work for Toyota. I have no strong feeling of identification with Toyota, even though I am an employee of the company. Rather, I try to maintain a certain sense of distance. But regardless of the stance I take, I still find that the Toyota schedule determines my lifestyle and that most of my thoughts are directed towards the company.

Without my being aware of what was happening, it gradually reached the stage where my private conversations too were concerned exclusively with the company or my workplace. You could say I was being unconsciously drawn into the company.

Other activities

30 July (Monday)

Yesterday was voting day for the House of Councillors election. Today at work they were collecting 'vote casting slips.' The union official wanted not only the workers' own slips, but also those of their family members. I'm ashamed to admit it, but I did not even know such a thing existed. When I asked, I learnt that the slips are given out at the voting booths. I was surprised to discover that this sort of thing goes on in the workplace.

29 August (Wednesday)

Since I arrived at Toyota not a single day has passed without my hearing the words 'traffic safety.' I suspect this is because it would damage the car company's image if any of its employees were to be involved in a traffic accident. Every day, messages on the in-house broadcast system, from someone or other in such-and-such a department, like 'I always make sure I put on my seatbelt' echo through the factory.

If one of the staff has an accident, then not only the person concerned, but all the members of the group are required to take joint responsibility and stand outside the factory before work holding traffic safety flags. We were told in our orientation training that we would have to undergo this 'punishment' even if one of us forgot to do up our seatbelt.

Even such drastic measures, however, cannot eliminate accidents or traffic infringements. According to a sign posted in our dormitory, on 10 and 21 July, employees of the company caused fatal accidents while driving under the influence of alcohol. A similar poster was displayed in the bath of the dormitory when we were undergoing training. It said that on the 20 July a member of staff from this dormitory had caused the death of a junior high school pupil by driving when he was intoxicated. A pamphlet I received on my way home the other day said, 'Recently there has been an increase in serious traffic accidents caused by "the six evils of the road" (*kōtsū rokuaku*, i.e. drink driving, speeding etc). We still have not been able to put a stop to drunken driving!! – Recent accident reports: 10 July, intoxicated driver collides with moped causing fatal accident. 2 June, hit and run accident while under the influence of alcohol. 27 May, accident while driving under the influence of alcohol causes property damage.'

21 September (Friday)

Today there was a workplace inspection by a vice president of Toyota and the factory manager. We had been preparing for this since yesterday. We repainted the walking course lines on the floor and wiped over any areas they would be likely to notice with cleaning fluid. Not only the route they were to follow on their inspection, but also the employees they were to talk to, had been decided beforehand. Tsuda (2 years service) was told yesterday that he should expect to be spoken to. We were told to have the trolley for the sub-assembly operation parked in its standard position for the period of the vice president's inspection, though normally we placed it a little away from the designated position.

From more than two hours before the vice president's visit, the bosses on the factory floor were on tender-hooks. Some of them kept rehearsing over and over again what to say, while others were constantly on their mobile phones impatiently checking the time of arrival of the inspection party. There were bosses all over the place, getting in the way of the transport operation. Somebody had taken it on himself to hide the pile of empty high-capacity component trays, presumably because he didn't want the vice president to notice them. I never did find those trays. I don't ask for any help, but at least I expect not to be hindered! The middle-aged fellow in charge of the transport on the previous process said sarcastically, 'That lot are our dependent relatives. They get paid for just shooting off their mouths.' Written explanations giving an overview of the factory and the various processes on the line were displayed on boards around the floor for the benefit of the vice president. He was being treated just like an important guest or a favoured customer. When the vice president finally appeared, he had a long procession of attendants following after him. After these came the workplace bosses. He also came to our prefab during the afternoon rest period, but just glanced at the computer and left again immediately.

Next to the prefab, there is a group at work comprised only of foreigners. I assume this is part of their staff training, as the company is planning to build a new factory in Poland. During the vice president's visit they tagged along too and listened to all the explanations about the operation of the line.

Incidentally, in the area surrounding the factory you often come across foreigners, but you don't see foreign workers resident in Japan working in this factory.

After the inspection, we had stocktaking. Because it was the end of the first half of the fiscal year, we all stopped our regular work early and involved ourselves in stocktaking. We had to accurately count all the parts left in the chutes to calculate our mid-term stock inventory.

It was a very busy day, what with the stocktaking on top of the visit of the vice president.

28 September (Friday)

Today we were all told to assemble at 3:20 p.m. in the prefab for safety training. We discussed with the opposite shift how we could thoroughly strengthen safety on the job. Safety is the driving concept for our assembly line and we take a great deal of care in getting it right.

The section leader Shimada (21 years with the company) co-ordinated the discussion and we were all encouraged to throw in our opinions. Shiraishi (19 years experience) also a section leader, was first to speak. 'I think it would be a good idea to do some simulation exercises. For example, using a dummy we could learn with our own eyes about the danger of getting caught up in the chain of a machine.' I was particularly impressed with what our group leader, Morita had to say, 'Other group leaders are now carrying out safety inspections, but frankly I can understand that you might not feel comfortable about that. For example, a worker in the sub-assembly unit might confirm the safety of the packing line and, conversely, one of the people on packing could check the sub-assembly unit. It would only take about ten minutes and it could be done in our normal working time.' In contrast to this approach, some were of the opinion that there should be closer management control. Yamashita, a section leader with nineteen years experience, said, 'In my previous workplace, every day we had to write a report that was checked by the boss. I think perhaps it might be a good idea to introduce that system into this workplace.' At the end of the day, it was only the bosses who said anything. The general workers just gazed silently at the floor.

Even with matters as straight-forward as safety policy, opinions differed from one worksite to another, and depending on the personality of the group leader, over whether to adopt a self-regulatory approach or a managerial solution. There is a degree of flexibility permitted in the running of the operation.

30 September (Sunday)

Today we have the debating competition of the section-leaders' committee. More accurately, 'The twenty-fifth debating competition: Let flaming passion resound in the heart! Inspiration 21 fulfilled.' Twenty section leaders from all divisions will be taking part. I'd quite like to go along, just to see what the atmosphere is like, but I can't persuade my body to make the effort.

4 October (Thursday)

Today we had an on-site inspection by the managing director. Just like the other day, the pressure of handling the visit fell on the 'top brass' of the factory floor. Again there was a spate of rehearsals. We were told to turn off the music and hide our CDs for the duration of the inspection. The workers on the inspection and packing line generally listen to CDs. They play Ayumi Hamasaki, Hikaru Utada, Ami Suzuki and SPEED, or some similar J-pop. The section leader with the punch perm is always moaning, 'Can't you play some traditional ballads (*enka*) occasionally!' Enoki brought her own ghetto-blaster from home to play the CDs on.

One of the bosses from another group came and told me not to pile the empty trays too high. If I don't, we can't get through the job in time. But this instruction was also part of the preparations for the manager's inspection.

25 October (Thursday)

Today in our lunch break, we had a workplace meeting of the union. The casual workers also took part. I'm not sure if we casual workers are officially members of the union. Nagata, the team leader, ran the meeting. The atmosphere was the same as that at our morning meetings. Here there are no clear boundaries between the company and the union, management and labour, or, for that matter, working hours and rest periods.

Dormitory life: From dormitory to factory and back again

1 August (Wednesday) – 6 November (Tuesday)

A total of seven hundred permanent and casual workers live in the dormitory for unmarried staff (Dormitory K). When we joined the company we filled the last vacancies in the dorm. Any casual employees who joined after us had to go to Dormitory A, the accommodation provided for staff of associated companies. It took them an hour each way to commute to and from the factory. We were well off in comparison, just five minutes away.

Most of the regular employees drove their own cars between the dormitory and the factory,[12] but the casual workers commuted in the shuttle bus. The bus would come to pick us up at ten minute intervals between 5:20 a.m. and 6:00 a.m. We could take the bus at any of these times, but I used to catch the first bus so I could have breakfast at the factory. To do so, I had to get up by 5:00 a.m. at the latest.

Incidentally, if you slept in until six o'clock, the supervisor of the dorm would come around and wake you up. Whenever you went out, you had to turn over the plaque on the board by the supervisor's booth from 'in' to 'out.' So, he could tell at a glance if anyone had slept in.

As autumn approached, the surroundings at that time of the morning grew darker day by day. By the time I was nearing the end of my contract, the sun still hadn't come up by five o'clock. I went off to work in the dark. In the bus, the atmosphere was gloomy, as everyone was locked in silence. Nobody said a word on the first shift. Every time the bus drove out of the dormitory gate, I couldn't help feeling depressed at the remnants of the barbed-wire entanglements that still surrounded the property. The tense high-pitched voice of the DJ on the radio playing on the bus also got on my nerves. But we were only five minutes away from the factory. We just turned off the highway into a side street and there right in front of us stood the gate of the factory. As soon as I saw the smoke rising from the chimney, I was all at once overcome by depression. I'd always be last off the bus, reluctantly dragging my dead weight off the seat after everyone had got off.

On the first shift, since the shuttle bus drives directly into the factory grounds, the driver checks the staff identity cards of all the passengers as they get on. On the second shift, the bus stops in front of the factory, so the guard on the gate checks the staff cards. If you forget your pass, you contact your superior and you have to go through a bothersome rigmarole to get in. There are even some workers who, if they forget their passes, go all the way back to the dormitory to collect them, because they don't want to come to the attention of the boss.

The first shift starts early in the morning. The dormitory dining room is still not open. If you want breakfast, you have to go to the factory cafeteria. You choose bread or rice and a few side dishes you like from the selection available. It costs ¥399 including tax – ¥120 for rice, ¥60 for miso soup and ¥200 for two side dishes. There is a greater variety to chose from for lunch and it is a little more expensive.

The cafeteria is run on an automatic payment system. You just place your tray on the reader machine and it displays the cost of your meal, the number of calories it contains etc. You hold your staff card over the machine. The amount is calculated and automatically deducted from your salary. Even here they have introduced automation. In the past apparently the company subsidized half the cost of meals for casual workers, but now they pay the full amount themselves. The company still pays half the cost of the meals for regular staff.

There is a television in the cafeteria and they always have the same morning news running. But from the instant I started working here, I lost any interest in news of the economy, or fluctuations in politics, or even in the weather forecast. The only thing I hear is the baseball results. I just sit there silently stuffing in the rice and miso soup.

After breakfast, I go to the locker room to change into my work clothes, then I head off to the prefabricated staff-room in the factory. They hold exercises before work, so we all try to gather in the prefab in time to join in. At 6:20 a.m. music starts playing throughout the factory and we do our exercises in time with the music. After that, all of us chant in unison the safety slogans, 'We work safely. Right!' 'We change our work patterns if required. Right!' 'We...' and so on. A representative reads out the 'five article safety charter.' After each article he shouts out 'Right!' and assumes the pose of one making a safety check. We all read out the slogans after the representative and assume the finger-pointing-safety-check pose. The representative is determined on a roster system and even I had to do it three times. The safety chant is a formalized procedure that few people take seriously. They tend not to say the slogans at all and simply release a half-hearted 'right' in the appropriate places. Then we move back into the prefab for a meeting. To this point, all the 'work' we have been doing is unpaid. But everyone joins in the exercises without a word of protest and attends the morning meeting as a matter of course. Thus begins a day's work on the factory floor.

As soon as I have finished work, I change my clothes and board the shuttle bus. The bus for the dormitory leaves at fifteen to thirty minute intervals. After work, most of the workers relax for a while in the prefab before they go home. Yamano, who joined with me, tells me that all his group 'hang around' in the prefab for about an hour to relax and unwind. He says he'd like to go home earlier, but the clubby atmosphere makes it difficult for anyone to leave before the rest.

In the bus everyone is glued to the display panel of their mobile phones. No doubt they are checking their e-mail messages. Thanks to mobile phones, we are able to maintain a tenuous link with the outside world. Only once was there a luggage inspection on the bus home. I was not on the bus at the time, but according to Yamano, an inspector got on and carefully went through all the workers' belongings.

If I was on the first shift and didn't have any overtime, I'd be back in the dormitory by a little after 4:00 p.m. The one pleasure I looked forward to in my daily routine was the bath. I enjoyed nothing more than relaxing there, soaking away in that vast bath without another soul around. That's why I made a point of getting back to the dormitory before everybody else. I couldn't afford to waste time relaxing in the prefab. Towards the end of the term of my contract, I would hurry to the bus without even changing out of my work clothes. I'd be sweaty, but not dirty like those working on machines. It was only five minutes back to the dorm. I'd hurry back to my room, then head straight for the bath. While I was taking a bath, I'd also be doing my washing. Even my trousers would be wet with perspiration, so I washed them every day.

There were two washing machines in each of the wings of each floor, a total of four machines per floor. You had to pay to use one of the washing machines and a dryer in each wing, so there was a good deal of competition over the use of the free machines. On the weekends the washing machines would be running constantly. The machines could only be used within the specified hours of 10:00 a.m. and 10:00 p.m. But this rule was not observed. Some people would even use it after the second shift in the small hours of the morning. I think the rooms near the washing machines must have been terribly noisy. There was no place to rest, neither in the factory nor in the dormitory. Fortunately, my room was on the fourth floor towards the back of the building. Yamano used to complain that there was 'some idiot who plays his guitar in the middle of the night' right near his room. It's a wonder that didn't cause any fights!

After my bath I'd go back to my room and, before having a rest, I'd write up a detailed account of the day's events in my diary. I found if I didn't write them down immediately, the details would quickly fade from my memory. But this was very difficult. Even while writing my diary I forgot things. I had brought along a laptop computer, so I could write up my diary in an hour or so, but I imagine it must have been a lot more difficult for Satoshi Kamata, the author of *Japan in the Passing Lane*. I would no longer have had the strength or the inclination to grip a pencil. Even tapping the keyboard my fingers would be shaking slightly. After writing up my diary I was so exhausted that I often dozed off. But if I slept then, I had trouble getting to sleep later at night when I went to bed.

After a short nap, I'd go off to a local shop with some workers I'd become friendly with, to buy a take-away meal for dinner. At first I ate dinner in the dormitory, but they served a lot of deep-fried food that did not agree with my constitution. You would hear the expression *agemono jigoku*, 'fried-food hell,' bandied around the place. According to Yamano, who had once run a restaurant, they used frozen ingredients. They had set meals for about ¥500. Shōji, who was planning to start a pub when his term was up, worked out the cost of ingredients and came to the conclusion that it was a rip-off. He said a convenience store lunchbox was cheaper. At first, as there was nothing decent to eat, I put up with what they had at the dorm. But my perseverance reached its limits and I ended up purchasing my food outside, even though it meant a round trip of one hour. As our physical strength is the only capital we have and we put our bodies on the line every day, you would think they could give a little more consideration to the food they provide.

When I was on the first shift, I'd be in bed before nine, but I found it hard to get to sleep. In the meantime, the people from the second shift would come back. I don't know how many times I was woken up by the sound of car engines and the noise of doors being opened and closed. So, I'd have to go off to work again the next day without having had a decent night's sleep. Right up to the end, I was never able to get used to this irregular lifestyle.

It was much the same when I was on the second shift. I wouldn't get back to the dorm until 1:00 a.m. at the earliest. That could be two or three o'clock if I had overtime. Then, by the time I'd had my bath, eaten and put myself to bed it would be after four in the morning. At about that time, the staff on the opposite shift would be getting up and making preparations to leave for work. It wasn't until they had all left and the sun was starting to come up, that I'd finally fall asleep. If I managed to sleep right up until the last minute when I had to prepare to catch the shuttle bus, I could get eight hours sleep, but apparently this schedule didn't suit my biorhythm and my body felt even more drained than it did on the first shift.

In addition, the change in shifts every other week put a great strain on me. The rotation from second shift back to first shift was particularly tough.

If you are on second shift on Friday night, you don't get back to the dormitory until the early hours of Saturday morning. In my case, I would sleep most of Saturday, then, on Sunday, go off with my friends to buy food supplies. I'd buy vast quantities of cup noodles, soft drinks, stamina drinks and health tonics. Amongst my acquaintances there were some who would go off and play *pachinko* pinball on their day off, but you can't stay out very late because the following week you are on the first shift again. You prepare to go to bed at eight or nine o'clock, but because your body is still working on the previous week's sleeping time, you can't just suddenly start going to sleep earlier. The body simply cannot adapt to these changes in shifts. Inevitably, I'd turn up for work on Mondays having had hardly any sleep the night before. Just when your body was getting used to the schedule, there would be another change of shift. This cycle was repeated over and over again for the whole time I was there.

Basically, Saturday was the only day off we got. But there were, in addition, special holidays. During the period of my contract, we got the Bon (all souls) festival holiday from the thirteenth to the seventeenth of August. In addition, there is the 'golden week' holiday in May and the New Year holiday. But we don't get time off for any of the other public holidays. We even worked through Physical Education Day (a national holiday held on the second Monday in October).

Sometimes we also got sudden unscheduled breaks. For example, 10 September was suddenly declared a holiday because of an impending typhoon. We got the message, 'there'll be no work today' just as we were preparing to leave for the factory. We could not do anything special with our day off. Outside the rain was bucketing down so we couldn't go out. To make matters worse, we were ordered to turn up for work on Saturday, 22 September, to make up for the day missed. That was a typhoon holiday we would have been happier without.

In the dormitory, everyone had their own single room equipped with a television set and an electric pot. We had air-conditioning, but you could only use the heating from after the end of November. The number one dormitory, where I was, had a mahjong table on the first floor and other dormitories had billiard tables, but there were no other entertainment facilities provided. The most inconvenient thing about living in this dormitory was that there were no shops nearby.

As they did not even have a kiosk in the dormitory, we had to go outside to purchase the necessities of life. But even the closest convenience store was more than fifteen minutes walk away. There were hardly any places to eat either. If you wanted to do any real shopping you had to take a train. It took twenty minutes to walk to the station.

Most of the regular workers had a car or a motorbike, or at least a bicycle, but it was rare to find a casual worker who owned any means of transport. There were several bicycles in each dormitory that you could borrow for up to two hours before 8:00 p.m. But on holidays, only the bikes in No.4 Dormitory (about ten bikes in all) could be borrowed. These would be out on loan all day from first thing in the morning. I would have thought that it is precisely on holidays when people would want to borrow a bicycle, but that's when there are so few available to be used. I felt like complaining, 'They make so many cars, you'd think at least they could lend us a car occasionally!'

Cars were always coming into and leaving the dormitory, not only during the day, but late into the night as well. The noise they made was a great inconvenience to those employees trying to get some sleep in the dorm, and to the residents who lived nearby. This dormitory and the factory are built on reclaimed land. Near the dormitory there is a quiet fishing port. Late at night on the 25 September, a Toyota employee driving home beeped his horn at the car in front that was slowly weaving its way along the road. This seemed to cause offence. When he was stopped at the next traffic lights, the driver of the car in front got out and came and beat him up. What's more, he was holding some kind of a hatchet in his hand, so the incident escalated into a case of grievous bodily harm. I remember hearing at our morning meeting about two or three similar incidents involving cars. I doubt if these would have occurred so often if we lived our lives at the same rhythm the locals do.

In principle, people other than employees are not allowed to enter the dormitory.

The pamphlet we received on entering the dormitory states, '1. Visitors are required to fill out a request slip and meetings are to take place in the first floor lounge. 2. In principle, family and friends are not permitted to stay in the dormitory overnight. N.B. Unless formal consent is obtained in advance, a woman may not enter a worker's room. Failure to observe this rule can result in expulsion from the dormitory.' Despite all this, strangers sometimes come wandering into the dormitory uninvited. Late at night and on holidays, when the supervisor is not around, we would get door-to-door salespeople coming in. I was approached by a life-insurance representative. Murayama said that some of the ones coming in looked like gangsters. The company has banned this kind of door-to-door sales, but they keep coming in anyway. There is a sign posted on the notice board at the entrance to the dormitory, warning about the huge amounts of money lost to door-to-door operators. Apparently, some workers in the dormitory have been signed up to buy expensive eiderdown quilts and accessories. A certain of my acquaintances, after being treated to dinner by one of his seniors in the factory, was badgered by a representative of a religious organization into buying a subscription to their newspaper. I told him he was wasting his money and should cancel the contract. He continued with the subscription, saying that he felt he couldn't refuse, and besides, it was not as if he was joining the religion or anything. He had unread newspapers scattered about everywhere in his room.

You can't expect the workers to be independent while the company continues to treat them as children. Those workers who wanted to travel to their homes over the Bon Festival break had to fill out a written request and those staying in the dormitory had to submit a health-check form every day. They put up a notice in the entrance hall saying that if the supervisor had not received the forms for three days in a row he would enter the worker's room to confirm that he was all right.

I don't know, if that actually happened, whether the supervisor would really go into a worker's room, but, at any rate, with the company even controlling worker's private lives, it is hard for them to become independent, responsible members of society.

Perhaps they no longer even feel the necessity to do so. Their entire lives revolve around the factory and the dormitory.[13]

Summary: The fine net of control

In this chapter we have had a glimpse at the aspect of integration into the enterprise through the management of labour. Management needs to achieve a stable and orderly workplace while maintaining the motivation of workers. To achieve a balance between the two, it skilfully employs the distinct strategies of 'selection' and 'integration.' In the process of being regulated, sometimes gently, sometimes strictly, the workers are gradually drawn into the fine net of control cast over and beyond the workplace.

7 Dynamism in the Workplace

In the previous two chapters we have been examining the net of control that stretches over the factory and to the world beyond and the way the workers caught up in this net carry out their work in accordance with the 'code' of the workplace, i.e. the group's rules of behaviour.

Does this mean, then, that here at Toyota the vast majority of workers are steeped in the company's management philosophy? Are they all so-called 'company men' who work obediently, always putting the company's interests ahead of their own?

Most of the research to date has paid little attention to aspects of instability in the workplace. In particular, from the 1980s on, one gets the impression that most of the research into labour in the automobile industry develops, as it were, from the *premise* that workers are indeed cemented into the company and imbued with management logic. However, given the high rate of separations from the company during this period, it is difficult to conclude that the entire workforce had soaked up the management line.[1] So, in this chapter, I would like to focus on conflict in the workplace.

Of course, I do not mean to suggest that there have been no others who have turned their attention to worker opposition and resistance.[2] Moreover, they have accurately taken worker resistance and opposition to be more in the category of 'negative resistance,' or 'letting off steam,' over dissatisfaction.[3] Certainly, the minor resistance seen in the workplace, does not lead to organized action or develop into a resistance movement. While it does play the role of letting off steam over dissatisfaction, I feel it also actually *contributes* to the maintenance of order in the workplace. It is difficult to see it as providing the impetus for the formation of the so-called 'agent of social change.' (Nohara et al. eds, 1988: 499–505).

But although workers on the factory floor might not employ open forms of resistance, they frequently manage to diffuse their dissatisfaction, by cleverly putting a different slant on the conditions imposed on them by management, and in so doing they can bring about change in the workplace. I would like to expand on this point here.

Conflict in the workplace

In our workplace, conditions are such that workers spend all their energy just to achieve their quotas for the day and it would be no exaggeration to say that they have virtually no spare time at all. In this atmosphere, bereft of normal human relationships, the slightest pressure or unreasonable request can quickly give rise to conflict. There are still 'weak points' on the line that have not been corrected and every day these lead to all sorts of problems.

Conflict between workers

31 August (Friday)

In the middle of the night after the second shift, Sawada, a casual worker on the opposite shift, came to see me in my room. He said he was having troubles at work.

I had a pretty good idea what the problem was, as I had heard from Segawa (casual worker) and Murayama (casual worker) about the workplace atmosphere on the opposite shift. From what Sawada was saying, only a young person could handle the sub-assembly operation. All the workers on the line were young. At twenty-six he was the oldest on the sub-assembly line. He said that, even at his age, he found the sub-assembly work very hard. He often fell behind the pace in his work and the regular staff member (23 years old) with whom he was paired, often put pressure on him with comments like, 'Can't you do it any faster?' He felt this criticism was unfair as he was doing the job properly. Unable to control his anger he lashed back with, 'Stop your bloody whining!' Then apparently he complained to his supervisor and asked to be assigned to a different job, as he could not work with his present partner. As a result, it seems, he succeeded in being transferred to the rear-end sub-assembly, a one-man task he could do alone.

3 September (Monday)

On my way home, I noticed Sawada sitting on the sofa talking to the group leader. I presume it was about his conflict with the regular employee. As it happened, Tahara, my contemporary casual worker, who sat next to me on the bus home, was also talking about trouble on the shop floor. He said a younger member of the regular staff was causing him problems because 'he never explains properly how to do things.' The average age of the casual workers assigned to this factory was around twenty-eight. They were often older than the regular employees working with them. It was difficult for the casual workers to have to kowtow to the younger staff and have them teach them how to do their jobs. This was one of the factors that led to conflict between regular employees and casual workers.

Of course, conflict of this kind did not only occur between regular employees and casual workers. It also often occurred between members of the regular staff. In the workplace, not only the older, inexperienced casual workers, but also even regular staff with years of experience, were not necessarily given the respect their age demanded. Quite the reverse, they were often made to feel as if they were getting in the way. I think this atmosphere reflected the tendency to undervalue expertise. On the factory floor, the emphasis was on those attributes in which the younger workers excelled, for example, speed, quick reflexes, strength, concentration, perseverance and, in particular, the flexibility to respond to change. The workplace is changing at a giddying rate. There are rumours going around that even this line might disappear in about three years if there is a downturn in sales. If that were to happen, then all of the workers here would have to start all over again learning new tasks and forging new interpersonal relationships. Behind this instability in the workplace, I think perhaps we can see a breakdown in the traditional pattern, in which the source of power in the workplace lay in skill developed through work experience.[4]

8 September (Saturday) (holiday)

Sawada and I watched the late-night program *Gaki no tsukai* (Kid messenger) on TV. It seems he had his job changed again today. He has only just this week changed over from sub-assembly to inspection and packing. But now, because Hashimoto (casual worker) on the cleaning round has hurt his back, he has been asked to take over Hashimoto's position. This means that, in the space of one month since he was assigned to his workplace (on the reverse shift to me), he has had some experience of every task in his group.

Sawada finally left the company at the end of September, without working out the full term of his contract. He said he found the cleaning round job 'ridiculous' and that he couldn't stand it any longer.

Problems are not confined to conflicts among the rank and file. You often see conflict between the supervisors and team leaders on the one hand and the general workers on the other.

Conflict between workers and supervisors or team leaders

4 October (Thursday)

Today, Nonaka, a casual worker who has been working as my partner, knocked off work early. He turned up at the factory, but his asthma was so bad he went back to the dormitory before the first work period. The bosses saw this as an opportunity to come over and tell me to do the cleaning round job by myself. When I asked them if they could move somebody across from another position, they said they couldn't, because they were also short of staff in sub-assembly. Recently, with increased production, the sub-assembly section has been chronically understaffed. So, apparently, they had been thinking for some time about reducing numbers on the cleaning round. The team leader, Nagata, said casually that I should just try it for the time being and, if it looked as if I could manage, I should continue doing it alone in future. From my point of view this was quite unacceptable. It might not have been so bad if some improvements had been introduced, but they were reducing the number of staff without making any other changes. Even without that, because of the increased volume of product going through the inspection and packing line, recently my job has become even harder than it was before. I made my dissatisfaction quite clear. My ugly mood soon spread out over the whole production line.

Fortunately, inspection and packing sympathized with my predicament. Yada (casual worker) interceded on my behalf, telling the team leader that he would step in and take Nonaka's place on the cleaning round. Kitamura, too, came over and said, 'Tell me as soon as you need high capacity trays.' Even among the regular employees, there were some who, in their own way, showed in their attitude that they were objecting on my behalf. Even Kawakami (8 years service), who normally would never utter a word of complaint to the supervisors, thought it was unreasonable for us to be moved to a different task every hour.

When I told the boss that I found the situation unacceptable, he counter-attacked with, 'They're doing it with just one person on the opposite shift, you know. If they can do it, you ought to be able to do it too.' When it was put to me in those terms, a mixture of competitive drive and pride in my work left me no choice but to accept the proposition. But I was too angry just to let matters ride, so I retorted, 'I know very well what happened on the opposite shift. The two casual workers who were in charge of the cleaning round are friends of mine. They both got injured. One hurt his back and had to be transferred to a different job. The person who stepped in to replace him found he couldn't handle the work and left the company at the end of last month without seeing out his term. Even on the opposite shift, you can't say that they are handling the cleaning round properly with just one man.'

But there was no way I could get out of doing the work. So, I tried laying down some conditions. I said that if I was to do the job, I wanted to finish at the end of regular working hours. I would not be able to cope with the additional physical strain of overtime work. I might be able to do it for a day or two, but in a week's time my body would break down. All the team leader said in reply to my request was, 'I'll think it over.'

Even as I was working, I could feel my resentment growing, to the point where I started handling the parts roughly. Putting the trays into the cleaning machine or onto the chute, I would bang them down angrily. The team leader, to his credit, must have thought he had gone too far, and after lunch he helped me with the transport of the front and rear units. I decided to work out a strategy with Takenaka (15 years service) about how to handle this problem. I requested the following.

1. That I would like the person on pre-inspection to help with the transport, if only with the front and rear units, which do not go through the cleaning process. 2. That I would like the empty trays returned from packing to be stacked in an orderly fashion so they are easy to carry. 3. As the morning is particularly busy, that I would like as much help as possible to get me through this period.

I succeeded in winning agreement over these points. But even though the work might be a little easier, there is no changing the fact that this is intensification of labour. I am virtually moving at trotting pace as I transport the trays.

16 October (Tuesday)

I shouldn't have complained about the reduction of staff on the cleaning round. It looks as if I might be transferred to assistant operator on sub-assembly. Apparently this is what the sub-assembly team leader wants. The new person on sub-assembly is to move to the cleaning round and I'm to go and help out in sub-assembly. My contract is coming to an end. I don't want to go on to another task. I let the boss know I was unhappy about it, saying, 'That's just playing musical chairs!' At which he retorted, 'Don't complain to me. It's the new guy. They say he's useless. If you have a problem with the move, complain to him.' That's not the sort of thing I can say to a new casual worker. The boss is just trying to turn a conflict between management and labour into a dispute between workers.

25 October (Thursday)
Yesterday I hurt my shin so I was taken off to the first aid room. Just before, I had been unleashing my pent up frustration on Takenaka, who has become section leader. I complained that it was unreasonable to be transferring me to another job so close to the end of my term, that there were no other casual workers being put on a different task every other work period, that I was not prepared to take the flak for other workers when there was nothing wrong with my own work, and that all this unreasonable pressure placed upon me had been the cause of my injury. In addition, I demanded to be sent back to the cleaning round. Takenaka immediately went to ask someone higher up and, as a result, I was finally able to be transferred back to the cleaning round.

Any increase in the overall workload is thrust onto some poor individual. The conflicts that arise from this process have to be sorted out on the shop floor. The supervisors have neither the time nor inclination to deal with them.

Here, workers are pushed to the limit and it is all they can do to meet their daily quotas. But, as far as possible, they avoid openly showing their dissatisfaction and the bosses are careful to prevent small incidents from blowing out into major conflicts. Even so, there is no end to the minor conflicts going on somewhere or other in the workplace.

Between acceptance and resistance

As we have seen, workers are not necessarily steeped in management ideology, nor is there always stability in the workplace.

By generally not letting their dissatisfaction surface directly and by reinterpreting the situation forced onto them by their bosses, it seems to me, the majority of factory workers are distancing themselves from management ideology.

The formation of the worker's internal world

Types of workers
Workers, employing various methods of their own, try to free themselves, no matter how slightly, from management thinking.

They can be loosely classified into four groups, depending on the methods they employ.

The first group is made up of those people who do not take shortcuts on the job, but who, internally reinterpret the 'situation' they find themselves in. To a casual observer, these people look as if they are working away extremely seriously, but part of their mind is far away from the company. At least, they themselves think so. By reinterpreting the situation they are in, these workers, compelled as they are to work obediently, are somehow able to maintain their self-respect as they carry out their work.

The second group is, fundamentally, like the first group, made up of serious workers. But when an opportunity arises, people in this group will take a shortcut in their work. They do this surreptitiously, so no-one standing nearby would notice. Either consciously or unconsciously, they act out the role of the diligent worker, even as they are cutting corners to save time. These people have a good understanding of the code of the workplace and they behave as if they are following the code. Let me give you a concrete example. If the person working on transport suddenly found he had some spare time, he wouldn't just stand around doing nothing. There are always the workplace eyes to contend with. So, although there is no need for it at all, he would go over and check the parts-storage chute, or pick up a part, making it look as if he were working. Unless he does this, he runs the danger of having some other task thrust upon him.

These two groups are mainly the regular workers, who plan to go on working here into the future. Some casual workers, here just for the wages and with no interest in anything else, also fall into these categories. In the main, workers go about their tasks uneventfully without causing waves, yet also remaining aloof from management ideology.

The third group contains those workers who operate just within the bounds of the workplace code. It is not as if the code, in the strictest sense, completely covers the workplace. There are also zones of ambiguity. It is these grey areas that are manipulated by members of the third group. In contrast to groups one and two, who operate within (or make it look as if they are operating within) the permitted range, this type works within the range that is *not specifically forbidden*. They talk dirty, flaunt their masculinity, bluff and boast, mimic their superiors, give nicknames to the bosses – in short, they do as they like, skirting along the boundaries of the code of conduct. So the degree of freedom they have is greater than that of the two former groups. Nevertheless, they never deviate far from the code. They behave like this to express their individuality and to parade their ability to do so before their colleagues. This kind of worker tends to be popular in the workplace.

The supervisors are comparatively tolerant of this kind of worker. This is because they operate with an awareness of the code and do not deny the validity of the code itself. At first glance, they appear perhaps to be diverging from the code. What's more, since most of them are good at their jobs and because they are active and energetic, there is a fear that they might influence the workers around them. But, they understand the cost of contravening the code. While they may occasionally put one foot over the line, they are not inclined to commit serious breaches of the rules.

These various characteristics are present to some degree in many workers. I would venture to say that you find many examples of this type in those workers situated between the core and the periphery. One example might be those casual workers who secretly wish to become regular employees of the company. While they have the ambition to be accepted into the core, at the same time, they desire to remain outsiders. On the one hand they criticize 'those guys' who have been integrated into the company, but, on the other, they are also attracted by Toyota's worldwide reputation. They are torn by ambivalent emotions. I can recall one fellow who would be heaping abuse on the company one minute and the next minute saying, 'I think I'll go home wearing my Toyota cap. I hope they put me on the permanent staff.' There was another who said he couldn't live down here permanently, but at the same time was keenly interested in any information regarding staff recruitment.

The fourth group was made up of those people who, while having won the trust of management, took it upon themselves to extend the ambiguous areas of the code. The code of practice embedded in the production technology is extremely tightly regulated so that every little movement an assembly line worker makes is controlled.[5] But the code becomes progressively vaguer and more ambiguous as you move further away from the assembly line. So it becomes possible for those who have reached the level of team leader to abuse the code to a considerable extent.

Let us take, for example, the situation where you leave the line during working hours. For workers on the assembly line to move way from their posts, except to go to the toilet, is clearly truancy. But a team leader might go off to check on progress in another operation, or go and help out where a problem has arisen somewhere else along the line. In actual fact, nobody notices if they move away from the line simply to take a break from the monotony of their work. A section leader in his mid-thirties once revealed to me that, 'When you've been working for a long time on inspection and packing, you find it hard to keep your eyes open. It's particularly bad in the afternoon. When I have to inspect small parts I leave the line and get someone else to take over.' The supervisors and team leaders often talk to the staff in other groups. Perhaps they might be fine-tuning between processes, but more likely they are simply having a chat. Actually, sometimes they would be talking about company events or club activities. The team leaders were in a better position than the rank-and-file workers to exploit the gaps and ambiguities in the code. They are able to take time off while making it appear as if they are working. The 'clever' ones amongst them do not try to gain freedom to move by deviating from the code. They obtain greater freedom by working within the code.

This type is particularly prevalent among the team leaders and others candidates aspiring to manager class. Only a small proportion of workers earmarked as elite employees belong to this group. These are the ones who seem to be most devoted to management philosophy, but in reality they are not. Rather, it is precisely because they are in a position to make best use of the vagaries of the code, that they can give the impression that they are seriously devoted to its principles. They need to do this to provide an example to those 'below.' Probably those concerned are hardly conscious of the fact that they are acting. True devotion and sham form a seamless whole. Such is the consummate *skill* of their performance.

Informal groups
Not only do workers in their various ways try to keep management ideology at arm's length, they also come together in informal groups to create their own world.

There are a number of small groups that spring up spontaneously among workers. These are not the so-called 'informal groups' that are *completely separate* from those organizations that have official management approval.[6] On the other hand, neither are they groups with a formal organizational structure. They might more appropriately be seen as groups formed through individual human relationships that grow up *within* a formal structure. It is not something confined to this Toyota workplace, but there are many grades, running from hot to cold, in the relationships between workers. It is only natural that in the same organization you find people you can get on with and people you can't. As you come into contact with specific people in your rest periods and the like, you find that over time these people naturally form into groups of mutually compatible individuals we might call friends. By becoming a member of one of these groups, you can give your own individual interpretation to the existing code, or extend the range of 'abuses' of the ambiguities of the code. Not only do these human relationships simply help to ease the physical pain a little, but they also let us experience the pleasure of the sense of play.

For example, on the transport operation, I sometimes cross paths with the other transport worker. It is just a few seconds, but in that time we often exchange jokes or grope at the other's crotch. As I go past, I protect my own crotch while leashing an attack on that of the other transport worker. But if you are guarding your crotch, you leave your backside open to attack. Then, you innocently continue transporting the parts as if nothing had happened. It's nothing really, and pretty childish. Normally, you wouldn't give this sort of thing a second thought, but because work on the line is so hard, conversely, even this kind of boisterous play becomes fun. It is all the more enjoyable when you can do it without the boss noticing.

This is how workers, through interaction with their workmates, can redefine the cruel reality of assembly-line work and create a world of their own.

We must be mindful of the fact, however, that this reinterpretation of the situation rarely goes beyond the worker's internal world and brings about very little change to the *reality* on the shop floor. So, ultimately, this reinterpretation leads to an acceptance of the harsh reality and contributes to order and stability in the workplace.

Tactics in the workplace

Are we to assume, then, that the rank and file at the end of the chain of command have absolutely no power to change the status quo? Do they have no choice, but to accept the current situation? To put the conclusion first, they can indeed bring about change. It is possible even for rank and file workers to gain substantial power through using 'tactics' aimed at destabilizing the order of the workplace. Even in a workplace that appears to be run in an entirely systematic manner, there are always 'weak links' and conflicts between departments. But because management expends a great deal of energy in trying to defuse problems of this kind, they rarely come out into the open. Workers can exert practical influence by probing away at the weak links and openly revealing underlying conflicts. Let us look a little more closely at how this is achieved.

Trouble on the line
It has been claimed that in the Toyota Production System any weaknesses on the line are repaired through implementing *kaizen*. But as we have seen, in the realities of work on the shop floor, weak points on the line are not always eliminated through improvement measures. Workers strive to keep weaknesses from surfacing, by weaving their own individual methods into their daily work and by carrying out fine-tuning between work processes. It is a great strain for workers to have to perform this symptomatic therapy. So those line-workers who feel unhappy about it, reinterpret the weak link on the line as 'unreasonable and impossible to handle.' If other workers accept this reinterpretation, a mood of resignation settles over the whole workplace, which, at worst, can lead to dysfunction. Even in our workplace, we saw the beginnings of this atmosphere emerging, when one worker put his own slant on a situation and started absenting himself from his post. The supervisor worked to calm the commotion down by putting the worker concerned on another task and reducing his workload. The source of dissatisfaction usually disappears when it is transferred to another worker, but incidents like this sometimes provide the impetus for change in the workplace.

In addition, workers can sometimes exercise a degree of control over the production process by intentionally manipulating trouble on the line. They can regulate the amount of overtime *to suit their physical condition*, by deliberately causing trouble themselves or by manipulating the time spent in correcting a problem. When trouble occurs, the time lost has to be made up through overtime work. So, workers generally do not welcome trouble with the machines. On the other hand, if they can convert line-stoppage time into rest breaks or opportunities to earn additional overtime money, they tend to react differently.

Of course, management is well aware of the situation. That is why they are always racking their brains about how many tasks they should give to this or that worker. If they define the content of a job too specifically, the worker doing that job will not do anything else. Anything slightly unexpected can soon lead to line dysfunction. If the boss says, 'Don't just stand there, do something!' the worker will reply, 'I haven't been told to do that job.' On the other hand, if a worker is put in charge of an overly complicated operation, managers need to consider the downside of increased training costs and the need for on-site supervision. Otherwise, a supervisor might say to a worker, 'What do you think you're doing there!' And the reply this time would be, 'I just thought I'd better fix it.'

Management on the factory floor is not just a simple matter of choosing between 'direct control' and 'responsible autonomy.' Mangers are constantly looking for the appropriate mix of both elements. Conversely, from the worker's point of view, if that delicate balance is lost it can lead to quite serious repercussions for the maintenance of order in the workplace.

The two faces of bottom-end supervisors

The rank and file see the supervisors on the shop floor as spokesmen for management. They impose the will of those above onto the worker below. That is how it seems to them. But even the supervisors at times act in opposition to the interests of management. The supervisors at the end of the line are the ones tasked to control the workplace, through their relationship with the general workers, but they in turn are controlled by their bosses higher up. The rank and file at the bottom of the heap can sometimes win minor concessions by exploiting the two-faced nature of bottom-end supervisors.

The reason bosses on the shop floor thrust additional work onto any worker who looks as if he has the slightest time to spare, is not because they have completely internalised management thinking. Even less is it that they are spiteful by nature. They are simply transferring the pressure they receive from above to those working below. They act, not through devotion to management ideology, but through self-interest and a sense of self- preservation. The factory supervisors themselves often violate management principles in areas those higher up cannot see.

Section leader Yamashita told me that the efficiency rate of each operation is calculated on the amount of overtime required – the higher the hours of overtime, the lower the efficiency rate. You would think, then, that supervisors, who control the operation, would do whatever they could to reduce overtime hours. But, in reality, this is not always so. If overtime hours are seen to be too low, they reduce your staff numbers. Loss of staff makes it difficult to run the operation and puts added strain on the supervisor.

Let us assume for the sake of argument, that the number of workers allocated to a line is predicated on thirty minutes overtime work per worker per day. Your manpower is reduced if the average daily overtime drops below thirty minutes. So, if this looks likely to happen, the supervisor in charge reports a slightly higher amount of overtime than was actually required. In fact, I was not the only casual worker to notice that there was more overtime indicated in the breakdown of earnings on our pay slip than we actually worked. This may have been due to thoughtful consideration on the part of our group leader, but I suspect it was more in response to the kind of situation described above. Once, when I tried to opt out of overtime and go home, the team leader let slip with, 'You want to earn a little extra cash, don't you? Come on. Work overtime. Besides, if our overtime is too low, we'll lose staff and it'll be worse for all of us in the long run.'

So even on days when it looked as if I'd be able to go home on time, the work would be dragged out and we would do 'point five' (i.e. 30 minutes) overtime.

The supervisors, who are charged with the task of controlling the workplace, to protect themselves, sometimes choose not to just unconditionally follow management's wishes. It is not obvious from the surface, but they subtly divert pressure from above.

Here is just one of a number of examples I could give you. At our meeting on the morning we were due to be visited by a work-efficiency project team, our supervisor gave us the following word of caution. 'Later, you might find a stranger with a stopwatch standing behind you. They are timing your work. If one of these people comes along, I want you to spend a little longer inspecting parts and to work more slowly than you usually do. Those of you on sub-assembly should be particularly careful. As we have just a little spare time before the cleaning machine, slow down on the processes before and after that area' (15 October). If, when they are recalculating the cycle time, members of the project team notice someone with free time, they interpret that time as waste and cut it out. This also makes it difficult for the bosses, who have to control and administer the operation on the factory floor. So, they direct the workers to make it look as if the work is taking up virtually all the allocated *takt* time. Shop-floor supervisors do not just unilaterally transfer pressure from above to those below.

The workers can sometimes put pressure on a supervisor, who is giving them orders along management lines, to pivot his stance a little closer to their position, by probing these contradictions, so to speak, of workplace supervision. Put in colloquial terms, perhaps we could say that this brings a 'we're all in the same boat' atmosphere into the workplace. In my case, it reached the point where, after I had been in the company a while, I could make up my own mind about whether I wanted to work overtime or not.

Conflict between departments

Even within the same company different departments have different interests. For example, while supervisors on site are not unaware of matters of safety, they place a higher priority on efficiency. Safety, on the other hand, is the principal concern of the safety management office. They send us warnings regarding the need to maintain safety, even if it means sacrificing efficiency. So, it is possible to constrain excessive rationalization in the workplace by pointing out inadequacies in safety provision to the person in charge of the safety management office.

Advantages of being on the periphery

You may be inclined to think that the casual worker, whose position is generally that of an expendable buffer, has less freedom than other workers, but, in the realities of the workplace, this is not necessarily so. There is some freedom in being a casual worker on the periphery that is not available to core company employees. One casual worker announced publicly, 'Daihatsu paid better and had a better atmosphere.' Another said, 'I'm not going to the factory. I can make more money playing *pachinko*.'

In particular, when casual workers are in the majority, this can lead to a breakdown in workplace order. It is thought that the more use that is made of casual workers, who can be laid off any time, the more flexible and more efficient the running of an operation becomes, but, in reality, this is not always the case. When, as in this workplace, casual workers make up around half of the workforce (as at 5 November, there are nine regular staff and nine casual workers), the proportion of the core category is reduced in size and the peripheral group becomes larger. Under these conditions, if several casual workers are all absent on the same day, it can cause major disruptions in the running of the workplace. This has repercussions up and down the assembly line. Given the scale of Toyota's production, even one day stoppage on an assembly line, results in a huge financial loss.

This is a hypothetical situation, but even if the casual workers do not actually take time off, once a supervisor's gets just a hint of the danger that they might do so, it brings about an immediate change in the dynamics of the workplace. Just because the casual workers are in the most marginalized position, it does not mean they are completely bereft of power in the workplace.

Even the rank and file at the end of the chain of command can destabilize order on the factory floor, through a skilful use of tactics. Though they avoid taking an openly defiant stance, they can gain a certain degree of practical power by cleverly reinterpreting the situation they find themselves in. The context of the factory floor is extremely fluid.

Finally, I would like to add just one more point. That is that, these 'tactics' require 'skill.' Furthermore, this skill is one that can be used, both to change the working environment, and to accelerate the rationalization espoused by management. The course followed depends on the temperament and thinking of the workers. The cohesiveness of their informal groups and the strength of their peer identity are also important factors. If a negative context (culture) of 'advancement by climbing over the backs of fellow workers' were to emerge on the factory floor, that skill would be turned towards changing the workplace. In the absence of this context (culture) of confrontation, workers deploy their tactical skill to seek a higher position to obtain greater authority in the workplace.

So, for workplace reform, it is not only reinterpreting the situation in the factory that is important. The possibility to reinterpret the situation is also regulated at a more macro level by the social context. At the same time, conversely, without directly observing the realities of the workplace, it seems to me, there is no way the social situation or context can be changed either.[7]

Summary: the essence of workplace dynamism

The factory workplace is not always run in a systematic fashion, despite its orderly appearance. There is a constant stream of minor problems. The battlefield aspect frequently shows through. But conflict rarely appears openly in the daily routine of the workplace. Workers accept the order of the workplace, but they are able to rock the boat by reinterpreting their situation.

What significance, then, can we find in this reinterpretation? It is neither an organized movement, nor does it have a political ideology. Consequently, it is unlikely to lead to sudden drastic change. Nevertheless, it certainly does have the actual capacity, gradually and within limited parameters, to bring about change in the workplace. We should not overlook the fact that, even though the workers themselves may not necessarily be employing this reinterpretation intentionally to bring about change, it may literally result in workplace reform.

Just before I left the company, they reverted to having two people on the cleaning round. After I left, apparently the top rack of the cleaned-item chute, which had been divided into upper and lower shelves, was reduced to just one shelf and a new machine was installed to make it easier to take the trays out of the cleaning machine. This should have considerably reduced the physical stress on the operator. Of course, it was not only the conflict on the line and reinterpretation of the situation that brought about this change, but the influence of these factors cannot be denied.

Research to date has portrayed the situation as one in which the 'evolution' of Toyota has been sustained, both directly and indirectly, by workers striving for *kaizen* in the strictest adherence to the management line and workers who leave the company without a single word of complaint. But these are not the only workers who exert influence on the shop floor. Change also occurs gradually through the jostling and struggle between management and labour and in workers reinterpreting the situation inflicted upon them.

Epilogue: The Labour Market and the Workplace

There is a close connection between the labour market and the workplace. When there is a seller's market for labour, this strengthens the worker's hand *vis-à-vis* management, not only in the market place, but also on the shop floor. Workers find it easier to express their dissatisfaction and managers try to resolve conflicts amicably. Conversely, in a buyer's market, workers find they have relatively less power in their dealings with management. Workers try not to complain so they can keep working with the company.

At present (2001) the market for labour is a buyer's market of unprecedented proportions. Even here in Toyota, workers themselves try to keep the level of complaint down to a bare minimum. Inuring themselves to the work by putting their own slant on the situation, they accept the status quo. They are too busy trying to maintain their own emotional balance to be lenient over their workmates' blunders. Neither do they want to hear complaints from their colleagues. It is more often fellow workers, particularly those in a weaker position, who are the target of complaint, not management.

I asked a number of the casual workers what the employment situation was like in their hometown and what sort of work they had been doing before they came to work for Toyota. All of them replied that they would not be able to find work if they returned to their hometowns. Most of the casual workers are from the countryside or small provincial towns. Casual workers from the country could not just up and leave, even if they did not have a positive reason to go on working in the company.

Tabata is twenty-three and single. He is from Ishikawa prefecture and is a high school graduate. Before coming to Toyota he was a labourer on public works projects. He wants to stay on working here somehow, as there is no work for him at home. If he got the opportunity he would like to become a permanent employee of the company.

Naganuma is eighteen, single and hails from Kumamoto prefecture in Kyushu. He left high school without graduating and immediately got a job building vinyl hothouses. But he thought the pay of ¥6,500 a day was too low, so he moved onto another job in the same line of work that paid ¥8,000 a day. Here, the work was physically beyond him, so he worked for a while as a labourer on construction sites for ¥6,000 a day, but he also found this work extremely hard. Most recently he had been working as a host in a women-only bar. He had escaped in a hurry by resigning and coming to work here.

Yada is a twenty-three year old high school graduate from Osaka. After high school he worked in community welfare and as a casual worker with Daihatsu. At first he considered becoming a full-time employee with Toyota, but later abandoned the idea. Several times he put his trust in his superiors and was let down every time. He doesn't want to stay long with this company. He says that if he had known what it would be like here, he would have been better off becoming a regular employee with Daihatsu. They had invited him to stay. He is thinking of going to Tokyo when he finishes here.

Kimata is twenty-seven, single and comes from Yamaguchi prefecture. He left university without graduating. Before entering Toyota he worked as a door-to-door salesman selling cleaners and educational materials. He also had a job where he acted as a kind of 'host.' He wants to run a cram school or something with the money he saves from working at Toyota.

Sawada is twenty-six, single and comes from Hyogo prefecture. He is a technical college graduate. He worked part-time with a sub-contractor to a TV company and as a gasoline station attendant. For a while after that he was out of work. When his money ran out he came to work at Toyota.

Kakegawa, twenty-five and single, comes from Oita prefecture in Kyushu. After graduating from high school he got a job with a provincial race-track, but the company went bankrupt and all the staff were dismissed.

Yamano is thirty-five and single. He comes from Fukuoka prefecture in Kyushu. After dropping out of university, he got an office job with an architectural design company. After that he had a range of jobs including clerical work in a life insurance company, running a food and drink establishment with two partners and working for a temp agency on painting and transport jobs. He came to work at Toyota because he needs a wad of money to help out his father who is sick in hospital.

Segawa is thirty-one, single and comes from Kagoshima prefecture in Kyushu. After graduating from high school he got a job as a salesman in a liquor company. After that, he worked as a truck driver and as a salesman for a tobacco company, but he gave up sales because he didn't want to be hounded by numbers (i.e. the sales quota). He decided to work at Toyota because he thought ¥300,000 in the hand was a good salary. But since coming here he feels he's been cheated. Only after meeting the tough working conditions, including working public holidays, doing overtime work, completing the term of his contract and so on, does he finally clear ¥200,000 a month. With these sorts of conditions you could probably get that sort of money elsewhere. But there's no work in Kagoshima. After this he thinks he might try nursing work or something in Tokyo or Osaka.

Shōji, thirty-eight and single, comes from Hokkaido. He has worked as a casual worker in other car factories. There is no work for him in Hokkaido. He has come to Toyota to earn enough money to open a food and drink business.

Nagase, thirty-five, comes from Hyogo prefecture. He has worked on and off at other car factories. Before coming to Toyota he was doing office work, but he was made redundant and laid off. He had been out of work for some time before coming here. At his age he can't expect to find work in his hometown.

Over a third of the casual workers are from Kyushu or Okinawa (Figure E.1). They can't easily resign from Toyota, as the prospects

Figure E.1: My contemporary casual workers in Plant K by place of origin

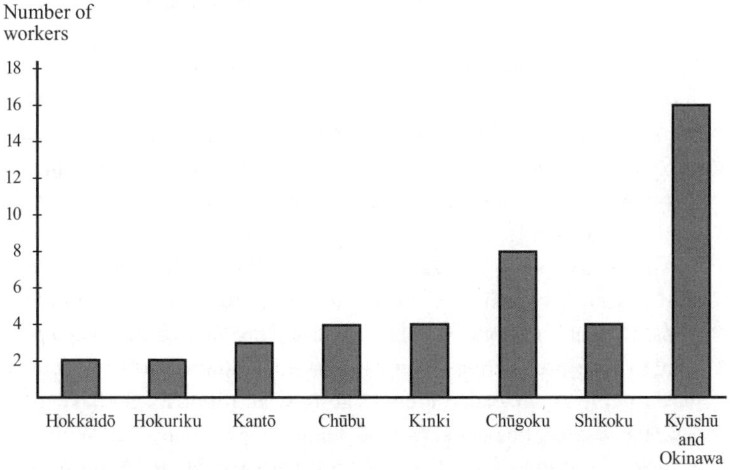

Number of workers

Note: The distribution of 43 workers, based on the list provided by the company.

of employment in their places of origin are bad. Deterioration of the job market keeps workers in their jobs and compels them to be obedient.[1] Management takes a cavalier attitude to workers, not only in the factory, but also in the labour market. One after another they employ large numbers of casual workers and one after another they turn them out. There were two hundred and ninety-two casual workers taken on at the time I joined the company, and two hundred and forty joined with Kitamura (though forty were sent home after the medical examination). When Tabata signed on, around eight hundred casual workers joined with him. Even since then, they have continued to employ a constant stream of casual workers[2] and, when their contracts are up, almost all of them leave Toyota as if nothing had happened. It is very easy for the company to replace them.

7 November (Wednesday) Time's up!

As the day ticks over from midnight to 8 November, I reach the end of the term of my contract. It's been a long time. You can't imagine how long! I think I did well to endure it. How I've been looking forward to this day! I don't have the energy now to go back and reflect over these past three and a half months. For a while, I just want to sleep and think of nothing.

In our lunch break last Friday we had a bit of a party. The group leader joined us. The company provided our lunch boxes. I got a propelling pencil from the personnel department as a memento for having reached the end of my contract. At the end of last week and the beginning of this week, two teams, sub-assembly and inspection/packing, put on farewell parties for me. In our midday rest period today, I gave a simple farewell speech. After work, I went around and personally said my goodbyes to each of the workmates I had become close to. I had a complicated mixture of feelings when one of my friends among the casual workers said, 'It's strange to imagine that tomorrow you won't be here any more. The place won't seem the same without you.'

Apparently they worked an hour and a half overtime again today. Half in jest, I was asked if I'd like to join in, because tomorrow I wouldn't be able to work even if I wanted to. I declined politely, saying I had to make preparations for my departure. I returned the key of my locker to the group leader. From tomorrow on, I'll no longer have to wear those safety boots that feel like lumps of lead on my feet. With a gesture of gratitude, I gently slipped my worn and tattered boots into the change room rubbish bin. Hardly anyone had finished at regular knock-off time. There were only three of us on the bus back to the dorm. Before, as soon as I had got on the bus, I would have shut my eyes and tried to steady my breathing, but today I spread myself out on the back seat and gazed out the window at the scenery outside. The dim shapes of the buildings and the on-coming cars were sucked up into the darkness as we passed.

After I got back to the dorm I had a last drink with Yamano. He joined at the same time as I did and is my closest friend in the factory. He has to work tomorrow, too. I felt sorry for him, but he said he wanted to give me a proper farewell. I don't know if I'd have been able to get through my term if he hadn't been around. We drank together until six in the morning and parted with a firm handshake. I returned to my room and had a light sleep. I woke at about nine and carried the things I'd be sending by mail and the bedding I had borrowed, down to the first floor. I tidied up my room and gave it a quick once over with the broom. This was all I needed to do before leaving the dorm. Just as I was about to go out the door of my room I paused and looked out the window – my last sight of the bench by the bus stop, the dorm cafeteria, the cars in the parking lot.

I left the dorm at 9:40 a.m. I handed the key of my room to the dorm supervisor. The cleaning lady said, 'Have a nice day' and I replied casually, 'I'll do my best.' I had often chatted with her, but today somehow I couldn't bring myself to say that it was all over. Once outside the dormitory, I saw that sometime, without my realizing it, the surrounding scenery had turned to autumn. When I arrived here it was the height of summer. Now, that time seemed like the distant past. It was a little chilly, but I enjoyed the feel of the clear, crisp air. I gave one mighty yawn as I made my way through the nearly empty parking area and headed slowly towards the gate. I suddenly came to a halt and turned back towards the dormitory. I immediately caught sight of the room that had been my home until just a few minutes ago. That room without an occupant seemed to stand out alone from the rest of the building. I put my headphones over my ears, turned the volume up full blast and set off at a brisk pace for H station.

Appendix I: Research Trends and the Skill Debate

Many researchers have surveyed the workplace in Japanese auto-mobile factories and produced a diverse range of findings, reflecting their disparate interests and methodologies. While acknowledging that I cannot cover them all, based on my own field of interest, I would like to trace the trends, and in so doing, to clarify problems and suggest issues for future research.

The 1960s: The start of comprehensive surveys of car factories

The first comprehensive report on a Japanese car factory was the Nihon Jinbunkagakkai (Japan Society for the Human Sciences)'s *Gijutsu kakushin no shakaiteki eikyō* (The social impact of technological innovation) published by Tokyo University Press in 1963, but covering the years of the survey, 1959–1960. From the mid-1950s there was a sudden increase in the productive force of Japanese enterprises and the country's economy expanded at an astonishing rate. Technological innovation was a major driving force. All industries strove to increase their competitiveness, raise efficiency and promote rationalization of the workplace through mechanization and automation. The investigating team from the Japan Society for the Human Sciences, aware of the current economic climate and the behaviour of certain enterprises, naturally chose Toyota as one of the targets of its research. This was because of Toyota's reputation at the time for pushing forward with modernization of machine infrastructure, changes in work management, enterprise rationalization, cutting of staff and putting down labour disputes. Consequently, the survey team established, as a major focus of its study, the need 'to investigate automation and its social impact' (p. 3) in Toyota. The impacts on the workplace that the team identified can be summarized as follows.

The impact of mechanization and automation on the workplace is that it has increased the intensity of labour through the 'simplification' and 'speeding up' of processes. In both machining and assembly, 'while there has been a reduction, in both the degree and volume, of physical strain and heavy labour, there has been, on the other hand, an increase in intensity of labour through shorter *takt* times, relocation of personnel, cutting of staff and increased production targets. It puts those working on the assembly line under great mental strain to have to work knowing they are directly responsible for the quality of the finished product' (p. 96).

Automation, with its concomitant simplification of work and intensification of labour, decreases workers' level of commitment to the enterprise. So, management earnestly introduces human relations (HR) activities to meet the need to integrate workers into the company. This is how the research team describes the form and function of these activities.

> Not only do supervisors have complete administrative control over workers on the shop floor, they also employ the auxiliary strategy of exercising their influence through groups. It is through groups, arranged in workplace units, or made up of employees who joined the company at the same time, or formed according to school background, and, on the basis of the regulations within the group, that workers are drawn into management thinking.

Further, it is not only in the workplace. 'Control extends beyond the workplace to leisure activities, research, education and to all aspects of life. The enterprise seeks to bind workers into a 'unified system of control.' It is at this point that, 'We can say that "autonomous groups" arise as an interim antidote to the various consequences of technological innovation' (p. 133).

The 1970s: building on the research results of the 1960s

The 1970s saw the publication of the research of a number of individual scholars like, Satoshi Kamata's *Jidōsha zetsubō kōjō: aru kisetsukō no nikki* (Automobile factory of despair: the diary of a seasonal worker) (Tokuma Shobō, 1973). (Translator's note: Tatsuru Akimoto's English translation appeared under the title, *Japan in the Passing Lane: An Insider's Account of Life in a Japanese Auto Factory*, Pantheon Books, 1982), Kiyoshi Yamamoto's *Jidōsha sangyō no rōshi kankei* (Labour and capital in the automobile industry) (Tokyo Daigaku Shuppankai, 1981), Hirohide Tanaka (1982, 1983) and his

Kaitai suru jukuren : ME kakumei to rōdō no mirai (Deskilling: the ME revolution and the future of work) (Nihon Keizai Shinbunsha, 1984), Ichirō Saga's *Kigyō to rōdō kumiai – Nissan Jidōsha rōshiron* (The company and labour unions – on management and labour in Nissan Motor) (Tabata Shoten, 1984).

Kamata's book is a journalistic account that attracted a great deal of attention for the unprecedented realism of his portrayal. It also greatly influenced researchers in the field. Its impact was such that it requires no further explanation here. The world he describes is nothing short of 'the automobile factory of despair' of the book's original title.

Yamamoto investigates the production technology that demands assembly-line operation and analyzes the method of efficiency control that reduces *takt* times, increases line speed and cuts staff members. He concludes, 'Work in auto factories is exceedingly cruel, in its monotony, in its lack of worker control, and in its high level of intensity' (Yamamoto, 1981: 111).

Tanaka gives this assessment of the trend towards a degradation of the traditional skill base in workplaces across the board.

> I think, first, that it is important for us to admit frankly that, as a result of this technological innovation, often dubbed the third industrial revolution, we are seeing a fundamental downgrading of traditional skill. This is not the first time that the advent of new production technology has destroyed traditional skills. This is precisely why the question of skill is called both an old and a new problem. But the new production technologies now about to come on line and the collapse of skill they will cause are fundamentally different from anything we have seen before.
>
> This is because the new micro-electronic technologies we are about to see, in essence, will not tolerate the situation we have had to date, in which blue-collar workers learn their jobs through long years of observation and physical experience in the sweat, grease and grime of the shop floor. The products of micro-electronics, like the IC (integrated circuit) and the LSI (large scale integrated circuit) and the NC (numerical control) machines and the MC's (machining centres) that use them, cannot be checked at a glance or pushed or probed into action at the touch of a hand. So far, we have not nurtured the new skills that will be required when that new workplace has become a reality. As a result, the new blue-collar worker we need may not come into being (Tanaka, 1984: 16–17).

In addition, in his interview with a former executive director of Toyota Motor company,[1] Tanaka cleverly drew out the Toyota management camp's real position on skill creation. When Tanaka confronted him with the current high rate of separations from the company, the former head replied, 'From the company's point of view, fundamentally, we are happy if we can keep the people who are keen and have ideas to contribute. I do not think the separation rate figures in themselves constitute much of a problem' (Tanaka, 1982: 73, f.n.2). Tanaka followed up this response with his view. 'Isn't it the case that, behind this attitude to separations, there is, as I pointed out before, a feeling within the company that accumulation of skill is not a particular priority?' (*Ibid.*). Large numbers join the company and large numbers leave, but management is happy as long as the 'superior' workers remain. Tanaka concluded from this that the company does not place much emphasis on technical training and skill formation.

Saga focuses not only on the influence the introduction of robots will have on workers, but also on the harsh reality that they may drive workers out of the factory altogether.

> After the introduction of robots, the work for human operators will be limited to peripheral and auxiliary tasks like the transporting and inserting of parts, checking for quality, maintenance, and on those tasks, such as welding, that robots still cannot do. The increased emphasis on this kind of auxiliary work may end up creating a new void for workers who, despite the inferior conditions they previously worked under, were at least engaged, in a sense, in skilled labour (Saga, 1984: 249).
>
> Industrial robots will also drive human labour that has become standardized and monotonous off the factory floor. Of course, in principle, it is impossible to get rid of human workers altogether, but the company will be able to be more discerning in its selection of staff and will reduce, even further, its need for skilled labour (*Ibid*: 219).

The research detailed above can be seen as pursuing in greater detail the negative issues arising from automation – the simplification of work, the degrading of skill, the increased intensity of labour, the reduction of staff – that had been presented in the report of the Japan Society for the Human Sciences in 1963.

The 1980s: New skills and non-standardized work

In the 1980s, particularly in the latter half of the decade when Japanese companies came to have overwhelming competitive power internationally, Toyota, or rather the Toyota Production System, attracted a great deal of attention as the epitome of Japanese-style business administration and systems of production. As a consequence, many researchers published studies of the company.[2] Situated within these general research trends, but slightly predating the formation of the research context of the late 1980s, were three comprehensive reports on Toyota.

Let us now clarify, for each of the groups involved, the issues considered, the survey results and the analysis of the Toyota workplace.

The first is, Koyama, Yōichi ed. (1985) *Kyodai kigyō taisei to rōdōsha* (The mega-enterprise system and the worker) Tokyo: Ochanomizu Shobō, a report on research carried out from 1978 to 1982.

This report is very much as the editor freely acknowledges, 'not in the strictest sense research aimed at proving a theory on the nature of work, but rather an on-site investigation to discover the facts and problems' (p. 7). Nevertheless, as the research progresses, major questions begin to surface. 'One of the big problems we faced in the process of carrying out our research, was how to explain why, despite the "harsh" realities of work on the shop floor, most Toyota workers, to a greater or lesser extent, said that they found their present jobs rewarding' (p. 618).

The investigating team set up several hypotheses in an attempt to find the answer to this conundrum. One possible solution concerns the workplace.

> In the factory, the work itself is simple and standardized and of a kind that can be mastered in a short time. But even so, 'the real work,' that workers must accomplish if they are to walk the career path within the company, is deep and complex and requires various capabilities that are formed over many years of training. It is, so to speak, a kind of 'skilled labour' and that is possibly why workers say they are satisfied with their current work (p. 622).

This hypothesis – the work enrichment and upgraded skill theory – is predicated on the following research findings.

Even in Division A³, in which it can be said they have achieved to a considerable extent the 'minimum requirement' of the goals of the Toyota Production System, which states that it can turn a new recruit into a 'a fully-fledged worker in three days,' there were many workers who answered that it took them much longer than we had expected before they felt that they 'knew everything about it' (p. 199).

In short, workers performing standardized work on the assembly line are able to perform their task within three days, but to reach the level where they 'know everything' about the job requires a fairly considerable period of time. This was probably why they considered the work as having depth and requiring a high level of skill. Further, the kind of skill they are talking about here is not the skill of the craftsman of the past, but 'the "social skills," needed mainly in the organizing of groups, such as leadership, ability to command and the ability to control human relationships, and the "intellectual skills" – creativity, the ability to put forward *kaizen* proposals and analytical ability' (p. 622).

In this way, the research group suggested the existence of 'new skills' workers acquire on the shop floor.

The second is Hikari Nohara and Eishi Fujita eds (1988) *Jidōsha sangyō to rōdōsha – rōdōsha kanri no kōzō to rōdōshazō* (The automobile industry and the worker – the structure of labour control and the image of workers) Hōritsu Bunkasha. The book is based on investigations carried out over the period from 1977 to 1981.

This research group, working on the Japan Inc. (Japan as a corporate society) model, first defines what it means by the concept of a corporate society (*kigyō shakai*).

In the society within the corporation, we have the goal (i.e. value) of economic efficiency, the fragmentation and flexibility of labour, and a model of behaviour that accepts competition on the basis of merit. These three categories are regarded as being of paramount importance. So, taking the argument a step further, we define a 'corporate society' as one that prioritises these three categories. Further, we call the tendency to highly value these qualities 'corporatization of society' or realization of the principle of 'corporate society' (p. 11).

Taking the concrete example of Motor Company A., they proceed to elucidate the internal company structure that has given rise to the ideal model of the corporate society and show how that structure relates to the world outside the company.

Seen at the macro-structural level, Motor Company A. as a whole, 'encourages competition for promotion within the company and works to eliminate elements that do not conform' (p. 510).

As a result, the workers who remain in the company tend to be of similar quality. This provides fertile soil for the cultivation of workers loyal to the company.

When you come down to the micro level,

> The Japanese economy and Motor Company A. have been able to achieve the high productivity they now enjoy, due to the fact that their workers work well autonomously. Let us consider how the company was able to accomplish this. First, we must not overlook the importance of the unilateral right of management to make decisions regarding wages and the allocation of staff. Without an enforceable framework of this kind, one cannot explain the success of the 'autonomous,' 'public-supported' approach, in achieving the kinds of increases in productivity we are seeing today. But, secondly, neither can one explain the secret of the success in implementing a mass worker autonomy system of that scale by such coercive means alone (*Ibid.*).

The research team on this project starts by acknowledging a status quo in which workers are fully integrated into the company line. Further, they put this integration down, in part, to management's administrative techniques which workers are coerced to follow. Yet, they consider that coercion alone cannot explain workers' devotion to the company. If that is indeed the case, why is it then, that workers accept the logic of 'corporate society' and that some of them are prepared to work autonomously? To answer this question the researchers pointed to the existence of 'new skills.'

> With mechanized production... and the fragmentation of labour, the work requiring direct human intervention, becomes increasingly simple and repetitive. On the other hand, along with the advances in systemization and integration of processes, first, the productivity of a process is not directly determined by the ability to perform it, so much as the capacity to improve the coordination of processes and the ability to organize people. Secondly, there is a greater danger of a minor slip by a worker resulting in a major fault in a product.

Consequently, it has become exceedingly important to prevent small mistakes before they happen. This is only possible through the concept of 'quality control woven into the production process,' which requires direct on-site operators to maintain constant, careful vigilance over the processes for which they are responsible. The skill required here is the power of observation.

After taking for granted, the production infrastructure, the division of labour and work organization of Japan's large modern factories, these attributes mentioned above – the ability to improve processes, the ability to organize, and powers of observation – have come to be seen as essential requirements in the manufacturing process.... In large Japanese factories, the workers themselves are demanding to be taught these skills, now regarded as necessary for factory work.

To respond to the technical demands of these kinds of workers on the shop floor, small-group activities, (QC Circles and the proposal system), tied in with multi-skilling, begin to appear. Moreover, the level of participation in these group activities becomes a factor in staff evaluation. So, even against the background of these compulsory mechanisms, since they are introduced to 'respond' to workers' requests, the enterprise's worker control strategies have been successful in drawing out and mobilizing 'autonomy' on the scale of a mass worker movement (p. 511).

The third is Hideo Totsuka and Tsutomu Hyōdō eds (1991), *Rōshi kankei no tenkan to sentaku – Nihon no jidōsha sangyō* (Changes and options in labour-management relations – the Japanese automobile industry), Nihon Hyōronsha. The research for this report was carried out between 1984 and 1987.

First, let us consider where the authors of the report focused their interest. This is what they had to say about the objectives of their research.

This research is an attempt to describe the actual conditions of the flexible and efficient system of labour that has underpinned the competitiveness of the Japanese automobile industry and to clarify the structure of labour-management relations that have made this system possible. We felt it important to deal with this issue because of its significance for the future direction of labour-management relations and for the labour movement in Japan today (p. 2).

They go on to say,

It is necessary to explain the basis upon which Japanese workers are able to accept a flexible, efficient system of labour utilization unlike any found elsewhere in the world (p. 6).

By focusing our attention on the processes management employs, not only to win agreement from workers over 'rationalization' measures, but also to go on to gain their active cooperation, we thought that perhaps we could arrive at a deeper understanding of the reasons why the efforts of management seem to be so successful. We hope at least to be able to find some clues to the solution of this problem (p. 7).

In their conclusions, the authors offer some answers to this question. For the reason management has succeeded in gaining 'acceptance and commitment' from its workers, we should not overlook the importance of the 'time and effort managers devote to the meticulous personnel administration system they themselves call "time-consuming down-to-earth personnel management"' (p. 261).

And the promotion system, particularly, the way in which 'a kind of relish for the work itself is transformed into commitment,' (p. 264) is also important in this regard.

On a production line based on the flowing assembly method seen in the car manufacturing industry, the repetitive tasks require no more than semi-skilled labour. But by providing employees with multi-skilling training through job rotation, there is an equitable sharing around of tasks.

Not only does this relieve workers from the monotony of always performing the same task, but it gives them the opportunity to experience a variety of jobs on the same assembly line, or, sometimes, even on another assembly line. This gives the workers a wider perspective on the work performed and can have the effect of nurturing an interest in the line as a whole (p. 256).

And,

It can be said that 'improvement of operation' activities and the QC activities that underpin them, are supported by the expansion of the skills and interest gained through multi-skilling under job rotation and the unique organization of the manufacturing division (p. 257).

In the analysis of their research data, the authors concluded that workers find their fulfilment in aspects of the performance of the work itself.

In the above, we have seen a very brief account of the topics of concern and the results of analysis of three field research projects. Comparing the three projects, all carried out during roughly the same period, we can see quite a few points they have in common.[4]

Namely, Japanese industry came through the oil shocks of the 1970s by implementing radical rationalization and went on from there to raise its international competitiveness. Behind this success, however, there was a stable system of labour-management relations and diligent workers, symbolized in the term *mōretsu shain* (fanatical company employees), some of whom, literally, died from overwork (*karōshi*). This was the image that was current among the general population at that time. We might imagine that this was also the view commonly held among most researchers. In fact, while all three groups of investigators acknowledge that work in the direct manufacturing division of Toyota is monotonous, demanding and inhumane, they all query how it is possible for workers to have high levels of job satisfaction, why they are prepared to work 'autonomously' and why they accept such harsh conditions.

In regard to the adverse survey findings on the high rate of separations from the company and strong dissatisfaction[5], while one may have reservations about the manner in which these topics were raised, it should be acknowledged, nevertheless, that the authors carried out their analyses on the premise that workers accepted these conditions. In answer to the questions they had set themselves, they referred to the uniquely Japanese work practices of job rotation, *kaizen* activities and QC circles and to the 'new skills,' – intellectual skills, the skill to observe work processes and organizational skills – those practices had created. In contrast to research of the 1960s and 1970s, which concentrated on the negative aspects of industrial technology, in the 1980s investigators, while acknowledging these aspects, focused on how a trend towards re-enriched work and the development of high levels of skill can emerge through work organization and systems of education.[6]

From the late 1980s to the early 1990s: the skill debate

From the latter half of the 1980s into the early 1990s, the researchers involved in the previous three studies each carried their arguments on the issue of skill a step further (Tsuji 1989, Yumoto 1989–90, Nohara 1992, Nomura 1993a, Sawada 1994).[7] As a result, the differences between them were thrown into relief and went on to develop into an open debate (Nohara 1994, Yumoto 1995, Nomura 1995). The debate was carried in the form of confrontations between Hikari Nohara and Masami Nomura on the one hand and Makoto Yumoto versus Nomura, on the other.[8] I shall not go into these here. Rather, I would like to take up the earlier debate between Kazuo Koike and Masami Nomura. I do so because Nomura claims Koike's theory forms the basis of the arguments of Nohara and Yumoto.[9]

First, let me very briefly confirm Koike's argument. In his various publications (1977, 1981, 1987, 1991 and 1993b) he claims that the quality of work can be divided into two concepts. These he calls '*tate no hirogari*' (vertical development) and '*yoko no hirogari*' (horizontal development). 'Vertical development' means that the worker develops by performing not only the 'routine work,' but also doing work outside the normal routine. This 'non-routine work' is 'responding to change' and 'dealing with abnormalities.' Responding to change includes dealing with each of a range of contingencies, including such things as, the introduction of new products, changes in the composition of a product, changes in quantity of production, changes in production methods and changes in group composition. 'Dealing with abnormalities' refers to *kaizen* activities and maintenance. To have the production workers deal only with routine work and put engineers in charge of non-routine work is to employ the 'separation method' (*bunri hōshiki*). The 'integrated method' (*tōgō hōshiki*) is the term used in the case where the production worker performs both roles. Horizontal development, on the other hand, occurs when the worker experiences a greater range of different tasks.

According to Koike, blue-collar workers in Japan's larger enterprises extend their working experience (i.e. career) through OJT (on-the-job training) both vertically and horizontally, and gain knowledge (i.e. intellectual skill) about the structure of machinery and the mechanism of production. It is this 'skill formation,' he claims, that gives Japanese companies their competitive edge internationally.

Nomura reels out a comprehensive refutation of Koike's argument.[10] Space does not permit me to deal with all his points here. I would, however, like to look at his criticisms from the viewpoint of 'division of labour,' which I consider to be the crux of his argument.

Nomura makes the criticism that Koike's claims are misleading because he ignores the existence of specialist mechanics and makes it sound as if the worker directly engaged in work on the assembly line does everything, including even, the work of the specialist mechanic.[11]

According to Nomura, employees are broadly divided into manufacturing staff and indirect staff (clerical staff, engineers and technicians). The former are subdivided into direct manufacturing workers and semi-direct manufacturing workers (simple mechanics and specialist mechanics). In Koike's theory, 'since labour is divided into the two broad categories of "manufacturing workers" and white-collar workers,' it is understood abroad that in Japan the category of 'direct manufacturing workers' lumps together specialist mechanics and direct manufacturing workers, which are kept separate in other advanced countries. So the idea, that 'in Japan they do not have the division, taken for granted in other advanced countries, between specialist mechanics and direct manufacturing workers,' has spread throughout the world. Further, since 'the abolition of division of labour' runs counter to the doctrines of 'Taylorism and Fordism,' the Japanese-style production system has gained a reputation for 'post-Taylorism and post-Fordism.' It is in this context that Nomura, by clearly showing the division-of-labour relationship between direct manufacturing workers and specialist mechanics, sets limits to the assessment of skill levels among direct manufacturing workers in Japanese companies.

In response to Nomura's criticisms, Koike said that, while he did not deny the existence of other divisions or their importance, he did stand by his particular claim that in Japan (direct) manufacturing workers clearly have higher levels of skill than their equivalents in other countries. 'Workers directly involved in manufacturing processes, such as machining, assembly, operation and monitoring of machines, have higher skill levels than those in other countries. It is probably this factor that has contributed most to the efficiency of shop-floor production in the Japanese manufacturing industry' (Koike, 1993a: 3).

In this debate, it could be said, there is virtually no point at which the arguments engage one another. There may be several reasons why this is so, but to cite just one, I think it may be because the researchers have based their assessments on different points of comparison. On the one hand, Koike asserts that, compared with the situation in companies overseas, (direct) manufacturing workers in Japanese companies have a higher level of skill. Nomura, on the other hand, points out, from the perspective of division of labour, that there are limits to the levels of skill achieved.[12]

At the same time, it must be said, despite the vehemence of the debate, there is very little difference between the two researchers as far as their 'fact-finding' is concerned. 'I too, consider that the skill of direct manufacturing workers in large Japanese enterprises, with the one proviso that those direct manufacturing workers (not specialist mechanics!) are male, is the same as Koike has indicated' (Nomura, 1993b: 31).

The mid to late 1990s: verifying points of conflict

It would be wrong to conclude that this debate over skill was of no significance. One outcome of the debate was to raise, as a new topic on the research agenda, the need to investigate the actual conditions of labour involved in the direct production division. Koike's theory provided a 'model' derived from comparison with industry abroad. In actual fact, his explanations, about the form 'responses to change' actually took, or exactly what the 'unexpected' in 'dealing with the unexpected' meant in practical terms, or just how actively QC activities were pursued, were not always necessarily based on sound empirical evidence. From the mid-1990s until the end of the decade, several scholars were stimulated by this debate to carry out investigative field research in this area.

Makoto Yoshida (1993 – investigation in 1992) conducted research through participatory observation during one month as a casual employee in a car factory, working in 'a team in charge of assembling mainly specially-equipped vehicles (street-sweeping vehicles, fire engines, snowploughs etc) but also trucks and buses' (p. 31).

'Basically, the job was simple work that required no specialist skills. But, simple though the operations themselves were, without experience, it was often difficult to do the job.' In addition, what Koike calls '"non-routine work," i.e. the need to respond to abnormal situations, cropped up quite often.' 'We would get the emergency response team to come and fix any problems that could not be handled on the shop floor, but for the most part the operator on the process concerned was able to deal with the problem' (p. 34). 'I emphasize the fact that, over time, the job came to call on skills beyond those of a so-called simple mechanic' (p. 35).

Takeshi Ōno (1997 – investigation 1992) carried out his research as a participant observer over the duration of one month, while he was working as a casual labourer at a car bumper-bar paint shop.

I would like to take issue with Koike's theory, in that he over-emphasizes the positive aspects, namely the depth and breadth, of skill (i.e. intellectual skills) in the Japanese automobile industry, at the expense of the opposite, negative view, i.e. that, 1. The skills acquired are shallow and narrow, and 2. There is a disparity between the career paths of on-line and off-line workers. In regard to 1, take the example of how in P1 (where Ōno was posted – Ihara) when it came to major improvements – like, say, fitting a smaller-diameter spray nozzle to cut down on the volume of wasted paint – an experimental group had to be called in. We had nobody in our workplace with the time or the accumulated know-how to do it. To illustrate the second point, factory workers show a great deal of interest in progressing their careers by moving into off-line work, like inspection or repair, but in Japan the path to off-line work is extremely narrow and is often closed (or, at least, no official, transparent career path has been established) (p. 155).

The clarification of these points of debate was not the principal objective of this participant observation. But even so, Ōno (1998 – investigation 1996) and Mitsuo Ishida et al. (1997 – investigation 1992–94) *Nihon no riin seisan hōshiki – jidōsha kigyō no jirei* (Japan's lean production method – examples from the car industry), Chūō Keizaisha, were both fairly conscious of the debate, as they carried out their on-site observations and interview surveys.

Takeshi Ōno, who worked for three months as a casual worker in a grand assembly plant, describes the 'change' and 'unexpected' he experienced as follows.

In A. Company workers have various kinds of non-specified tasks imposed upon them. The performance of these jobs – such as, quickly restoring a minor breakdown of equipment, or detecting faulty products – presumably plays a significant role in raising the productivity and quality of A. Company. But, we cannot say that these non-specific tasks raise the quality of work (skill) or enhance worker motivation. To describe the special characteristics of A. Company, we would probably have to look to its mechanisms for achieving high productivity and high quality – the mechanism of mutual observation which makes the detection of faulty products 'autonomous' and the strict personnel administration system based on 'stress.' By and large, you would have to say, in regard to the work in A. Company, that its significance has been greatly overestimated (Ōno, 1998: 31).

In regard to QC activities, he points out the 'stagnation or stultification of small group activities' (*Ibid*. p. 27) and 'the dearth, or low quality, of *kaizen* content in QC activities' (*Ibid*. p. 28). Instead, he emphasizes their 'human relations-type role in fostering smooth communication on the factory floor' (*Ibid*. p. 29). In conclusion he states, 'On the whole, in my frank opinion, I would say that the value of QC activities in A. Company has been overestimated' (*Ibid*.).

Mitsuo Ishida and his co-authors 'observed and described three representative workplaces; body shop, machining and final assembly, plus the maintenance section associated with them' (Ishida *et al*. 1997: 230). As a result of his research, it has become clear that skill levels vary from one workplace to another.

'The workplace requiring the highest level of skill was the machining section followed in decreasing order by final assembly and the body shop' (*Ibid*. p. 234). His assessment of skill levels overall is positive, 'There is an accumulation of skill in the manufacturing workplace, that props up the meticulous efficiency-management system. To see this combination in action, really gives one an appreciation of the considerable competitive strength of the Japanese automobile industry' (*Ibid*. p. 264).

On QC activities, he takes a similar line to Ōno (1998) highlighting the fact that they tend to be rather low-key. 'First it needs to be pointed out that the participation of general workers, both in actual attendance and in terms of their effectiveness, is modest, yet the QC activities are indispensable because of the role they play in mid-term staff development' (*Ibid*. p. 31).

Although we tend to lump them all together as factory work in the automobile industry, there are considerable differences in the work and skill levels required, depending on what is being made under what process. The situation varies from one company to another, or depending on whether we are talking about machining or sub-assembly/assembly/painting. Consequently, it is inherently impossible to assess the quality of factory workers' work and their levels of skill, as a single whole. Furthermore, the evaluation of skill is a relative matter. It is quite natural for observers of the same phenomenon to assess it differently.[13] Even in the simple description of work, differences arise, depending on the observer's area of interest and analytical frame, or on the image of assembly line workers that observer had originally formed. So we must be cautious about coming to a single conclusion from these research findings. Nevertheless, as the survey results accumulate, it has become clear that we can, to a certain extent, add qualifications to our assessment of the quality of work and the level of skill on the bipolar oppositions of complex/simple or high/low.

When we remove all the rhetorical padding from the various research reports cited above and extract just the concrete descriptions, what emerges is, as it were, a common picture of the level of 'unexpected' work factory workers are required to perform. We can say that the debate over skill moved a step forward from the earlier stalemate as a result of these workplace investigations.

The end of the 1990s: mass production skill

We can say that the various studies on skill from the second half of the 1980s into the first half of the 1990s, all took it for granted that skill was not required for, to borrow Koike's term, '*fudan no sagyō*' (routine work). They held that it was formed through participation in '*fudan to chigatta sagyō*' (lit. 'work different from usual,' i.e. 'non-routine work'), *kaizen* activities, QC circles and job rotation.

However, at the end of the 1990s, Fukuyama (1998) and Tsuji (1998) cast doubt on this common understanding and proposed, 'to shed light on an area that has previously been left as a virtually untouched void' (Tsuji, 1998: 114).

Tsuji (1998) looking back over previous research on workers in the automobile industry, points out, 'Until very recently, the common understanding and the generally accepted position among researchers into labour in the Japanese automobile industry has been that the "core work" of assembly-line workers requires no technical expertise and that there is no skill in this area' (*Ibid*. p. 116). Basing himself on the opinion of Fukuyama, who had had thirty years experience as a machining operator with a major finished vehicle assembly company, Tsuji asserts, 'Once we accept that mass production labour in an automobile factory, in both the peripheral work (dealing with abnormalities) and the core work (repetitive work) involves high levels of skill, we need to conceptualise this fact in the term "mass production skill (*ryōsangata jukuren*)."' (*Ibid*. p. 111). He goes on to state that 'not only recognizing the skill in "peripheral work," but clarifying the fact that high levels of skill are also found in "core work"' brings 'coherence into the skill debate' (*Ibid*. p. 117).

Research on the 'Toyota Reformation' from the 1990s

To date, many researchers have carried out their investigations, analyses and assessments around their interest in the issue of skill. But even as they have been doing so, there has been a major change in the target of their research. That has been the so-called Toyota Reformation.

At a time when Japan was reeling in the ecstasy of the economic bubble, Toyota was confronting a difficult economic environment. It faced staff shortages and was having trouble recruiting younger workers. There was a drop in morale on the shop floor and an increase in the numbers leaving the company. In response to these problems, from the end of the 1980s into the early 1990s Toyota aggressively pushed through its policy of implementing even greater levels of automation. But the measures pursued at this time did not bring the results the company had hoped for. On the contrary, they spawned a whole raft of new problems. The excessive automation resulted in a blowout in capital investment, more time spent on repairing machines, difficulty in changing vehicle models and increases in the salaries budget because of the need to employ more maintenance staff. In addition, the excessive simplification of work exacerbated the factory workers' feelings of alienation.

So, at this point, Toyota made an about-turn and groped with the idea of easing back on automation. It raised the developmental concept of 'automation in which people and machines co-exist' and devised the idea of 'in-line automation.' In addition, it implemented improvements in the organization of work. To relieve the pressure of line stoppages, each group was given a certain degree of autonomy ('autonomous completion process').

In addition, by quantifying the difficulty of assembly-line work and improving those tasks that were most demanding, they were able to increase the retention rate of younger workers. They also worked towards the creation of workplaces where older workers and women could work.

Starting with Uichi Asō et al. *Shakai kankyō no henka to jidōsha seisan shisutemu – Toyota shisutemu wa kawatta no ka* (Changes in the social environment and the automobile production system – has the Toyota system changed?) (Hōritsu Bunkasha, 1999), a large number of researchers have written on the background to the Toyota Reformation (Kojima 1994, Ogawa 1994, Shi 1994, Mine 1994, Fujimoto 1994, 1997, Shimizu 1995, 1999, 2001, Nohara 1997a,

1997b, Imada 1997, 1998, Fujita 1997). Assessments of the raft of reforms vary from one scholar to another, but the trend overall seems to be that the majority have been positive, with most agreeing that the working environment has improved.[14]

Problems and issues for the future

In the above, I have tried to bring together an overview, based on my own research concerns, of the trends in field-based research of labour conditions in automobile factories.

Here, to wrap things up, I would like to add just one personal opinion of my own concerning these research trends.

In recent years, the discussion of labour in car factories has focused on the major theme of skill. Many researchers have been engaged in surveying and analysing this issue and, as I indicated above, there has been a constant advance in research findings.

But, I would like to probe a little further into why the issue of skill came to become one of the main topics of research.

The reason it has gained so much attention is because it is a matter of concern to both management and labour. For the worker, it is the source of power – the power to negotiate inside and outside the company, the power to control the labour process and the power to constrain workloads. For management too, it is a compelling issue, relating to control within the workplace and beyond. At the same time, skill is an important theme in relation to productivity. That is why conditions on the shop floor are thrown into view by focusing on skill. In fact, with the progressive build-up of research findings on the issue of skill, we have come to understand the multi-faceted nature of the factory workplace.

But that is not the whole story. I cannot help thinking that, in recent years, those engaged in the skill debate have forgotten the starting point of interest in this issue. They are not approaching the question of skill in order to elucidate the substance of actual working conditions on the factory floor. On the contrary, they are investigating and analysing managerial behaviour or patterns of work to ascertain whether or not these are in any way related to skill. At least, that is the impression I have been getting. With the increasing elaboration of the argument, the skill debate has become formalized and removed from the logic of the shop floor. To such an extent, I feel, that it has come to take on the role of a shield, hiding from view the real conditions in the workplace. I can't help feeling that the skill debate today has embraced what can only be called a paradoxical approach to the problem.

Let me give you an example. In the earlier research, claims were made for a 'reintegration of conception and execution,' on the basis of the fact that assembly line workers in Toyota (Toyota Production System) also have responsibility for work beyond the simple tasks of the line.[15] Given that the doctrine of Taylorism stood on the principle of 'separation of conception and execution,' this would mean, researchers claimed, that Toyota (Toyota Production System) was based on something else. This is obviously in antithesis to Braverman's theory.[16] But the point at issue here is not to evaluate the arguments surrounding Braverman's proposal. Regardless of how we assess the Braverman thesis, if we become too absorbed in the formulaic representation of the theory, this has the undesired effect of concealing from us the actual conditions on the shop floor. That is the point I wish to make here.

Originally, Braverman demonstrated the trend towards separation of conception and execution in order to bring out the essence of capital's desire to exert its control over the labour process. In contrast to this, the debate over his theory concentrated only on minor differences in types of skill or patterns of work – important though the assessment of these areas might be – rather than dealing adequately with the underlying issue of control.[17] Management is continually trying to suppress workers' power as it surfaces from time to time against the background of work or skill.[18] If we are to get an accurate picture of conditions on the shop floor, we must be careful not to be drawn into considering workers' skill formation alone. We need to understand the complicated power relationships involving management, engineers and factory workers as they struggle for control or skill in the process of design and introduction of technology.[19]

We can also see the same problem of researchers distancing themselves from the actualities of the shop floor in studies analysing the connection between skill and competitive power. Work incorporates the two aspects of quality and quantity. Workers respond to these with skill and endurance respectively. We cannot necessarily tell which of these contributes to productivity. But even so, the source of competitive advantage is invariably put down to skill and the focus is always on the relationship between skill and productivity. As a result, the aspect of quantity as a component of work is excluded from the outset.[20] Moreover, the problem does not end there. There is always the danger that researchers will not only see just one aspect of reality, but that they will interpret that reality arbitrarily.

For example, let us consider the 'abnormal' case of removing a part that has become jammed along the line. Is that work of high quality? Is it an opportunity for skill formation? Or, rather, is it a hindrance that slows down the speed of production and disrupts the rhythm of work? In reality, there is a range of possible interpretations. Yet, a researcher, focusing only on the relationship between competitiveness and skill formation, is likely to conclude that, in companies with a competitive edge, 'dealing with abnormalities' *as a whole* is considered high quality work.[21] This also applies to those researchers who have sought to explain the reasons behind workers' acceptance of the status quo. They tend to consider the mode of work as providing opportunities for skill formation and interpret factory work as high quality labour. Of course, regardless of where you place the main focus of your research, you cannot avoid the issue of interpretation. But, if you are seeking to describe the actual state of work as it is performed on the factory floor, it is necessary to go back and investigate work as a whole, considering both its aspects, i.e. quality and quantity.[22]

I think there have been more than a few occasions in the past when a hypothesis set up to explain how society works, or an analytical model devised to elucidate some social phenomenon, have, paradoxically, been apt to conceal the actual conditions in the field. Now, to bring to light the real conditions in the workplace, what we need is not just a one-off, unilateral focusing of our research questions and analytical model on the field, but to keep going back and forth to the field, constantly amending our model. In recent years, the majority of investigations into Toyota's reformation have been based on interviews with management. These have provided valuable research findings in their own right. But, rather than deducing work conditions from what the managers tell us, I feel perhaps there is a need now to go back and unravel the context of the factory floor. This is our task for the future.

Appendix II: Subsequent Developments in the Toyota Workplace

I am writing this additional appendix at the end of September 2006. Five years have passed since the initial investigation. Given that the world of economics and management moves so quickly, I would like to take the opportunity afforded by the publication of this English edition to briefly comment on trends in Toyota over the five years since I worked in the factory.

Moving into the twenty-first century, Toyota has gone on from strength to strength. Although signs of recovery are emerging within the Japanese economy, on the whole most companies are exhibiting lack-lustre performance. Toyota stands out as the one company that is progressing vigorously. For six years in a row since the fiscal year of 1999, Toyota has had the highest reported income of any public corporation in Japan. It is firmly entrenched as the leader of the automobile industry in Japan with over a forty per cent share (44.3% in 2005) of the domestic car market (excluding light vehicles). The company's sales figures (consolidated accounts) topped ten trillion yen (approx. US$85.6 billion at the November 2006 conversion rate of around 117 yen to the US dollar – the dollar conversions below calculated at 2006 rates are provided as a rough guide only), in 1996 and have continued to grow steadily since. By the time of my investigation in 2001 the figure had risen to 15.1 trillion yen ($128.5 billion). By 2005 it had risen to 21 trillion yen ($178.6 billion). In 2001 Toyota made history by becoming the first manufacturing company in Japan to top one trillion yen (approx. $8.5 billion) in profits (consolidated accounts). In 2005 the company's profit had risen to 1.87 trillion yen (just over 16 billion US dollars).

A recent business trend within Toyota worthy of note is the emergence of the Lexus brand on the domestic market. From 30 August 2005, the Lexus, which was already being sold abroad as Toyota's luxury model, was also launched in Japan. Determined not to rest on its laurels, the company continues to take an aggressive stance. Although it has been a hard struggle for the company and sales for the year after the release of the Lexus on the domestic market are barely half the target figures, in September 2006 Toyota sought to turn its fortunes around by releasing its top-of-the-range LS model. It already had pre-sale orders for over nine thousand of the ten thousand vehicles it expects to sell in the first year. But it is probably still too soon to tell whether Lexus has succeeded in establishing itself as a new brand.

Internationally Toyota's performance has been equally impressive. In the fiscal year 2003 the company overtook Ford Motors in worldwide vehicle sales and jumped to number two in the international league of carmakers. Toyota's hybrid cars like the Prius have been selling well, riding the crest of the wave of rising oil prices. The company now has the top position, occupied by GM, well and truly in its sights.

Based on the figures, Toyota management is running extremely favourably. In recent years it has enjoyed skyrocketing growth. The 'Toyota Production System (TPS)' and the 'Toyota Way' are experiencing a revivalist boom and Toyota management methods are back in the spotlight. Are we to assume then that there are no blemishes in this fine performance – that there are no problems at all on the shop floor?

As we have seen in these pages, the context of the workplace is complex and fluid. Even minor variations in the environment inside and outside the factory can result in major changes to the workplace. In the limited space available to me here I would like to make a few observations, focusing on the recent tendency to increase casual workers and on the influence on 'quality,' said to be the source of Toyota's competitive edge.

From the late 1980s to the late 1990s there were times when no casual workers were employed at all and even during peak periods the figure was under three thousand per year. But from 2000 there was a sudden growth in casual employment. In 2003 the number passed six thousand and in 2005 broke through the ten thousand mark. The proportion of fixed-term contract labour in the workplace regularly exceeded thirty per cent and in some cases accounted for half the workforce. At present the number of casual employees seems to have reached a peak.[1]

From the viewpoint of the workers, the large-scale employment of casual staff means deterioration in working conditions including salary levels, career development and job security. But it enables management to cut costs by providing the flexibility to increase or decrease the number of workers employed in response to changes in the volume of production. It increases productivity. If that is the case, does raising the level of casual employment increase management efficiency?

One issue that immediately springs to mind is that of diminishing levels of skill. When the proportion of non-tenured employees increases, there is a fall in the skill levels of the workplace as a whole. If that occurs Toyota's '*monozukuri*' (lit. 'making things,' i.e. manufacturing), long heralded as its strength, is placed in jeopardy.

That is not to say that work on the Toyota production line requires large numbers of workers with the manual skills of the artisans of the past. We confirmed this fact elsewhere in this volume. But, no matter how precisely the Manufacturing Management Division (*seisan kanribu*) may design a process, uncalculated mishaps are bound to occur in the workplace. So it is also essential to have in the workplace the skill to deal with these unpredictable incidents. Skill is accumulated and disseminated through people. Once a person with a certain skill has gone, it is difficult to regain that skill. Consequently, over the long-term situation, there is a need to maintain a number of workers with high levels of technical skill.

Further, on top of the increase in non-tenured workers, there will be a mass exodus from the company over the years 2007 through 2009 when employees of the so-called *dankai no sedai*[2] (baby-boomer generation) retire. Those veteran workers who over the years have been the mainstay of Toyota factories will all leave at once. When that happens it will further weaken Toyota's '*monozukuri*' base.

There is nothing particularly unusual about this argument. Many commentators have pointed out these trends. But, if we observe carefully from the tail-end down on the shop floor, we can see that it is nothing as grand as 'skill,' but a more insignificant change in 'consciousness' that is having a major effect on quality. Here I would like to delve a little more deeply into this point that has thus far been largely overlooked.

Assembly line work is a simple operation. Standardized procedures have been designed to ensure that the same part can be made regardless of who is in charge. The Toyota line, too, is organized along the so-called principles of Taylorism. In that case, can anyone produce exactly the same part? Can we produce a part of the same quality by following the directions of the standard procedures manual? To put the conclusion first, the answer is 'No!' Simple though the work is, individual differences inevitably arise.

Variation in quality in assembly-line work arises from truly minute differences in the decision whether or not to let a part pass on to the next stage in the manufacturing process. Powers of concentration tend to falter when you are producing hundreds, or even thousands of parts per day. Large variations in product quality can result from slightly different mental responses to these periods of psychological stress. On the one hand, there are those who pay little attention to minor details and adopt the attitude, "What the hell, let it through!" while there are others who respond firmly with, "Wait a minute! I must be more careful."

Differences in powers of concentration and endurance may well vary from one individual to another, but there is also considerable variation according to the employment status of the worker concerned. As a general rule, we can say that regular employees have a stronger sense of responsibility. Workers who intend to work a long time with the company have a greater sense of self-discipline and a strong conviction that faulty parts should not pass through the assembly line. Consequently, increasing the number of non-regular employees inevitably results in a rise in the rate of faulty and imperfect parts coming off the line.

Moreover, individual personality differences and employment status are not the only factors affecting quality. The overall atmosphere of the workplace also exerts a major influence. This very important point tends to be overlooked. We find situations in which workers keep one another in check through a system of mutual surveillance operating within the group. In contrast, there are also workplaces where workers support and encourage each other in an atmosphere of friendly cooperation. In either case, the atmosphere of the workplace is a powerful regulator of quality levels.

It is for precisely this reason that the Toyota management camp devotes a great deal of effort to personnel management, from the level of regulation of interpersonal relationships in the workplace to the uniting of workers of the company as a whole. However, with the recent increases in the proportion of non-regular employees, the 'kakoikomi' (enclosure) method employed up to now no longer works. As I indicated above, in the average workplace non-regular staff account for over thirty per cent of the workforce and in some cases this proportion increases to over half those employed. In terms of numbers alone, it is difficult to say that non-regular workers still occupy a peripheral position. So the limitations of the method whereby the central core of regular workers win over the minority group of non-regular workers are beginning to become apparent.

Further, the proportion of graduates of the Toyota Technical Skills Academy (*Toyota Kōgyō Gakuen*) who occupy a central position within the core itself, is tending to decline. Whereas in the past the academy turned out several hundred graduates every year, in recent years this number has fallen to below one hundred. This results in a further weakening of the centripetal force provided by the Toyota Technical Skills Academy graduates at the core and a strengthening of the influence of the non-regular workers at the periphery.

Sooner or later most of the non-regular workers will leave Toyota. Their commitment to the company is relatively weak. When the proportion of workers of this kind increases, it is very easy for an atmosphere to develop in the workplace that is just the opposite of management expectations. And the mentality of the casual worker and his (or her) patterns of behaviour become diffused through the workplace as a whole, extending even to the regular workers.

Management is taking this problem very seriously. When I inspected a Toyota factory in October 2005 and asked someone from the PR department what he felt the influence of increased employment of casual workers might be, he let slip that 'we're groping about wondering where the explosion might come.'

The increase in non-tenured workers lowers the level of perseverance of the entire workplace. And a lack of endurance invites deterioration in quality. Recent events underline the reality of this observation. There has been a spate of large-scale recalls (replacement or cost-free repair). It is claimed that over the five-year period to the end of fiscal year 2005 the number of recalled vehicles had swollen to forty-two times the number at the beginning of the period.[3]

To give just a couple of concrete examples, in October 2005 faults arose in the light switch mechanism of sixteen models, including the Corolla sedan etc., totalling 1,272,214 vehicles manufactured between May 2000 and August 2002. It was the biggest single recall in the history of the Japanese auto manufacturing industry.[4] In April 2006 there was even a recall of the Lexus, a luxury vehicle with a reputation for superior quality. Toyota reported to the Ministry of Land Infrastructure and Transport the recall of 11,109 vehicles manufactured between July and December 2005 on the grounds that faults had been discovered in the manufacture of the seat belts.[5]

Of course, not all the increase in large-scale recalls over recent years can be attributed to the increase in non-tenured labour. Unreasonable cost-cutting plans and the move towards the use of common parts are also contributing factors. The use of a common part in a number of different models immediately increases the number of vehicles involved in a recall. In addition, we cannot ignore the influence of Mitsubishi Motor's run of 'hidden recalls.' Mitsubishi's mistake that had threatened the very survival of the company was seen as a lesson to others in the industry and led to greater openness and voluntary disclosure of problems. But it is an undeniable fact that simple errors that would have been inconceivable in Toyota in the past are occurring in the workplace.[6] From the investigation of the workplace detailed in this book it is also easy to imagine how an increase in non-regular workers could directly and indirectly lead to the deterioration of product quality.

To have a continual stream of new casual workers coming into a workplace where everyone is struggling to meet their own daily quotas puts an additional strain on staff. They have to contend with the added responsibility for training, increasingly complicated interpersonal relationships and falling morale. In the latter half of this book I have portrayed in some detail from my own direct observation of the situation on the shop floor, how a workplace can be on the verge of blowing apart. Some of the recent recalls include parts manufactured during that period. At present there are a lot more non-tenured workers than there were then. I suspect there is also considerably more confusion in the workplace.

Moreover, a worsening of the atmosphere in the workplace does not only result in a drop in quality. As I have repeated many times in these pages, the 'minimum duty' required of assembly-line workers is no more than the performance of simple, repetitive tasks. But in order for the factory to keep running, they also need to make minor adjustments between manufacturing processes.

Under the tightly regulated Toyota Production System, with no 'play' or 'room to move,' line workers have been virtually forced to perform these tasks. It is a 'tacit rule' of the workplace that they take on these duties in addition to their simple basic jobs. However, when non-tenured workers constitute a majority, many of them do only what they are told, so it becomes difficult to keep the line running.

Currently Toyota is suffering from a lack of 'smart, resourceful' workers and the system is nearing the limit of its tolerance.

Of course, the Toyota management is not sitting on its hands in the face of these problems. It is doing all it can to come up with counter measures like extending the length of the period of employment for casual workers[7] and increasing the numbers it appoints to the regular staff.[8] Toyota's ability to respond to changes in the external environment, i.e. its 'power to evolve,' has been cited as a source of Toyota's strength. We have been given just a glimpse of that ability. But now that Toyota has become such a giant enterprise, will it be able to maintain that ability as strongly as it has in the past? Is it not possible that we are already witnessing a weakening of that very ability?

We need to keep a close eye on future developments in Toyota.

Ryōji Ihara.
September 2006
Gifu

Postscript

Already one and half years have passed since I left Toyota. When I was working in the factory I thought how nice and free the life of an academic is, but when I started writing the manuscript for this book, I began to feel work in Toyota was easier. I suppose my lazy disposition is going to catch me out whatever I do.

This book would not have taken its present form without the advice and encouragement of many people. I cannot name them all here, but I would like to convey my heartfelt thanks to every one of them.

I particularly regret that, given the nature of this book, I have not been able to name the friends and workmates who worked with me during my time at Toyota. I cannot forget how we worked together in a lather of sweat, joked with one another under extreme conditions or occasionally even held serious conversations. Though I only worked there for three short months, several different groups threw farewell parties for me, and insisted on paying for everything. I am very happy I was able to experience that warmth of friendship from the men and women I worked with.

Since I entered graduate school I have benefited from the support of my supervisor, Professor Masao Watanabe. It was Watanabe sensei who gave me the chance to resume my studies when I was wandering about at a loose end, having quit my job as a 'salary man' (i.e. white collar employee). He was also the one who helped me overcome my tendency to become bored easily, so that I even got to the point where I could sit down and confront the classics.

I had had the benefit of Professor Hiroyuki Itami's guidance during one of my undergraduate seminars. At the time, as I recall, we did not always see eye to eye and there were occasional clashes, but Professor Itami was kind enough to take me in despite all that. If I have been at all successful in seeing things in a broader perspective, I think that must be my reward from the confrontations (one-sided attacks from my quarter) with Itami sensei. For that, I thank him most deeply.

Professor Emeritus Takayoshi Kitagawa, a pioneer in the field of labour research in the automobile industry, gave me the opportunity to present this research and provided useful comments. On other group research projects, I was able to learn about research methods under the painstaking guidance of Professor Kitagawa and other scholars. I hope some of their 'skill' in this area has rubbed off on me.

I am grateful to Professor Takehiko Hayakawa, who, from just after the time I entered university until today, has taught me just what a researcher and educator should be. Forever modest and unassuming, Professor Hayakawa would probably deny that, but I cannot imagine how much I have learned in the course of the candid conversations I have had with him. I thank him from the bottom of my heart.

I thank Professor Takuji Yanagida, who was also my senior in my undergraduate days, for explaining modern management and economic theory in terms that even I could easily understand. He always hastened to point out whenever the opportunity arose, that it is not just a matter of learning the technical formulae; you must look at the management and economic thinking behind them. I cannot say how much encouragement it has brought me to see Professor Yanagida, a man of my own generation, applying himself so assiduously to his research.

Mr Yoshitaka Nakamura read through the manuscript of this book and gave me his valuable comments. Mr Nakamura and I hold an autonomous seminar once a month. We frequently have heated debates that go on till dawn. If I have finally learned something about social theory, it is entirely thanks to him. Further, I would like to take this opportunity to express my thanks to my research colleagues, Ms Haruka Ōtake, Mr Hiroaki Obitani and Ms Chisako Katō for their constant warm encouragement.

Mr Kaoru Sakurai of Sakurai Shoten kindly agreed to publish this book, for which I thank him most sincerely.

Finally, if I may be excused for introducing a personal note, I would like to give my heartfelt thanks to my parents, Kikuko and Kōsuke, and siblings, Ikuko and Ren'ichi for their perseverance in putting up with my wilful, irresponsible antics.

Ryōji Ihara.
31 March 2003
Tokyo

Notes

Prologue

1 All names used in this book, with the exception of my own (Ihara) are fictitious.

Chapter 1

1 'In reference to the Toyota Production System, the word for automation should always be written as "autonomation," with the character for "to work" rather than with the usual character for "to move." This is because "to work" is written with a Chinese character containing the man radical, signifying that "autonomation," as it is used by Toyota, conveys the sense that machines are endowed with the intellect of human beings. The idea of *jidōka* (autonomation) using the character for "to work" for the second element (*dō*) is the concept of the founder of the Toyota company, Sakichi Toyoda, who applied it to his automated loom. That is to say, the machine was designed so that if the threads in the warp broke, or the supply of yarn to the weft were to run out, it would come to an immediate stop. In other words, the ability to determine whether things were running smoothly or not was built into the machine' (Ōno, 1978: 217).

2 The term 'process' is commonly used to signify the manufacturing stages in the course of production, such as, casting, forging, sintering, processing, heat-treatment, assembly and so on. But in Toyota, it is also used to refer to each individual worker's post on the assembly line. You refer to your own position as your 'own process' and the positions on the assembly line immediately before and after you as the 'process before' and the 'process after.'

3 I refer to the permanent staff (*honkō*) as 'regular employees' (*ippan jūgyōin*) and the short-term contract workers (*kikankō*) as 'casual employees' (*kikan jūgyōin*). The term *honkō* is seldom heard in this factory and while I did hear the term *kikankō* from time to time, it often carried a slightly pejorative connotation. In this book I use the terms that were used in the factory.

Chapter 2

1 Kojima (1994), Ogawa (1994), Shi (1994), Mine (1994), Fujimoto (1994, 1997), Shimizu (1995, 1999, 2000), Nohara (1997a, 1997b), Imada (1997, 1998), Fujita (1997), Asao et al. (1999) and others have dealt with the Toyota 'reformation.' In addition, some of these include research on Toyota Kyushu.

2 Most researchers of labour in the automobile industry have used similar terminology to point out the existence of this phenomenon. The terms used are based on Kazuo Koike's concepts of labour, for a detailed explanation of which see, Koike (1991 and 1993b).

3 The average male stride is generally said to be around 75 cm. Here it is perhaps appropriate for me to give a brief description of my own physical characteristics and ability. I am twenty-nine years old, 185 centimetres tall and weigh 74 kilograms. When I was a student I could run fifty metres in just over six seconds and bench press eighty kilograms. My ability has fallen away a little since my student days, but I think my physical ability is still above the average for an adult male.

4 From what I've heard from the casual workers, it seems that, even so, Plant K is on the easier side. News about which factories were easier somehow filtered through to us even before our assignments were announced. Probably the source of this information was the repeaters among the casual workers. The rumour went around that assembly in Plant T was the toughest. After we had been assigned to our positions I heard from one of my contemporary casual workers who had been sent to Plant T that it was indeed extremely hard. Several times my supervisor told me, 'You're better off in this factory; it's clean, safe and the work's easy.' Of course, I had to take what he said with a grain of salt because there was an ulterior motive behind his words. He was telling me not to complain about the status quo.

5 The symptoms disappeared soon after I left Toyota.

6 In chapter 4, 'Worker Autonomy,' I deal in detail with 'change' as it affects the entire workplace, as, for example, in the rearrangement of work organization. This also applies to dealing with the 'unexpected,' which we shall be considering in the next section, at the level of the workplace as a whole.

7 Here I am referring to the young leader charged with on-site management. This is not a formal position.

8 In our workplace there were three to four off-line workers for the inspection/packing line and the sub-assembly process line combined. As the off-line workers also fill in for employees on annual leave, the number of people working off-line is not fixed. The off-line workers are drawn from those who play a central role on the factory floor, like the team leaders and some of the section leaders. The personnel can change from day to day, but Shiraishi (Section leader, 19 years experience), Shimada (Section leader, 19 years experience), Nagata (Team leader – inspection/packing line, 13 years experience) and Ogawa (Team leader – sub-assembly, 10 years experience) frequently worked off-line.

9 The tools of trade of the QC circle are; the Pareto graph, the characteristic factor chart, the histogram, the hierarchy of control diagram, the scatter graph and the check sheet. See Imai (1991: 378–99).

10 In the following, for the sake of clarity, the author has made some very minor changes in reporting the comments of other workers.

11 According to Komatsu (2000) in his 1997 and 1999 interview surveys of staff in the Personnel Department of Toyota Motor, he found that, 'In the process of job rotation, a higher priority is placed on acquiring skill in the

job in which workers are currently engaged than on becoming proficient in a variety of tasks. As far as possible, precipitous multi-skilling is avoided. Further, casual and short-term contract workers in all workplaces are assigned tasks designated "beginner processes" and new members of staff also start with these jobs' (p. 285). In my workplace the situation was as I have described.

12 So far, I have been using the term 'rotation' in the general sense of 'alternation of workplace,' but Suzuki (1983) drawing on his experience as deputy head of the general affairs division of Plant K, divides rotation into the following three types.

1. Rotation. Transfer from one workplace (mainly one group) to another at intervals of several years. In this case there is a complete change in the type of work performed, the employee's affiliation and human relationships. In the case of supervisors (from section leader up) this is called 'management rotation.'

2. Intra-group rotation. Movement within the group as the need demands. Here there is very little change in the type of work, affiliation or human relations. OJT (on the job training) is essential to develop multi-skilling.

3. Job rotation. Planned alternation of jobs at regular intervals of from two to four hours (pp. 222–3).

In my workplace there was no regular, planned rotation of the type described by Suzuki. If called to put a name to it, I suppose 'irregular rotation' might do. But regardless of what we might call it, rotation here did not have the slightest hint of educational consideration.

Chapter 3

1 The field research of the 1960s and 1970s was, Nihon Jinbun-kagakkai (Japan Society of Human Sciences) ed. (1963), Kamata (1973), Yamamoto (1981), Tanaka (1982, 1983, 1984) and Saga (1984). From the 1980s on we have, Koyama ed. (1985), Nohara et al. eds (1988), Totsuka et al. eds (1991) and the published work of the individual researchers involved in the investigations. For a detailed account see Appendix I.

2 A representative paper is that of Kazuo Koike (see Ch.2, n.2). Koike's argument covers the whole of Japanese industry, but automobile labour theory of the 1980s has been heavily influenced by Koike's work. For an assessment of skill among workers in the automobile industry and its conceptual framework see, Tsuji (1989), Yumoto (1989–90), Nohara (1992), Sawada (1994). For a skilful summary of the various arguments on skill, see Yumoto (1994).

3 Fukuyama (1998), Tsuji (1998).

4 In this book I have used the term 'standardized work' rather than 'routine work.' My reason for doing so will become clear later, but the divisions 'routine work' = 'fixed-pattern work,' 'non-routine work' = 'non-fixed-pattern work' = response to 'change and the unexpected' are not always appropriate terms when seen from the reality of work on the factory floor.

5 Lave and Wenger (1991) based on painstaking observation, is a detailed analysis of the process of skill formation in a wide range of jobs. This

research clearly shows that workers learn through interaction with their working environment. We can say that assembly line workers probably also go through the same process.

6 Asakawa (1987) taking his examples from a fitting-out assembly line, also indicates that it was the older workers who commented that the work was hard (*kitsui*) and that they had no time to spare (pp. 126–9).

7 Since the 1990s, with the aging of assembly-line workers, coping with the physical and mental burden has become a progressively more urgent problem. Management is desperately struggling to find a solution to this problem, not only to secure the labour supply, but also to strengthen production by reducing line stoppages and the number of imperfect products (e.g. Mitoma et al. (1999). Given these circumstances, you cannot help wondering whether it is really wise to go on insisting that 'skill' (= accumulated experience) should be regarded as an indispensable attribute for all assembly-line workers across the board.

8 This is surprisingly close to what Satoshi Kamata was saying almost thirty years ago. This is what he wrote then.

'In the time it takes for one worker to become "established" many others drop out. I do not believe that we can simply dismiss as "unskilled" those conveyor-belt workers who, like me, take a full month before they can keep up with the unilaterally imposed speed requirement. There are only three workers; the group leader, section leader and assistant section leader, who fully understand the entire process of transmission assembly. These three are not unskilled workers, but neither can they really be called skilled, or even semi-skilled. From the outset they are placed outside the boundaries of the concept of "skill". I think it would be more appropriate to call them "anti-skilled" workers. They are also called "single-skilled workers" (*tannōkō*) but should we really describe their capabilities as skill at all? They are simply performing a taxing job' (Kamata, 1973: 110–11).

This is really an individual opinion, but I feel what we have here is another example of an 'automobile despair factory.' [Note: The original Japanese title of Kamata's book that appeared in English as *Japan in the Passing Lane* was *Jidōsha Zetsubō Kōjō* (Automobile Despair Factory).] Of course, different individuals may view the same experience in different ways. So I expect some readers will criticise my subjectivity. But for anyone who has been through the experience, the reality is so harsh that any criticism of this kind is ineffectual. We see the same kind of thinking reported in Kawasaki (1998–99). He spent nine months working as a welder in a Honda body-assembly plant. I quote him here at some length.

'In his *Japan in the Passing Lane*, the author, Kamata, repeatedly vents his anger at the harshness of conveyor-belt labour. When I read that, I had a suspicion that Mr Kamata must not have been particularly strong physically. In addition, he was especially sensitive to labour problems. So, I had some reservations that he might have gone sneaking into Toyota intending from the outset to write an exposé and consequently painted the work in a particularly bad light. I'm different. I'm confident of the physical strength I have built up through sport and manual labour. I've been crazy about cars since I was a kid, even though I don't have one of my own. (I read all the

books in the *Machigaidarake no kuruma-erabi* (How not to choose a car)
series as soon as they came out). Apart from geographical considerations,
the reason I applied to be a casual worker with Honda was because that
was the Japanese carmaker that impressed me most. So, I can see things
objectively from both sides without bias. My view of work on the conveyor-
belt is bound to be different from Mr Kamata's. That's what I thought. But as
soon as I started working there I discovered that Mr Kamata's descriptions
were extremely accurate. It was not simply a matter of physical strength
and mental attitude' (Kawasaki, 1998 [vol. 2]: 178).

In addition, there are first-hand reports of experience working as casual
labour in Japanese automobile plants including, Shiomi (1978–79), Sagawa
(1980) and Fukui (1999). Shiomi (worked in 'A' automobile factory on the
outskirts of Tokyo, on machining and a milling lathe) and Sagawa (worked
in the Zama factory of Nissan Motors, on a pressing machine) both give
similar assessments. Of course, it depends a lot on the job you are assigned.
On the other hand Fukui (Toyota Motor's Tawara factory, forming section,
painting), whose task was to mask the side mouldings of sedans to keep the
paint off, saw the job as, 'like a student's basic part-time job, requiring no
special skills or brainpower, the sort of job you can easily start from middle-
age. For anyone with reasonable physical endurance, this is a highly paid
job with good conditions.' Of course, he stresses the quota, 'so high that
virtually no-one ever attains it' and the fact that 'worries over interpersonal
relations are greater than those over the work.' I shall be dealing with the
latter in detail in due course.

9   For the 'career' debate, see Koike (1981, 1991, 1997).
10 I do not deal with the connections between skill and off-the-job-training
    (Off-JT). Rather than trying to guess what level of skill has come through
    the education system, I seek to clarify the kinds of skills actually formed
    in the workplace. Komatsu (2000), mentioned before, touches on the latest
    'professional skills acquisition system' (revised in October 1999).
11 I am prepared to admit that QC Circles essentially do have a positive aspect
    (for the worker). *Nihon Kagaku Gijutsu Renmei* (The Union of Japanese
    Scientists and Engineers) ed. *Genba to QC* (QC on the factory floor), *FQC*,
    and *QC Sākuru – shokuba to QC* (QC circles – QC in the workplace) list
    numerous instances that show this to be so. For example, Toyo Industries
    (*Genba to QC*, No. 95, 1971), Toyota Motor (*Ibid.* No. 99, 1971), Toyota
    Motor (*Ibid.* No. 103, 1972), Nissan Motors (FQC. No. 114, 1973), Hino
    Motors (*Ibid.* No. 118, 1973), Mitsubishi Motors (*Ibid.* No. 119, 1973),
    Toyota Motor (*Ibid.* No. 131, 1974) and Toyota Motor (*Ibid.* No. 132, 1974)
    despite the undeniable fact that all are reports of 'ideal employees,' all
    emphasize the positive aspects of QC activity. Further, Kobayashi (1987)
    one of the few field survey studies of small group activity in the automobile
    industry, casts an analytical eye over not only the supervisory aspects of QC,
    but also its role in QWL, 'humanization of work' and character building
    (pp. 180–3). But we should be concentrating our attention on the way QC
    functions in the context of the workplace and the significance it has in
    the lives of the workers overall. In this respect, there are limitations to
    analyses that focus on QC alone. In my workplace, for most workers, their

involvement in QC Circles was in a state of inertia – a far cry from active participation. Previous research also points out the inactivity of QC. 'The level of worker participation has also declined in QC activities. There are conspicuous cases of management concocting reports just before the QC conferences and the tendency in some quarters is for QC to become just a hollow formality' (Kimura, 1990: 216).

12 'Even for a simple assembly line process a fairly high level of skill *is demanded* to grasp the essential knack and key points of a task and put them into appropriate words for the training of new recruits. The acquisition of this skill is seen as a *prerequisite* in the promotion process for workers at Toyota' (Koyama ed., 1985: 201. My italics). '"Process improvement skill," i.e. the ability to lower costs and raise quality through reorganization of work mechanisms, and improving methods and infrastructure, "organizational skill," or the ability to co-ordinate small group activity in the workplace, and even "educational skill," which relates to the other two skills, are regarded as the most important *requirements* of on-site managers. There are considerable differences in the allocation of administrative tasks depending on whether or not one has these skills' (Nohara et al., 1988: 383–4. My italics). I cannot help feeling that most of the previous research has either, assumed that the skill formed through career building is that demanded of managers, or confused the distinction by substituting what is theoretically required with what actually exists in practice. There is no necessary correlation between the skills demanded of managers and the skills they acquire over the course of their careers. At very least, we cannot say that the connection between the two is self-evident. Consequently, I have chosen to explore this point below.

13 Here I confine myself to a few brief remarks, as I deal with the (young) team leaders in detail in the next chapter.

14 The reason for this is that they have already been 'sorted' according to the different paths through which they were recruited into the company. There is a detailed discussion of the mechanisms of 'competition and selection' in Chapter 6.

15 Other researchers have also drawn attention to this point. 'The skill management wants is a keen ability to detect areas for improvement. Of course, it is necessary *to understand* the jobs in the workplace, but there is no need *to have mastered the work itself.* Consequently, when a worker moves up into a managerial position, he does not necessarily take charge of the workplace in which he was previously involved' (Ishida, 1997: 234. My italics).

16 For an account of intensive training for managers, see Koyama ed. (1985: 297–301).

17 Most previous research seems unaware of this point. Of those who have taken it up, we can say that Asanuma in the main follows Koike's theory but he also makes the following point. 'There are also cases where workers experience other types of work in a supporting role. But this usually happens as the result of a temporary internal staff redeployment to avoid laying-off employees faced with a downturn in demand for the specific item they had been producing. *It is not done with the primary aim of skill formation* (Asanuma, 1997: 92–3. My italics).

Chapter 4

1 For example, Monden (1989, 1991). 'In Toyota, in every factory they have introduced small group activities called "QC circles." In these circles they debate measures to introduce workplace autonomy and *kaizen* activities so that any conflicts that may arise with workers over productivity targets can be resolved' (1989: 219–20).

2 See, for example, Saruta (1995). 'You can say that Toyota's "autonomous" "QC circles" are nothing more than a means to raise productivity by making workers, under management control, pay the sacrifice of taking responsibility for product quality, cost and safety procedures' (p. 121).

3 Although it is taken from a study of Japanese factory labour overall, I give the following as a representative example of this view. 'I would like to throw into relief this two-sided nature of small group activities, namely the positive and negative aspects' (Kyōtani, 1982: 96). 'In reality, in QC activities the gap between the "hawks" and the "doves" or between the "model" QC Circles and those formed by workers is no more than "the thickness of a single sheet of paper." By this I mean that Japanese workers continue to display the dual attributes of being faithful "employees," while at the same time being thoroughly "organized labour"' (Kumazawa, 1993: 178).

4 For a discussion of the above manpower saving procedure see Monden (1991: 302).

5 'Sometimes the reduction in staff numbers is represented as a means to force the remaining workers to work harder, with little regard at all for their basic humanity. But this criticism either fails to comprehend the nature of job improvement or is voiced when an inappropriate procedure has been followed. When a process in the factory undergoes improvement, all workers involved must understand that getting rid of unnecessary work will definitely not result in intensification of their workloads. It is not intensification, *but the work improvement plan adds value to the work by keeping the workload at the same level as it was before*' (Monden, 1989: 131–2. My italics).

6 We also find this argument in Burawoy (1979). Through his analysis as a participant observer of factory work, Burawoy clearly shows that there is a mechanism (making out) that guarantees that this will happen while at the same time obscuring the surplus value created. 'Making out' means 'performing well' in the unofficial 'game' of work on the factory floor. As an example of this kind of game, Burawoy cites the competition among workers to produce the greatest excess accumulation of products. The employees become engrossed in this game because it helps to relieve the boredom of their monotonous tasks and it provides the opportunity for them to win the esteem of their fellow workers. Burawoy stresses the point that these games seen in the labour process are certainly not entirely the result of autonomous action, nor are they contrary to the interests of management. Although workers strive to hone their skills in this game solely to gain the consent of their colleagues, the creation of this consent gives rise to surplus value, which, seen in the light of macro-economic theory, contributes to the reproduction of the capitalist system.

Moreover, in our workplace, participation in these games resulted in an even harsher outcome for the workers than that Burawoy observed. This was because participation for us did not stop at the preservation of order in the workplace, but actually encouraged intensification of our workloads.

7 See, for example, Sakakibara (1988). 'It seems correct to say that the Japanese production system, as represented in Toyota, has been able to inject dynamism towards growth of the enterprise as a whole by institutionally encouraging continuous learning at the level of the factory floor' (p. 150).

8 Consequently, when this burden is taken into account, you cannot necessarily say that work on our line is easier or more humane than it would be with a conveyor belt assembly line. Yamano (fixed-term, joined with me), who works on a conveyor-belt line, says that when you get used to it, perhaps it is easier to work on a conveyor belt. That is because there is no troublesome human interaction. You just do what you are told.

9 According to Friedman, 'Broadly, there are two major types of strategies which top managers use to exercise authority over labour power – Responsible Autonomy and Direct Control. The Responsible Autonomy type of strategy attempts to harness the adaptability of labour power by giving workers leeway and encouraging them to adapt to changing situations in a manner beneficial to the firm. To do this top managers give workers status, authority and responsibility. Top managers try to win their loyalty, and co-opt their organisations to the firm's ideals (that is, the competitive struggle) ideologically. The Direct Control type of strategy tries to limit the scope for labour power to vary by coercive threats, close supervision and minimising individual worker responsibility' (p. 78). Friedman claims that there has been an historical progression from direct control to responsible autonomy.

10 Koike (1976, 1977a, 1977b) has the following observation to make about regulatory control in a 'semi-autonomous' workplace. 'The labour unions play no role at all in the distribution of workloads or movement of staff between processes within the workplace or related workplaces. But management intervention is also limited in those areas in which the unions are not involved. These decisions are generally made by the foreman, but there is also an element of factory floor practice involved. As evidence of this, we can cite the fact that even within the same factory, movements are determined differently from one workplace to another. This is indeed "egalitarian workplace distribution" and the "semi-autonomous groups" that exercise this regulatory power represent the highest level of workplace participation.'

   In regard to this workplace, I must say that Koike's view is extremely superficial and his interpretation arbitrary. Kumazawa (1977), Nomura (1993b) and Kyōtani (1993) make the same criticism.

11 This method is also used in CAMI, the joint venture set up by Suzuki and GM. A manager in CAMI is quoted as saying, 'In Japan for example they say, "the line speed today is one and a half minutes, by the end of tomorrow I want to see that reduced by three seconds." As if to say that, after that there will be a few points we should check, they often raise the speed of the

line without increasing the workforce. This method has hardly been used at all in North America, but we have introduced it into our CAMI factory.' (CAW/TCA ed., 1996: 54). Raising the speed of the line takes priority.

12 This question can also be reinterpreted as follows. For each worker, the 'job' demarcation is vague so the actual task (i.e. burden) they are obliged to take on increases. Whether it be in the form of fine-tuning between processes, in 'spontaneous' quality meetings or in work taken home. Fundamentally, the assembly line worker's job is to do only the standardized work assigned to them, but in practice they have no choice but to do all the peripheral 'jobs' as well.

In addition, it should be pointed out here that it is not necessarily to the workers' advantage for them to be given greater scope to exercise their autonomy. Workers have a very strong consciousness of their own domain and a keen sense of independence. So increased autonomy can, paradoxically, lead to stress over interpersonal relationships and intervention between processes on the line. In general, assembly line work is treated as 'labour alienated from human relations,' (e.g. Blauner, 1964), but the fact is that factory workers do not necessarily want to have interaction with their fellow workers while they are working. Apart from touching base with close workmates, workers find it a nuisance to be compelled to communicate with their fellow workers. Consequently, semi-autonomous workplace management based on group participation cannot be judged as an unequivocally positive development. In the past, conflict arising over the sense of independence of deskilled operators was simply not an issue to be considered. But, Mulcahy and Faulkner (1979) clearly illustrate this point with actual examples from overseas.

13 Here, I did not deal with 'regulation through the unions,' but this almost never happens. I do not deny the indirect influence of the unions, but in our workplace direct intervention by the union did not exist. Kamii (1994) has a detailed account of the role of the unions in workplace regulation.

Chapter 5

1 Monden (1989, 1991) and Sakakibara (1988) etc. As a whole, 1980s research into labour in the Japanese automobile industry shares the view that as the company meets the demands of workers, even concerning their very work *per se*, workers are prepared to work positively and accept the status quo despite the controls they are under. See Appendix I for a detailed discussion of this point.

2 Control measures of this kind are often raised, not only by labour researchers in this field, but also, more generally, by researchers in Japanese-style management and production systems. It is a system of salary and rank incentives. See, for example, Kagono (1988).

3 Some researchers of Japanese production and management systems have made elaborate analyses of the relationship between control (coercion) and autonomy; 'coercive autonomy' (Kumazawa, 1993), 'the structure and logic of "control" and "acceptance"' (Kyōtani, 1993), 'controlled

participation' (Suzuki, 1994), 'coercion and autonomy as mechanisms of control' (Maruyama, 1995) etc.

4 Now that the Toyota Production System has been established these '*kanban*' are no more than tools of production, but they were first introduced with the expressed intention of labour management. Taiichi Ohno (Ōno) the father of the Toyota Production System, explains as follows. 'At the time, the site of production was run by the foreman (a craftsman). Division and section heads had no control over work on the factory floor. All they did was make excuses for delays in production. To counter this, first we made a manual of standardized working procedures and displayed the standardized working procedures above the workers on each process. The *kanban* originated from these boards displaying the standard working procedures. That is to say that the *kanban* started as "supervision through the eyes." The "eyes" concerned were *not those of the workers, but the eyes of the supervisors and managers who could see by glancing at the boards* whether or not the workers were following the standardized procedures. That is to say, as is the case with a shop sign, the *signboards were there for people outside the operation to see*. (Note: What is being discussed here is different from what is generally called the Toyota *kanban* system)' (Shimokawa et al. eds, 2001: 11. My italics).

5 This working environment resembles the 'panopticon' (panoramic observation system) Michel Foucault deals with in his *Discipline and Punish: Birth of the Prison*. At least, it seems to me, it results in the same effect. The panopticon is a prison complex devised by Jeremy Bentham.

'We know the principle on which it was based: at the periphery, an annular building; at the centre, a tower; this tower is pierced with wide windows that open onto the inner side of the ring; the peripheric building is divided into cells, each of which extends the whole width of the building; they have two windows, one on the inside, corresponding to the windows of the tower; the other, on the outside, allows the light to cross the cell from one end to the other. All that is needed, then, is to place a supervisor in a central tower and to shut up in each cell a madman, a patient, a condemned man, a worker or a schoolboy. By the effect of backlighting, one can observe from the tower, standing out precisely against the light, the small captive shadows in the cells of the periphery. They are like so many cages, so many small theatres, in which each actor is alone, perfectly individualized and constantly visible. The panoptic mechanism arranges spatial unities that make it possible to see constantly and to recognize immediately' (Foucault, 1975: 201–2. English here from Alan Sheridan trans., 1977: 200).

Also, from the 1990s there was a considerable volume of research into the labour process using the analytical framework of Foucault's *Subjectification of Power*. Examples include Clegg (1989), Knights (1990), Sakolosky (1992), Sewell and Wilkinson (1992) and McKinlay and Taylor (1996).

Incidentally, it is difficult for workers in this environment to control the labour process in ways other than those recognised by management. In Toyota it is strictly forbidden to add modifications to the working area without the permission of the supervisor or a team leader. Far from making changes to the working of any machine, workers are not even permitted to touch the machines. Even if a worker were to attempt to make a change without the boss's permission, it would soon be discovered, as the glass partitions of the workplace leave everything open to the full view of any observer. Permit me to give you one trifling example. You are even reprimanded for leaving a pair of cotton work-gloves at your work post. Gloves are to be discarded after use and replaced by new ones after each break. A fixed number of pairs of gloves is allocated to each group and these are kept in a box outside the prefab. As I took my break on a bench near my work position it was a nuisance to go all the way to the prefab just to pick up a new pair of gloves. So I hid a few pairs of gloves above the parts-storage chute. For a while nobody noticed them. But when the leader of another group was making a safety inspection he noticed them. He was constantly going along the line checking everything carefully and making sure it was neat and tidy.

Consequently, if a worker wants to make any change to his working environment he must go through the formal procedures. It is not a matter of Toyota workers also being able to make changes through the system of creative proposal and QC circles, the fact is, they can *only* make changes to their workplace through these channels.

6 If the employment relationship is seen in terms of agency models, then the employer becomes the principal and the worker is the agent.

7 You may be wondering how many faulty products come through to the inspection and packing line. According to Yada, about ten 'suspicious-looking' parts come through in an average day. Of these three or four would definitely be faulty. He would make a point of getting his boss to confirm the status of the remainder. Workers on inspection and packing have to find the ten faulty parts among a few thousand parts they check each day.

8 'Giving equal weight to authority and responsibility is often cited as one of the main principles of management. But because of the difficulty of measuring the variables of performance, which constitutes a subordinate's responsibility, it is extremely difficult to obtain a complete match between authority and responsibility. In practice this leads to the creation of a system that demands greater responsibility than the level of authority given. Moreover, this phenomenon is virtually universal in those enterprises commonly dubbed *the excellent companies*' (Itami, 1986:52. My emphasis). Toyota is the epitome of an *excellent company.*

9 This is the case in other auto factories. 'It is a fact that the workers have also asked for regular planned rotation. While CAMI sees the rotation process as part of its policy to promote flexibility, the workers, for their part, use rotation in an attempt to control their work and limit the latent capriciousness of management's flexibility policy. As there is no mechanism to recognize ownership of work, nor any written rules to limit or protect an individual's job, rotation itself has come to assume the form of a set of rules governing work on the factory floor.' (CAW/TCA, 1996: 60). CAMI is a joint venture between Suzuki and General Motors.

10 In chapter three I touched upon the organizational and administrative capabilities of workers. If I were to make a link with what I said there, it would be to point out that the special capability workers acquire when training other workers is not organizational and administrative skill, but the logic, critical gaze and world-view of those who manage them. By

being placed temporarily in managerial roles, general workers gradually begin to see things through the eyes of management and little by little yield their foothold on the factory floor to the administrators. It would make a mockery of the whole concept of skill formation if we were to refer to this capability as a skill.

11 Makino (1996), which focuses on small-group activity in the automobile industry, analyses the link between communication and skill formation. In addition, there are researchers in the fields of management theory and economics who point out the importance of communication in the workplace from the viewpoint of efficient 'knowledge creation' and increased 'information efficiency.' Aoki (1988) proposes the 'Japanese model,' in which a decentralized information management system is complemented by an incentive system (rank hierarchy). Nonaka (1990) says that information and knowledge is efficiently created by the organization as a whole, through what he calls 'middle-up-down management.'

However, none of these arguments says anything about power relationships. There is no mention of the fact that workers are controlled through 'shared information.' Power is exercised even in organizations that have, or at least appear to have, a decentralized power base or flattened-out structure and workers are controlled in workplaces that at first glance seem to have done away with power relationships.

Chapter 6

1 There have been previous studies written from the worker's viewpoint (Yoshida 1993, Ōno 1997 and 1998). These studies, like mine, elucidate the actual situation on the factory floor through participatory observation, but, unlike me, these researchers limit themselves to the labour process and do not go on to deal with the lives of the workers themselves.

2 Tsuji (2002) in his 2001 follow-up study building on his workplace survey of 1982, clearly shows the trend towards aging of the factory workforce. His surveys indicated that while the average age of group leaders (16 in his sample) in 1982 was 43 years and 9 months, by 2001 this had risen to 51 years and 3 months (based on a sample of 10) (pp. 96–7).

3 Nohara et al. (1988) states, 'Competition within groups or between groups is organized on the basis of commonly agreed issues and assessment criteria' (p. 405) and 'It is a strategy to eliminate square pegs through the encouragement of competition for promotion within the enterprise as a whole' (p. 510). It is claimed that workers are integrated into the company through 'fierce competition for promotion' based on 'merit.'

4 According to the recruitment advertisement in the *Asahi Shimbun* (22 September 2002) applicants should be, 'aged between eighteen and fifty-nine and be available for a period of at least four months (initial contracts are four months). However, applicants over forty-five years of age must have had previous experience on an automobile production line.' The length of contract and the age of applicants are a little different from when I applied. At that time they were only taking applications from people up to forty-five.

5   According to Yamamoto (1978), Toyota has created a variety of social clubs
as part of its human relations activities. These are based on place of origin,
manner of recruitment, gender and so on. For example, there is the *Hōyōkai*
for graduates of Toyota Industrial Academy (*Toyota Kōgyō Kōtō Gakuen*),
the *Hōshinkai* for university graduates, the *Hōseikai* for high school
graduates, the *Hōryūkai* for experienced appointees, the *Hōeikai* for former
Self Defence Force personnel, the *Hōsenkai* for graduates of technical
junior colleges and the *Hōkikai* for graduates of junior colleges. (Note that
the *Hō* in the names of these associations is an alternative reading of the
first character in the name, Toyota. Translator's note). I didn't really get to
know anyone from the Toyota Industrial Academy (the name was changed
to the Toyota Technical Skills Academy – *Toyota Kōgyō Gijutsu Gakuen*,
in 1996) or any former Self Defence Force personnel, but several times I
saw Toyota Academy students who lived in the same dormitory as me and
caught the same bus to the factory. I presume they were going through a
period of on-the-job training or something. A senior employee, a man in his
fifties, from another workplace told me that when he was young the Toyota
Academy graduates were the elite employees. Some of the brighter ones
even went to Nagoya University. He said that his own younger brother also
went to the academy, but these days the system of workplace associations
has broken down and there is no longer any sense that the graduates are an
elite group.

6   In our workplace there were section leaders who had been outside appointees,
but Shiomi writes that in the factory where he worked, 'Staff appointed
from the workforce are at a disadvantage compared to those taken on as
high school graduates. As things stand at present, it is exceedingly difficult
for them to be promoted to section leader' (Shiomi, 1978 (1): 87).

7   It was not until the 1990s that Toyota as a whole began employing female
factory workers.
     'Toyota first employed female staff to work on an assembly line in April
1991' (*Nihon Keizai Shimbun* 22 April 1993, evening edition). 'In response
to Japan's falling birth rate and aging society, Toyota has decided to actively
recruit women workers for its production plants. Of 1,470 blue-collar
workers employed by Toyota this spring, 260, almost double last year's
intake, were woman. This is roughly 18% of the total.' 'As of this spring the
total number of women factory workers employed by Toyota has reached 650'
(*Ibid*. 7 April 1999). Incidentally, in Toyota Motor Manufacturing (TMM),
Toyota's American operation, women comprise approximately 25% of the
workforce (Besser, 1996: Ch.7).

8   When it comes to setting the standard work time, the thinking in European
and American companies is to add a little extra to the net time it takes to
complete the job, but in Toyota no leeway is included. For a detailed account
see Nomura (1993a: 60–3).

9   'In the course of reviewing its production lines, the company is vigorously
promoting a policy of "creating friendly factories, sympathetic to women
and older workers".' (*Nihon Keizai Shimbun* 4 February 1992, Central
Japan edition). 'Toyota Motor has embarked on the construction of new
production systems with any eye on extending its recruitment of women

factory workers. Along with the progressive development of a new-style production line incorporating lower shelves for parts and a range of lighter tools, from next spring the company will be bringing forward the finishing time for late night shifts.' 'By providing a working environment considerate to the needs of women, the company hopes to increase its annual recruitment level from two hundred at present to one thousand in two or three years time' (*Ibid.* 7 April 1999).

10 There is also a distinction made between Toyota Academy graduates and normal high school graduates. Komatsu (2001) states, 'The total number of Toyota Academy graduates at the end of the 1998 fiscal year had reached 14,439, of whom 7,642 worked at the company. As the total number of factory staff employed by Toyota in 1999 was about forty-five thousand, the percentage of these positions occupied by graduates of the Toyota Academy amounts to around 17 per cent. The ratio of Toyota Academy staff to those from regular high schools was, at the time of my investigation (20 October 1999 – Ihara), one to six. At the same point of time sixty per cent of the supervisory positions from section leader up were occupied by Toyota Academy graduates. There are 114 Toyota Academy graduates among the 276 staff at the level of section head on site in Toyota Motor as a whole. This constitutes 41% of the total. Higher up, there are 22 Toyota Academy graduates, amounting to 76% of the total, counted in the ranks of the 29 staff who have been promoted to deputy division head on site. In addition, from the 1998 fiscal year, a new career path was introduced to make it possible for factory workers to rise to the rank of division head (*buchō*). As at 1999, three members of the factory staff had risen to this position. All were graduates of Toyota Academy' (pp. 119–20). These statistics make it very clear that there is a difference in status between the Toyota Academy graduates and recruits from regular high schools. It is not only in opportunities for promotion. They are also favoured from the viewpoint of skill formation. According to Tsunekawa (2002) 'Many of the Toyota Academy graduates have traditionally been allocated to positions, such as the maintenance division, which call for higher levels of technical skill.' In addition, the career paths of personnel in maintenance never cross with those in the direct production division.

Tomita (1998) in his detailed investigation of the influence of the move to ME (micro-electronics) in a car body assembly plant, elucidates the clear division of labour and the disparity of career paths between the two groups. 'There is a clear demarcation line drawn between the direct production workers and the staff of the maintenance division, not only in the nature of the work they perform, but also in the quality of the work and the type of training they receive' (p. 216). Further, Koike et al. (2001) in their questionnaire survey of enterprises relating to the automobile industry discovered that there is very little movement of personnel between the production area and the maintenance/preservation area. 'The number of workplaces that answered that there was no movement of personnel (54.4%) greatly outnumbered those that said there was (21.1%)' (p. 296). In regard to Toyota, Komatsu (2002) claims that 'you can't say there is absolutely no exchange of staff between direct production and maintenance operations.'

(p. 110). But as far as I could tell from my position on the shop floor, at present any such movement is very limited indeed.

The Toyota personnel department denies that the Toyota Academy graduates receive privileged treatment as career-course employees. (Komatsu, 2001: 120). But the facts show that, in essence, the career course for academy graduates has become firmly institutionalized.

11 Apparently, casual workers with over six months continual service are entitled to a number of days of paid recreational leave.

12 As you would expect, the overwhelming majority of employees drove Toyotas. This was not only because employees got a discount on the purchase price, but apparently 'because the company would not give a single yen in petrol allowance to employees who commuted to work in anything but a Toyota or a Daihatsu (Daihatsu is a Toyota subsidiary)' (Fukui, 1999: 126).

13 It goes back ten years, but there is an article related to this question. 'The Toyota Co-operative (with approximately 170,000 members in Toyota city) comprising mainly members of staff of the Toyota Motor Group, this month started a permanent marriage counselling service and an *omiai* (match-making) corner. It is a program aimed at the young co-op. members who, in commuting between the factory and the unmarried staff dormitory, have few opportunities to meet members of the opposite sex, to help them find their lifelong partner. Mr A. from Toyota headquarters laments the fact that, "In our daily working lives opportunities to meet members of the opposite sex are virtually non-existent"' (*Nihon Keizai Shimbun* 12 February 1991 Nagoya, evening edition. City page). Further, some of the regular employees also live in company-owned housing. In our group, Nishiyama (17 years service), Ogawa (10 years service) and Shiroki (8 years service) all live in the same company housing complex.

Chapter 7

1 'Revealing a separation rate of around 50% over a period of approximately three years' (Koyama, 1985: 618).

Incidentally, this lack of attention to 'resistance,' is not only a feature of research into the Japanese automobile industry. It is also prevalent overall in workplace studies outside Japan.

When Braverman's *Labor and Monopoly Capital: the Degradation of Work in the Twentieth Century* was published in 1974, it received a deal of attention as a 'rediscovery of the labour process,' but at the same time it came in for criticism from a number of quarters. One of these criticisms was that it underestimated the importance of worker subjectivity and resistance.

'The root of the problem is seen as stemming form Braverman's deliberate exclusion of the dimension of class struggle and consciousness. While this is prioritised by him as a means of painting a picture of the working class in work "as it really is," it is argued that this involves a neglect of the important effects of worker resistance and organization on technology and labour processes' (Thompson, 1982: 87).

After that, research dealing with the issue of resistance begins to appear, but by the end of the 1970s, the focus of analysis of the labour process seems to shift to the areas of 'acceptance and integration' and, once again, 'resistance' moves off centre stage.

In the 1980s the mainstream of research, examining the industry in Italy, Germany and Japan, points to the enrichment of labour, the raising of skill levels, and also to the high level of worker motivation. 'Flexible specialization' (Piore and Sabel, 1984), 'new production concept' (Kern and Schumann, 1984) and 'lean production method' (Womack et al., 1990) are representative keywords of the research of this period. Further, this tendency can also be seen in the concepts of post-Fordism and the *théorie de la régulation*.

In the 1990s numerous studies based on the work of Foucault appear (See Chapter 5, note 5). These hold that workers are bound up in an elaborate system of close control and have no opportunity to resist. This applies in particular to operators working under the JIT (just-in-time) and TQM (total-quality-management) systems. It is held that workers in Japanese car factories outside Japan work obediently under close control (Delbridge et al., 1992, Garrahan and Stewart, 1992, Stewart and Garrahan, 1995 etc.).

Here I have given just a very brief sketch of trends in workplace-based research abroad, but overall, I think you can say that the general tendency has been to neglect the issue of worker resistance. For a detailed account of international research on the labour process, see the papers included in; Zimbalist ed. (1979), Knights and Willmott eds (1988, 1990), Sturdy et al. eds (1992), Ackers et al. eds (1996) and Wardell et al. eds (1999).

2 Yoshida (1993) and Ōno (1997, 1998) both cited before, treat not only acceptance, but also touch on resistance. Nohara et al. eds (1988) also has a section on 'Resistance and self-defence in the workplace' (pp. 499–503).

3 'Even conduct I have labelled "negative resistance" should be interpreted as not going beyond the sphere of self-discipline' (Yoshida, 1993: 45). 'As I have argued in the body of the text, the implicit rules of the workplace can be regarded as functioning, to a certain extent, to keep dissatisfaction under the surface – their role is, so to speak, that of a "safety valve"' (Ōno 1997: 154).

4 To be acknowledged in the workplace is not simply a matter of building up years of experience. You need to have gained a position with a title, or have got hold of some real authority as a team leader. After actually seeing the situation with my own eyes, I find the 'career' argument even less convincing.

Of course, not all workplaces have developed this atmosphere where accumulated service is undervalued. The company newspaper had a special feature on workers who have continued working on the shop floor. It was full of phrases like, 'master craftsman,' 'consummate skill,' 'words alone cannot convey the world of creation' (*Toyota Jidōsha Shanaihō Kurieishon*, September 2001). In addition, the union newsletter carried an article explaining the 'new skilled partner system' to be introduced from April 2001. 'This is a system targeting factory workers (CX class) approaching retirement, to allow them to continue, even after retirement, to exercise in the workplace the vast experience and high level skill that they have cultivated at Toyota' (*Toyota Jidōsha Rōdō Kumiai – Haai* (Hi!) October 2001).

But the following points need to be borne in mind. 1. I think workplaces requiring a 'consummate' level of skill must be exceedingly rare. The examples taken up in the company newspaper were of employees engaged in the machining of engines and in the forming of bumper bars. 2. It is possible that this emphasis on technical expertise has been implemented in reaction to the current tendency to undervalue skill. A cynical view might be that behind this emphasis on skill lies the reality that it tends to be given very little attention. 3. Management talks about the re-utilization of high-level skill and mouths the slogan 'varied and flexible patterns of employment,' but in reality, it is only when the wishes of the individual and the needs of the company coincide, that people are re-employed. They will simply be using the retirees as a buffer. This becomes obvious when you consider how the system was developed. The union wanted the system to apply to anyone who wanted to be re-employed, but management refused. 'At first, labour and management were some distance apart on the issue, but after a frank exchange of views, discussion moved on to the creation of the system itself.' The result of all this boiled down to re-employment only in cases in which 'needs coincide.' According to the union newspaper, 'about ten per cent of the total will be employed.' What is more, the highest priority in the selection criteria is, 'the ability to cooperate' (*kyōchōsei*). Management is more interested in having people who will continue working well on the factory floor just as they have been doing in the past, than in employing highly skilled retirees.

5 By 'code incorporated into technology' I mean the historical and social elements in technology. Feenberg (1999) calls this the 'technical code.' Technology is not neutral. Neither are advances in technology autonomous. Dominant social forms are reflected in technological design. Noble (1984) clearly demonstrates the social relationships incorporated into production technology. For a detailed discussion of both these arguments, see Ihara (2001).

6 The so-called 'informal groups' ('informal organizations') refers to groups of friends separate from corporate organizations, as was clearly demonstrated using the Hawthorn experiment in Mayo (1933) and in Roethlisberger and Dickson (1939). Within these informal groups, restriction of production was employed to prevent cutting of staff, lowering of wages and increasing workloads. (The Hawthorn experiment refers to an experiment carried out over several years from 1927 by Mayo and others at the Hawthorn plant of the Western Electric Company. Their initial purpose was to investigate the relationship between the physical working environment and productivity. Their results, however, clearly showed that productivity is greatly influenced by the informal personal relationships formed among fellow workers. The experiment became the theoretical cornerstone for the later 'human relations debate.')

7 Here, in regard to this point, I would like tentatively to consider an idea about the influence of consumers.

This does not apply just to cars, but what consumers demand in a product changes over time. Consumers a generation ago did not consider environmental-friendliness a feature they looked for in a car. But now, this and safety are included alongside design and functionality as factors to be considered when buying a car. If, in the future, 'products of worker-friendly companies' were to become a condition of purchase for consumers, or even if this were not made a condition, but just became an important factor in the creation of the image of a company and its products, then management would have no choice but to be more sensitive to the working environment and this would possibly result in improved conditions for workers. It is quite plausible to think of 'worker-friendliness' being added alongside 'environmental-friendliness.'

Of course, for consumers, quality and design are most important. But there does not necessarily have to be a trade-off between quality and worker friendliness. On the contrary, over-reliance on automation can result in deterioration in product quality. It should be perfectly possible to produce high quality products in a worker-friendly factory.

The necessary prerequisite for the creation of this kind of social environment is for society as a whole to share information about conditions on the factory floor. Dissemination over the Internet is likely to be effective in this respect. Opportunities for workers to send out information electronically have increased and it will be difficult for managers to completely stop this flow.

Epilogue

1 Even so, there is a constant stream of casual workers who resign before their term is up. As we have seen, in this workplace alone, the contract workers Sawada and Hashimoto left before the end of their contract. According to Kitamura, of the fifty casual workers who joined the company on 28 August and were assigned to their positions on 1 September (Dormitory A) five had already left (13 September). This is probably a higher proportion than in Dormitory K. It can't be easy for the workers in Dormitory A to have to spend nearly two hours in travelling time to and from the factory in addition to the gruelling work they perform.

For reference, investigation of the place of origin (i.e. where they were living before they joined Toyota) of the regular workers in this group reveals that they come here from all over the country, not necessarily just from this local area. Nagata is from Saga prefecture, Kawakami from Kanagawa prefecture, Shiroki from Hiroshima, Tsuda from Osaka and Kuramoto from Tokyo. From what I could ascertain about the recruitment process from Shiroki, there are employment quotas for various high schools and that, after getting a letter of recommendation from their school, candidates have to pass an exam, which they take in their local area, but is held at a number of locations across the country. Apparently Shiroki took the exam in Okayama.

2 This casual attitude on the part of management seems to have got worse since I left. At the end of December 2001 I asked an acquaintance about

the situation in the factory. Apparently it had changed considerably even in the month since I left. They are predicting a drop in production on the line I was on, from the spring of 2002. As a result, they don't need casual workers, so there will not be any extensions for those workers who come to the ends of their contracts around March. Up until about six months ago they were flat out employing as many contract workers as they could get hold of, but in the space of less than a year they'll reach the point where they won't need any at all. In addition, apparently the scheme of appointments to the permanent staff will also disappear. It is already being phased out. Management treats the casual workers anyway it likes.

However, seen at the level of the company as a whole, there will be an increase in the employment of fixed-term contract workers from 2002 onwards. According to the *Nikkan Kenmin Fukui* (Fukui Prefecture Daily) of 23 January 2003, 'Toyota Motor announced on 22 January, that, at the beginning of this month, 6,100 casual workers will be employed to work in its factories in Japan. This is the highest number in the company's history and the first time the number of workers employed at the same time has topped six thousand. The policy is to constrain the employment of permanent staff and raise the proportion of contract workers, a flexible workforce, easily increased or decreased at will, in order to meet the increased production of cars for export to buoyant markets abroad, mainly in North America. As a general rule, casual workers at Toyota work on a four-month contract. In the first half of last year this was at the level of around 3,800 workers, but the figure increased gradually, so that between July and September it had risen to 4,800 and to 5,700 for the period October to December. The figure of 5,900 reached in December last year was a record at that time, but this has been broken by the new record created this month.' 'Given the expectation that this trend will continue, we will see a strengthening of the policy of making use of contract labour, to keep pressure on wages and respond to temporary increases in consumer demand. "Casual worker numbers will remain at a high level for some time" (Management).'

What then of the regular staff? Is their position any more stable? Apparently not. There is talk about putting the inspection and packing line out to sub-contractors. If that happens, all the workers currently on that line will be moved to another workplace. They'll have to move within a year. Management is also cavalier in its treatment of full-time employees.

Not only in the factory, but outside as well, management is inconsiderate in its treatment of staff. I heard that the casual workers who had been commuting from Dormitory A were moved to Dormitory D (like Dormitory A, the dormitory of an associated company) in Okazaki on 15 December 2001. Apparently workers from Plant T will be taking their places in Dormitory A.

To accommodate management's flexible response to fluctuations in demand, some workers are obliged to leave the company. Others are all too simply moved out of jobs they know and like or made to vacate accommodation they have come to consider home. These are the realities that lie behind management's 'superb performance.'

Appendix I

1 In 1982 Toyota Motor Co. Ltd (*Toyota Jidōsha Kōgyō KK*) and Toyota Motor Sales Co. Ltd. (*Toyota Jidōsha Hanbai KK*) amalgamated forming the present, Toyota Motor Corporation (*Toyota Jidōsha KK*).

2 Many researchers unconditionally put forward Toyota management as the archetype (*tenkei*) or as representative (*daihyōteki*) of Japanese-style management (Japanese production systems). Satake (2000) points out the issue of confusion in the use of these terms and discusses their commonalities and differences.

3 Here let me briefly explain the divisions within Toyota. In general factories there are three divisions, 1. The indirect division (the administrative/clerical and engineering departments), 2. The manufacturing support division (the production engineering department, machine department, technical affairs and inspection departments, and 3. The direct manufacturing division (the various manufacturing processes). But in Toyota these three divisions had been respectively called division D, division C and A/B division. Division A was 'a division that could make technical production plans according to the number of vehicles to be produced etc. Consequently, in regard to personnel management, it could make macro staffing estimates for the division as a whole by taking into account factors such as working capacity.' Division B was, 'an indirect division in the factory workplace, able to make approximate staffing estimates in line with workplace production' (Tanaka, 1982: 69, f.n. 2). Incidentally, this divisional structure was changed in July 1992. All the manufacturing staff in the factory became members of Division P, the manufacturing staff in the Engineering Division and the Production Engineering division went into Division E and Division D became division S (Ishida, 1997: 48).

4 Of course, there are also differences between them. There are differences in research methodology and even within the same research group there are differences of opinion. Endō et al. (1989) contains a mutual evaluation carried out by the two preceding groups.

5 I shall not discuss the individual arguments here as they fall beyond the aims of the present study, but Koyama ed. (1985) points out, 'a rate of separations equivalent to loss of half the staff over a period of roughly three years' (p. 618). Nohara et al. (1988) also deals with a large number of actual examples illustrating 'the resistance and defensive behaviour to be found in the workplace' (pp. 499–503).

6 Further, in the 1960s, at the same time as changes in industrial production were about to bring about the demise of the old craftsman skills, Nihon Jinbunkagakkai ed. (1963) was already aware that 'new skills' were coming into demand. 'It is often stressed that technological reform makes skills redundant and leads to deskilling of labour across the board. But, what is actually happening in industry is a little different from this' (p. 6). 'Changes in production processes accompanying technological innovation are calling for the ability to adapt to new technology and make logical judgements on operations' (p. 95). The skills indicated here are the same 'intellectual skills' commentators were asserting in the 1980s.

7   For a succinct summary of this and other theories about skill in factory
    workers in the automobile industry see Yumoto (1994).
8   At the same time, in overseas research on labour in the Japanese automobile
    industry, we see a similar pattern of opposition. Broadly, foreign researchers
    may be divided into those who focus on 'new skill' and 'autonomy' on the
    one hand, and those who emphasise 'deskilling' and 'coercion' on the other.
    Kenny and Florida (1988), Womack *et al.* (1990) and Coriat (1991) fall into
    the former category and Dohse *et al.* (1985), Katō and Steven (1990), Parker
    and Slaughter (1988) and Berggren (1992) are included in the latter.
9   Koike is not a specialist in this field, but recently he has been surveying
    labour in automobile factories. Koike (1998), Koike *et al.* (2001).
10 Nomura levels his criticism at all Koike's publications. His papers
    criticising Koike are collected together into Nomura (1993b). Looking at the
    progress of the debate we see that Nomura makes his general criticisms of
    Koike's research output in chapters one and two of Nomura (1993b). Koike
    defends himself and counter-attacks in Koike (1993a). Nomura comes back
    with a refutation of Koike and a further attack in chapter three of Nomura
    (1993b).
        Incidentally, Nomura has recently opened a further attack on Koike's
    'intellectual skills' theory, taking into account research since the original
    debate (Nomura, 2001).
11 For the argument from here see Nomura (1993b: 97).
12 I also get the impression that in Nomura's debates with other scholars the
    arguments tend to pass one another by without ever engaging. I think one
    reason for this is confusion between the assessment of skill on the one hand
    and the definition of skill on the other.
13 The assessment of skill is extremely vague. This is because both socially
    and historically it is a relative concept. 'The distinction between skilled
    and unskilled labour rests in part on pure illusion, or, to say the least, on
    distinctions that have long since ceased to be real, and that survive only
    by virtue of a traditional convention; in part on the helpless condition of
    some groups of the working-class, a condition that prevents them from
    exacting equally with the rest the value of their labour-power. Accidental
    circumstances here play so great a part, that these two forms of labour
    sometimes change places' (Marx, 1968: 259. The English here is from
    Samuel Moore and Edward Aveling's 1887 translation, *Capital* vol.1, pt.3,
    ch.7, f.n.18). Skill is defined within a socio-historical context and the
    assessment of skill is influenced by questions of social interest. Yamashita
    (1995) surveys the arguments over the relativism surrounding the concept
    of skill.
14 Arai (1996) brings together the early arguments on the Toyota reformation
    and summarizes the differences in researchers' assessments.
15 'The reorganization of work and processes we see here, in the context of
    the separation of "conception and execution" in human work, was to re-
    engage the issue of "conception" of production methods.' (Nohara, 1992:
    96). *Kaizen* in operation in the factory and the QC activities that support
    them result in workers themselves rationally bringing together work plans
    and their implementation' (Totsuka *et al.* eds, 1991: 255). Nakamura makes

this same point in regard to companies subcontracted to the automobile industry and Maruyama applies it to the Japanese-style production system as a whole. 'Given the premise that work may be separated into conception and execution, it may be said that work organizations are formed on the principle of the worker's involvement in the conception component. But, this involvement in the conception component should not be regarded as a minor change or a slight difference. The gap between this and the "separation into conception and execution" is incomparably large' (Nakamura, 1996: 237–8). 'The work organization in the Japanese factory is based on the principle of "integration of conception and execution," the antithesis of "Taylorism." This, and the fact that workers expand their work to cover many fields without losing sight of the goal of their labour, can be cited as characteristics of the work organization in a Japanese factory' (Maruyama, 1995: 11).

16   'Thus if the first principle is the gathering and development of knowledge of labor processes, and the second is the concentration of this knowledge as the exclusive province of management – together with its essential converse, the absence of such knowledge among the workers – then the third is the *use of this monopoly over knowledge to control each step of the labor process and its mode of execution*' (Braverman, 1974: 119).

17   From Braverman on, we find the same confusion in the debate over the labour process. After running his eye over the numerous arguments indicating the raising of skill levels and the enrichment of work, Thompson (1983) concludes as follows.

    'It is possible to identify technical aspects of work enrichment whereby job satisfaction and commitment may be increased by modifying marginal aspects of work organization. But the key focus remains control' (Thompson, 1983: 117).

18   They are dealing, it must be said, with the influence of micro-electronics (ME) in manufacturing workplaces overall, but Akino (1991) and Kamibayashi (1995) while recognising the move to multi-skilling of operators (raising the level of work) show that this is not necessarily in conflict with management control.

    'Raising the level of the work they perform does not necessarily mean that workers gain autonomy from management control. Neither can it be said that only unskilled workers can be adequately controlled. When workers here say that they have had the level of their work upgraded, that does not necessarily mean that they have gained any autonomy in power relationships'(Akino, 1991, 1: 46). 'There is not necessarily any contradiction or conflict between the multi-skilling of factory workers and the autonomy they have in their work on the one hand, and the control they are under on the other. ... The trade-off between multi-skilling/autonomy and the authority to control, which had been the tacitly accepted premise in theories to date, could not be confirmed in our data. ... At the level of work organization, we found, that while managers gave factory workers several jobs and were fairly tolerant in allowing them autonomy, they tended, on the other hand, to maintain close control over them' (Kamibayashi, 1995: 13).

19 The same applies to research that employs Koike's analytical frame of 'modes of integration' and 'modes of separation.' Isa (1997) and Muramatsu (1996) analyse a number of actual examples, mainly from the automobile industry, using his schema. Tsuchiya (1996) applies the model to other industries. There probably needs to be more investigation to discover whether modes of integration of skill are linked to the workers' control over their workplace and beyond.

Further, Hiraga, following the process from when new technology is introduced into a car factory to when it becomes established, seeks to elucidate the relationships between production technology, skill, work organization and authority (Hiraga 1995, 1997, 2000). His work deserves further attention, though I don't think it has been taken up in the field of labour research on automobile factories. Recently, there has been a tendency in the debate over skill to focus attention on the aspect of the subjectivity of work, but in order to keep analysts' arbitrary interpretations to a bare minimum, the need now is to go back and get a firm grasp on the objective conditions of industrial technology.

20 'I do not think it is at all possible for me to explain the great disparities in efficiency through longer hours or greater density of work. I do not believe the claim that Japanese factories work much longer hours than companies in America and Europe do, but I shall not deal with that issue here' (Koike, 1993b: 7).

21 Here is an example. 'Even though mass production appears at first glance to be just repetitive work, when you actually get in and take a closer look, you come to understand that a surprising number of problems occur. Generally the trouble is caused by irregularities in quality or a breakdown of equipment. The skill to deal with a problem must greatly influence efficiency. A skilful response can stop the flow of faulty products immediately. A poor response can result in the continued production of faulty products or a lengthy stoppage of the line. There is a huge difference in efficiency. So we estimate how much know-how they can find, or what will happen if that is not available and we measure the size of the effect that will have on efficiency, in short, we measure the level of skill' (Koike et al., 2001: 5). Even in responding to a minor problem, there is a big difference in efficiency depending on whether or not it can be done on the spot on the shop floor. I recognize that, but responding to a problem is not necessarily directly related to the level of skill. What we have here is an unjustified leap of logic.

22 In the tide of research dealing with quality and skill, there are also some theorists who go back to the issue of quantity. Chida (1993), Chida and Kajiyama (1996) and Maruyama et al. (2000) all remark on the heavy workload under the Toyota Production System. Hiranuma (1996) following on from his criticism of intrinsic weaknesses in Koike's intellectual skills argument, makes the point that, 'In the automobile industry, what most needs to be changed in the typical mass-production workplace is, first and foremost, the inhumanity of the system of management' (p. 127). Ōno (1998) also emphasises the harsh work conditions rather than skill. 'I cannot avoid mention of the cruelty of the work speed (work density) enforced upon

workers in this way.' 'The speed (work density) on a U-shaped assembly line far exceeds the general imagination. It is raised to what can only be called an inhumane level' (p. 23).

Appendix II

1 Recently there have been several reports focusing on non-tenured workers in Toyota. For a study of the history and present state of Toyota's non-tenured workers see, for example, Komatsu (2005a, 2005b) and Date (2005).
2 The term *'dankai no sedai'* (literally: 'the clump generation') refers to those born in Japan between 1947 and 1949, also known as 'the first baby boom.'
3 *Jiji Tsūshin* (Current Affairs Press) 19 July 2006. *Shūkan Tōyō Keizai* (East Asian Economic Weekly) 29 July 2006 included a chart of recent recalls in their feature editions on Toyota's recalls.
4 *Asahi Shimbun* (morning edition) 19 October 2005, p. 1.
5 *Ibid.*, 13 April 2006, p. 33.
6 Even Mr Watanabe, the President of Toyota, in his management briefing meeting on 20 September 2006 considered that the causes of the recent recalls 'stem from both design and manufacture' http://response.jp/issue/2006/0920/article86152_1.html.
7 In accordance with the revision of the Labour Standards Law that came into force in January 2004, Toyota extended the maximum term for a continuing contract for casual employees to two years and eleven months.
8 'There were 958 casual employees appointed in the 2005 fiscal year, a 60% rise over 2004. The company is planning to appoint 900 in 2006' (*Nihon Keizai Shinbun* 7 July 2006 (morning, Chūbu (Central Japan) edition) p. 7). Approximately six times the figure of three years ago.

Bibliography

Ackers, Peter, Chris Smith and Paul Smith eds (1996), *The New Workplace and Trade Unionism: Critical Perspectives on Work and Organization*, London and New York: Routledge.

Aichi Rōdō Mondai Kenkyūjo (Aichi Labor Research Institute) (1990), *Toyota gurūpu no shinsenryaku – "kōzōchōseika" no jidōsha sangyō* (New strategies of the Toyota Group – the automobile industry under 'structural regulation'), Tokyo: Shin Nihon Shuppansha.

Akino, Shōji (1991), 'ME-gijutsu ni yoru rōdō no henka to kanri – ME-gijutsu to rōdō no henka o meguru giron no kentō' (parts 1 & 2) (Management and changes to work under ME technology – an investigation of the debate surrounding ME technology and changes in work), *Rikkyō keizaigaku kenkyū* (Rikkyo economic review), 44 (4), pp. 93–112, 45 (2), pp. 25–48.

Aoki, Masahiko (1988), *Information, Incentives and Bargaining in the Japanese Economy*, Cambridge: Cambridge University Press. Japanese translation by Kōichi Nagayasu, *Nihon keizai no seido bunseki: jōhō insentibu kōshō geemu*, Chikuma Shobō, 1992.

Arai, Hisao (1996), 'Yakusha kaidai: Nihongata seisan shisutemu e no Furansu kara no issekkin' (Translator's commentary: A French approach to the Japanese-style production system), in Hisao Arai's translation of Boyer, Robert and Jean Pierre Durand (1993), *L'aprés-fordisme*, Paris: Syros.

Asakawa, Kazuyuki (1987), *Rain rōdōsha no tokuchō to 'jobu kontorōru' – A-jikō M-seisakusho gisō kumitatejo ni okeru jirei kenkyū 1* (Characteristics of line workers and 'job control' – research on actual examples in a fitout assembly line in M plant of A Motor Industries), Sapporo: Hokkaidō Daigaku kyōiku gakubu kyōiku-shakaigaku kenkyūshitsu (Educational-sociology research unit, faculty of education, Hokkaido University).

Asanuma, Banri (1997), *Nihon no kigyō soshiki – kakushinteki tekiō no mekanizumu* (Japanese company organization – innovative adaptation mechanisms), Tokyo: Tōyō Keizai Shinpōsha.

Asō, Uichi, Masaki Saruta, Hikari Nohara, Eishi Fujita and Haruhiko Yamashita eds (1999), *Shakai kankyō no henka to jidōsha seisan shisutemu – Toyota shisutemu wa kawatta ka* (Changes in the social environment and the automobile production system – has the Toyota system changed?), Tokyo: Hōritsu Bunkasha.

Berggren, C. (1992), *Alternative to Lean Production*, New York: ILR Press.

Besser, Terry L. (1996), *Team Toyota: Transplanting the Toyota Culture to the Camry Plant in Kentucky*, New York: University of New York Press. Japanese translation by Yoshiji Suzuki, *Toyota no Beikoku kōjō no keiei – chiimu bunka to Amerikajin*, Hokkaidō Daigaku Tosho Kankōkai, 1999.

Blauner, R. (1964), *Alienation and Freedom – The Factory Worker and His Industry*, Chicago: The University of Chicago Press. Japanese translation by Yoshiyuki Satō, *Rōdō ni okeru sogai to jiyū*, Shinsensha, 1971.

Boyer, Robert and Jean Pierre Durand (1993), *L'après-fordisme*, Paris: Syros. Japanese translation by Hisao Arai, *Afutā fōdizumu*, Mineruva Shobō, 1996.

Braverman, Harry (1974), *Labor and Monopoly Capital: the Degradation of Work in the Twentieth Century*, New York: Monthly Review Press. Japanese translation by Kenji Tomizawa, *Rōdō to dokusen shihon*, Iwanami Shoten, 1978.

Burawoy, Michael (1979), *Manufacturing Consent: Changes in the Labor Process under Monopoly Capitalism*, Chicago and London: The University of Chicago Press.

CAW-CANADA Research Group on CAMI (1993), *The CAMI Report: Lean Production in a Unionized Auto Plant*. Japanese translation by Yoshinari Maruyama, *Riin seisan shisutemu wa rōdō o yutaka ni suru ka – Kanada jidōsha kōjō repōto*, Taga Shuppan, 1996.

Chida, Tadao (1993), 'Toyota seisan hōshiki to rōdō no arisama' (The Toyota method of production and the state of labour), *Keizai kagaku tsūshin* (Letters of economics science), 74, pp. 48–55.

Chida, Tadao and Masatada Kajiyama (1996), 'Nihonteki seisan shisutemu to kamitsu rōdō – Toyota no gendaiteki rōdō futan' (Japanese-style production systems and the over-intensification of work – Toyota's modern workloads), *Keizai* (The Economy), 7, pp. 51–67.

Chūnichi Shinbunsha *Nikkan kenmin Fukui* (Fukui prefecture daily).

Clegg, S. R. (1989), 'Radical Revision: Power, Discipline and Organization,' *Organization Studies*, 10, pp. 97–115.

Coriat, B. (1991), *Penser à l'envers: travail et organization dans l'entreprise japonaise*, Paris: Christian Bourgois. Japanese translation by Masanori Hanada and Yoshinori Saitō, *Gyakuten no shikō – Nihon kigyō no rōdō to soshiki*, Fujiwara Shoten, 1992.

Date, Hironori (2005), 'Sengo Nihon no jidōsha sangyō to rinjikō – 1950–60 nendai no Toyota jikō o chūshin ni' (Casual mechanics in the postwar Japanese car industry – focusing on Toyota Automobile Manufacturing in the 1950s and 1960s), *Ōhara Shakai Mondai Kenkyūjo zasshi* (Journal of the Ohara Institute for Social Research), 556, pp. 12–23.

Delbridge, Rick, Peter Turnbull and Barry Wilkinson (1992), 'Pushing Back the Frontiers: Management Control and Work Intensification Under JIT/ TQM Factory Regimes,' *New Technology, Work and Employment*, No. 7, pp. 97–106.

Dohse, Knuth, Ulrich Jurgens and Thomas Malsch (1985), 'From "Fordism to Toyotaism"? The Social Organization of the Labor Process in the Japanese Automobile Industry,' *Politics and Society*, 14(2), pp. 115–46.

Endō, Hiroichi, Eishi Fujita, Katsuji Tsuji and Jun'ichi Arai (1989), 'Toyota kenkyū no tōtatsuten to kadai – Tōkai Kyōto ryōgurūpu no sōgo hyōka to tōron,' (The current state of and future issues for Toyota research – mutual assessment and debate of the Tōkai and Kyoto groups), *Ritsumeikan sangyō shakai ronshū* (Ritsumeikan review of industrial society), 25 (2), pp. 71–8.

Feenberg, Andrew (1999), *Questioning Technology*, London and New York: Routledge.

Foucault, Michel (1975), *Surveiller et punir: naissance de la prison*, Paris: Gallimard. Japanese translation by Hajime Tamura, *Kangoku no tanjō – kanshi to shobatsu*, Shinchōsha, 1977. English translation by Alan Sheridan, *Discipline and Punish: the Birth of the Prison*, Vintage Books, 1977.

Friedman, A. (1977), *Industry and Labour: Class Struggle at Work and Monopoly Capitalism*, London: Macmillan.

Fukui, Kōji (1999), *Toyota no himitsu – kore wa bikkuri! seisan genba hōkoku kikan jūgyōin ga minasama o sekai san'i no jidōsha kōjo e goannai* (Toyota's secret – What a surprise! Report from the factory; we casual employees welcome you all to the world's third largest automobile factory), Tokyo: Eeru Shuppansha.

Fujimoto, Takahiro (1994), *Jidōsha sangyō nijū-isseiki e no shinario – seichō-gata shisutemu kara baransugata shisutemu e no tenkan* (Twenty-first century scenarios for the car industry – the change from growth to balance), Tokyo: Seisansei Shuppan.

Fujimoto, Takahiro (1997), *Seisan shisutemu no shinkaron – Toyota jidōsha ni miru soshiki nōryoku to sōhatsu purosesu* (Evolution of systems of production – organizational capacity and the processes of creation in Toyota), Tokyo: Yūhikaku.

Fujita, Eishi (1997), 'Jidōsha sangyō to jinji-rōmu kanri – seisan taisei no henbō' (The automobile industry and management of personnel and labour – the changing face of production), *Nihon rōdō shakaigakkai nenpō* (Annual review of labor sociology), 8, pp. 3–35.

Fukuyama, Hiroshi (1997), *Ryōsan ni okeru ginō – ginō shiron – ryōsan kōjō sagyōsha kara mita ginō* (On skill in mass production – An hypothesis on skill seen from the viewpoint of operators in a mass production factory), Tokyo: Henshū Kōbō Tabi to Yu to Kazesha.

Fukuyama, Hiroshi (1998), '"Ryōsan ni okeru ginō" ni tsuite – kensaku-kakō no jirei' (On 'skill in mass production' – examples from grinder processing), *Ritsumeikan sangyō shakai ronshū* (Ritsumeikan review of industrial society), 34 (1), pp. 121–32.

Garrahan, P. and Stewart Paul (1992), *The Nissan Enigma*, London: Routledge.

Hiraga, Ryūta (1995), 'Seisan gijutsu to ginō' (Production technology and skill), *Hitotsubashi Daigaku kenkyū nenpō – Shōgaku kenkyū* (Hitotsubashi University research series. Commerce and management), 3, pp. 117–61.

Hiraga, Ryūta (1997), 'Kenkyū nōto – jidōsha tosō no saizensen – Nissan jidōsha Kyūshū kōjō no jirei' (Research notes: at the forefront of car painting – examples from the Kyushu factory of Nissan Motor, *Ikkyō Ronsō* (Hitotsubashi Reviews), 1(18), pp. 768–79.

Hiraga, Ryūta (2000), 'Forukusuwāgensha ni okeru shokunō-tōgō shisō – setsubi sōsakukō o chūshin ni shite (The concept of functional integration in Volkswagen – focusing on plant operators), *Ikkyō Ronsō* (Hitotsubashi Reviews), 124(5), pp. 591–616.

Hiranuma, Takashi (1996), 'Nihon ni okeru jukurenkeisei mondai no mondaisei – Koike Kazuo kyōju no "chiteki jukuren ron" ni taisuru hihanteki kentō' (The problematicality of skill formation in Japan – a critical analysis of Prof. Kazuo Koike's 'intellectual skills theory'), *Keiei ronshū* (Meiji Business Review), 44 (1 and 2 combined edition), pp. 113–37.

Hokkaidō Daigaku kyōiku gakubu kyōiku-shakaigaku kenkyūshitsu (Hokkaido University Faculty of Education Educational Sociology Research Center) (1987), *Genka ni okeru jidōsha kigyō no shokuba kōzō to rōdōsha seikatsu – A jikō M seisakusho ni okeru jirei kenkyū* (The structure of the workplace and the lives of workers in present-day auto factories: a study of examples from M plant of auto factory A).

Ihara, Ryōji (2001), 'Yakusha kaisetsu' (Translator's commentary), Noble (1995), in Watanabe et al. translation.

Imada, Osamu (1997), 'Gendai Nihon jidōsha kigyō no kumitate rain ni okeru aratana dōkō : seisan gijutsu bumon no kinō o chūshin ni' (New trends on the assembly line in the modern Japanese car industry – focusing on the function of the production technology division), *Ritsumeikan keieigaku* (The Ritsumeikan business review), 36 (2), pp. 1–20.

Imada, Osamu (1998), *Gendai jidōsha kigyō no gijutsu kanri rōdō : gijutsu hatten to kanri kigyō rōdō no kenkyū* (Skill, control and work in the modern car industry: research on management and labour with advances in technology), Tokyo : Zeimu keiri kyōkai.

Imai, Masaaki (1991), *Kaizen : Nihon kigyō ga kokusai kyōsō de seikō shita keiei nouhau* (*Kaizen*: the management know-how that led Japanese companies to success abroad), Tokyo : Kōdansha.

Isa, Katsuhide (1997), 'Nihon kigyō no seisan shokuba ni okeru "ginō kanri" : kikitori chōsa ni motozuku "chiteki jukuren" ron no ichi kentō' (Skill management in the manufacturing workplace in Japanese companies: an investigation of 'intellectual skills' based on interview surveys*), Nihon rōdō kenkyū zasshi* (The Japanese Journal of Labour studies), 450, pp. 62–73.

Ishida, Mitsuo, Fumito Matsumura, Tokuo Hisamoto and Hiroyuki Fujimura eds (1996), *Jidōsha kigyō no rōdō to jinzai keisei* (Labour and staff development in the automobile industry), Tokyo : Nihon rōdō kenkyū kikō (The Japan Institute of Labour).

Ishida, Mitsuo, Hiroshi Fujimura, Tokuo Hisamoto and Fumito Matsumura eds (1997), *Nihon no riin seisan hōshiki : jidōsha kigyō no jirei* (Japan's lean production system: examples from the car industry, Tokyo : Chūō Keizaisha.

Itami, Hiroyuki (1986), *Manejimento kontorōru no riron* (The theory of management control), Tokyo: Iwanami Shoten.

Itami, Hiroyuki, Tadao Kagono, Takao Kobayashi, Kiyonori Sakakibara and Motoshige Itō (1988), *Kyōsō to kakushin: jidōsha sangyō no kigyō seichō* (Competition and innovation: company growth in the car industry), Tokyo: Tōyō Keizai Shinpōsha.

Itami, Hiroyuki, Tadao Kagono and Motoshige Itō eds (1993), *Riidinguzu: Nihon no kigyō shisutemu daisankan: jinteki shigen* (Readings: Japanese company systems vol. 3 : human resources), Tokyo: Yūhikaku.

Kamata, Satoshi (1973), *Jidōsha zetsubō kōjō: aru kisetsu rōdōsha no nikki* (Automobile factory of despair: the diary of a seasonal worker), Tokuma Shoten. Translated by Tatsuru Akimoto and with an introduction by Ronald Dore, *Japan in the Passing Lane: An Insider's Account of Life in a Japanese Auto Factory*, Pantheon Books, 1982.

Kamii, Yoshihiko (1994), *Rōdō kumiai no shokuba kisei : Nihon jidōsha sangyō no jirei kenkyū* (Workplace regulation of labour unions: a study of examples from the Japanese car industry), Tokyo: Tokyo Daigaku Shuppankai.

Kanbayashi, Norio (1995), 'MEka shokuba ni okeru genba sagyōsha no shokumunaiyō to kanri shisutemu: Nihon kigyō no jittai chōsa kara' (Work content and systems of control of factory workers in the ME workplace – actual examples from Japanese enterprises), *Ōhara shakai mondai kenkyūjo zasshi* (Journal of the Ohara Institute for Social Research), 440. pp. 1–15.

Katō, Tetsurō and Rob Steven (1990), 'Nihon shihonshugi wa posuto-fōdoshugi ka' (Is Japanese capitalism post-fordism?), *Mado*, 4, pp. 230–56.

Kawasaki, Sangyō (1998–99), 'Boku wa Honda no kikan rōdōsha to shite hataraita: kikankō no kyūkagetsu' (I worked as a casual labourer for Honda:

nine months as a casual mechanic), vol. 1–11, *NAVI*, 1998 (6), pp. 212–17, 1998 (7), pp. 178–83, 1998 (8), pp. 196–202, 1998 (9), pp. 176–81, 1998 (10), pp. 210–15, 1998 (11), pp. 190–5, 1998 (12), pp. 190–5, 1999 (1), pp. 196–201, 1999 (2), pp. 180–5, 1999 (3), pp. 162–7, 1999 (4), pp. 228–30.

Kenney, Martin and Richard Florida (1988), 'Beyond Mass Production: Production and the Labor Process in Japan,' *Politics and Society*, 16(1), pp. 121–58. Japanese translation by Yoshiyuki Ogasawara, 'Tairyō seisan o koete – Nihon ni okeru seisan to rōdō katei,' *Mado*, 3, 1990.

Kern, Horst and Michael Schumann (1984), 'Work and Social Character: Old and New Contours,' *Economic and Industrial Democracy*, 5, pp. 51–71.

Kimura, Takao (1990), 'Toyota keiei senryaku no shintenkai to "gōrika" no genkyokumen' (New developments in Toyota management strategy and the present state of 'rationalization'), in Aichi Rōdōmondai Kenkyūjo (1990).

Knights, David (1990), 'Subjectivity, Power and the Labour Process,' in Knights, David and Hugh Willmott eds (1990).

Knightts, David and Hugh Willmott eds (1988), *New Technology and the Labor Process*, London: Macmillan

Knights, David and Hugh Willmott eds (1990), *Labour Process Theory*, London: Macmillan.

Kobayashi, Hajime (1987), 'Rain shokuba shakai no kōzō to kihan – A jidōsha M seisakujo gisō kumitate shokuba ni okeru jirei kenkyū, 2' (Structure and norms of assembly line society: a study of examples from the fit-out assembly line of factory M of A Motor Co., 2), in Hokkaidō Daigaku kyōiku gakubu kyōiku-shakaigaku kenkyūshitsu (Educational Sociology Research Center, Faculty of Education, Hokkaido University) (1989).

Koike, Kazuo (1976), 'Waga kuni rōshi kankei no tokushitsu to henka e no taiō' (The characteristics of labour-management relations in Japan and the response to change), *Nihon rōdō kyōkai zasshi* (The monthly journal of the Japan Institute of Labour), 207, pp. 61–7.

Koike, Kazuo (1977a), 'Kigyōbetsu kumiai no hatsugenryoku – Kumazawa Makoto shi no hihan ni kotaete' (Enterprise comparison of union bargaining power – a response to Makoto Kumazawa's criticism),' *Nihon rōdō kyōkai zasshi* (The monthly journal of the Japan Institute of Labour), 217, pp. 31–5.

Koike, Kazuo (1977b), *Shokuba no rōdō kumiai to sanka – rōshi kankei no Nichibei hikaku* (Labour unions and participation in the workplace – a comparison of labour relations in Japan and America), Tokyo: Yūhikaku Sensho.

Koike, Kazuo (1981), *Nihon no jukuren – sugureta jinzai keisei shisutemu*

(Japanese skill – a superior system of human resource creation), Tokyo: Yūhikaku.

Koike, Kazuo (1991), *Shigoto no keizaigaku* (The economics of work), Tokyo: Tōyō Keizai Shinpōsha.

Koike, Kazuo (1993a), 'Chiteki jukuren sairon – Nomura Masami shi no hihan ni taishite' (Intellectual skills revisited – in response to Masami Nomura's criticism), *Nihon rōdō kenkyū zasshi* (The Japanese journal of labour studies), 402, pp. 2–11.

Koike, Kazuo (1993b), 'Nihon kigyō to chiteki jukuren' (Japanese companies and intellectual skills), in Itami *et al.* ed. (1991, vol. 3 ch. 2).

Koike, Kazuo (1997), *Nihon kigyō no jinzai keisei – fukakujitsusei ni taisho suru tame no nouhau* (Human resource creation in Japanese companies – know-how to respond to uncertainty), Tokyo: Chūkō Shinsho.

Koike, K. (1998), 'NUMMI and Its Prototype Plant in Japan: A Comparative Study of Human Resource Development at the Workshop Level,' *Journal of the Japanese and International Economies*, 12, pp. 49–74.

Koike, Kazuo, Hiroyuki Chūma and Sōichi Ōta (2001), *Monozukuri no ginō – jidōsha sangyō no shokuba de* (The skill of manufacture – in the automobile industry workplace), Tokyo: Tōyō Keizai Shinpōsha.

Koike, Kazuo and Takenori Inoki eds (1987), *Jinzai keisei no kokusai hikaku – Tōnan Ajia to Nihon* (An international comparison of human resource creation – Southeast Asia and Japan), Tokyo: Tōyō Keizai Shinpōsha.

Kojima, Takenori (1994), *Chō riin kakumei* (The ultra-lean revolution), Tokyo: Nihon Keizai Shinbunsha.

Komatsu, Shirō (2000), 'Jidōsha kigyō ni okeru ginōkei jinzai yōsei (Training a skills-based workforce in Japanese industry),' *Ritsumeikan keieigaku* (The Ritsumeikan business review), 39 (1), pp. 237–63.

Komatsu, Shirō (2001), 'Nihon jidōsha kigyō ni okeru ginōkei yōsei gakkō no genjō' (The present state of skill-training schools in the Japanese automobile industry), *Ritsumeikan keieigaku* (The Ritsumeikan business review), 40 (1), pp. 105–52.

Komatsu, Shirō (2002), 'Jidōsha seizō ni okeru rōdō no henshitsu to aratana nōryoku keisei – chokusetsu seisan sagyōsha no TPM-hozen gyōmu e no shinshutsu to nōryoku keisei' (The changing quality of work and new capacity building in the Japanese automobile manufacturing industry – capacity building with the move of direct production workers into TPM and maintenance work), *Ritsumeikan keieigaku* (The Ritsumeikan business review), 41 (2), pp. 105–37.

Komatsu, Shirō (2005a), 'Toyota seisan hōshiki ni okeru hi-tenkeikoyōka no gan'i' (Jō), (Ge), (Implications of atypical employment in the Toyota Production System 1 & 2), *Chingin to shakai hoshō* (Wage and social security), 1401, pp. 17–47 & 1402, pp. 16–29.

Komatsu, Shirō (2005b), 'Toyota seisan hōshiki ni okeru hi-tenkeikoyōka to rōdō kanri' (Atypical employment and labour management in the Toyota Production System), *Rōdō shakaigaku kenkyū* (Journal of labor sociology), 6, pp. 1–40.

Koyama, Yōichi ed. (1985), *Kyodai kigyō taisei to rōdōsha* (The mega-enterprise system and the worker), Tokyo: Ochanomizu Shobō.

Kumazawa, Makoto (1993), *Shinpen Nihon no rōdōshazō* (The image of the Japanese worker : new edition), Tokyo: Chikuma Gakugei Bunko.

Kyōtani, Eiji (1982), 'Shokuba ni okeru shōshūdan katsudō no genjitsu to seikaku' (The nature and present state of small group activities in the workplace), *Mita gakkai zasshi* (Mita journal of economics), 75 (2), pp. 203–19.

Kyōtani, Eiji (1993), *Furekishihibiritii to wa nani ka – gendai Nihon no rōdō katei* (What is flexibility? – the labour process in Japan today), Tokyo: Madosha.

Lave, J. and E. Wenger (1991), *Situated Learning: Legitimate Peripheral Participation*, Cambridge: Cambridge University Press. Japanese translation by Yutaka Saeki, *Jōkyō ni umekomareta gakushū: seitōteki shūhen sanka*, Sangyō Tosho, 1993.

McKinlay, A. and Phil Taylor (1996), 'Power, Surveillance and Resistance: Inside the "factory of the future"' in Ackers et al. eds (1996).

Makino, Yasunori (1996), 'Shōshūdan katsudō no yakuwari (2) – chokusetsu bumon rōdōsha no jukuren keisei to QC' (The role of small group activities (2) – skill formation of workers in the direct production division), *Ritsumeikan sangyō shakai ronshū* (Ritsumeikan review of industrial society), 32 (3), pp. 97–111.

Marukusu, Kāru (Karl Marx) (1968), *Shihonron* (Capital), Vol. 1, Tokyo: Ōtsuki Shoten.

Marx, Karl [1867] (1887 English translation of *Das Kapital*) by Samuel Moore and Edward Aveling is available on-line at http://www.marxists.org/archive/marx/works/1867-c1/index.htm.

Maruyama, Yoshinari (1995), *Nihonteki seisan shisutemu to furekishihibiritii* (Japanese style production systems and flexibility), Tokyo: Nihon Hyōronsha.

Maruyama, Yoshinari and Toshitsugu Takamori eds (2000), *Gendai Nihon no shokuba rōdō – JIT shisutemu to chōkamitsu rōdō* (Labour on the shopfloor in Japan today – the JIT system and ultra over-intensification of work), Tokyo: Shin Nihon Shuppansha.

Mayo, Elton (1933), *The Human Problems of an Industrial Civilization*, New

York: Arno Press. Japanese translation by Eiichi Muramoto, *Sangyō bunmei ni okeru ningen mondai: Hōson jikken to sono tenkai*, Nihon Nōritsu Kyōkai, 1967.

Mine, Manabu (1994), 'Sagyō soshiki to rōshi kankei – Nihon no jidōsha sangyō no ba'ai' (The organization of work and labour relations – the case of the Japanese car industry), *Shakai rōdō kenkyū* (Society and labour), 41 (1–2), pp. 60–98.

Mitoma, Toshiharu, Hitoshi Kōnosu and Yoshinori Eri (1999), 'Hataraku hito no kareika ni tekiō suru jidōsha kumitate kōtei o mezashite' (Towards a vehicle assembly process suited to the aging workforce), *Jidōsha gijutsu* (Review of automotive engineering), 53 (12), pp. 42–7.

Monden, Yasuhiro (1989), *Toyota shisutemu – Toyota-shiki seisan kanri shisutemu* (The Toyota system: Toyota-style production management system), Tokyo: Kōdansha Bunko.

Monden, Yasuhiro (1991), *Shin-Toyota shisutemu* (The new Toyota system), Tokyo: Kōdansha.

Mulcahy, S. D. and R. R. Faulkner (1979), 'Person and Machine in a New England Factory,' in Zimbalist, ed. (1979).

Muramatsu, Kuramitsu (1996), Ryōsan shokuba ni okeru chiteki jukuren to tōgō-bunri no keikō – daikigyō to chūshōkigyō no jirei kara' (Intellectual skills in the mass production workplace and trends in inte-gration/separation – from examples of large and small-to-medium-sized enterprises), *Nihon rōdō kenkyū zasshi* (The Japanese journal of labour studies), 434, pp. 2–11.

Nakamura, Keisuke (1996), *Nihon no shokuba to seisan shisutemu* (The Japanese workplace and systems of production), Tokyo: Tōkyō Daigaku Shuppankai.

Nihon Jinbunkagakkai (Japan Society for the Human Sciences) ed. (1963), *Gijutsu kakushin no shakaiteki eikyō* (The social impact of technological innovation), Tokyo Daigaku Shuppankai.

Nihon Kagaku Gijutsu Renmei (Union of Japanese Scientists and Engineers) ed. *Genba to QC* (QC and the shopfl oor), *FQC* (FQC – Field quality control), *QC sākuru – shokuba to QC* (Quality control circles – QC in the workplace), Tokyo: Nikka Giren Shuppansha.

Nikkan Jidōsha Shinbunsha, *Nikkan jidōsha shinbun* (Nikkan automobile news).

Noble, David (1984), *Forces of Production: A Social History of Industrial Automation*, New York: Oxford University Press.

Noble, David (1995), *Progress without People: New Technology, Unemploy-ment, and the Message of Resistance*, Toronto: Between the Lines. Japanese translation by Masao Watanabe and Ryōji Ihara, *Ningenfuzai no shinpo – atarashii gijutsu, shitsugyō, teikō no messeeji*, Kobushi Shobō, 2001.

Nohara, Hikari (1992), 'Nihon no "furekishiburu" seisan shisutemu no saikentō' (Japan's 'flexible' production system revisited), *Shakaiseisaku gakkai nenpō* (Annals of the Society for the Study of Social Policy), 36, pp. 77–98.

Nohara, Hikari (1994), 'Toyota shisutemu no atarashii tenkai to teirārizumu no yukue – Nomura Masami-cho *Toyotizumu – Nihongata seisan shisutemu no seijuku to hen'yō* ni yosete' (New developments in the Toyota system and the future of Taylorism – in connection with Masami Nomura's *Toyotism – maturity and change in Japanese-style production systems*), *Ōhara Shakai Mondai Kenkyūjo zasshi* (Journal of the Ohara Institute for Social Research), 431, pp. 16–35.

Nohara, Hikari (1997a), 'T. jidōsha M. kōjō daini kumitate kōjō no jittai chōsa – shakai kankyō no henka to shokuba soshiki no saihen (1), (2)' (Survey of the actual conditions of no. 2 assembly factory of M. plant of the T. motor company – changes in the social environment and rearrangement of workplace systems), *Hiroshima hōgaku* (Hiroshima law), 20 (4), pp. 201–40, 21 (1), pp. 159–91.

Nohara, Hikari (1997b), 'Bungyō shinka : seisanryoku no hatten wa shinwa datta no ka? – Nihon jidōsha sangyō ni okeru kōjō sagyō soshiki hensei no dōkō to Sweeden – Borubo-Uddebara moderu' (Evolution of the division of labour; was the advance in productive power a myth? – Trends towards changes in the organization of factory work in the Japanese automobile industry and the Swedish Volvo-Uddebara model), Keizai riron gakkai dai yonjūgokai taikai (45th conference of the Japan Society of Political Economy).

Nohara, Hikari and Eishi Fujita eds (1988), *Jidōsha sangyō to rōdōsha – rōdōsha kanri no kōzō to rōdōshazō* (The automobile industry and the worker – the structure of labour control and the image of workers), Tokyo: Hōritsu Bunkasha.

Nomura, Masami (1993a), *Toyotizumu – Nihongata seisan shisutemu no seijuku to hen'yō*'(Toyotism – Maturity and change in Japanese-style production systems), Tokyo: Mineruva Shobō.

Nomura, Masami (1993b), *Jukuren to bungyō – Nihon kigyō to teirāshugi* (Skill and the division of labor – Japanese companies and Taylorism), Okayama: Okayama Daigaku Keizai Gakubu (Faculty of Economics, Okayama University).

Nomura, Masami (1995), 'Toyotizumu no hyōka o megutte – Yumoto Makoto shi no komento e no repurai' (On the assessment of Toyotism – a reply to Makoto Yumoto's comments), *Nihon rōdō shakaigakkai nenpō* (Annual Review of Labor Sociology), 6, pp. 103–10.

Nomura, Masami (2001), *Chiteki jukurenron hihan – Koike Kazuo ni okeru riron to jisshō* (A critique of the intellectual-skills theory – theory and substantiation in Kazuo Koike), Tokyo: Mineruva Shobō.

Nonaka, Ikujirō (1990), *Chishiki sōzō no keiei – Nihon kigyō no episutemorojii* (The management of knowledge creation – the epistemology of Japanese companies), Tokyo: Nihon Keizai Shinbunsha.

Odaka, Kōnosuke and Tsuyoshi Tsuru eds (2001), *Dejitaruka jidai no soshiki kaikaku* (Organizational reform in the digital age), Tokyo: Yūhikaku.

Ogawa, Eiji ed. (1994), *Toyota seisan hōshiki no kenkyū* (A study of the Toyota production system), Tokyo: Nihon Keizai Shinbunsha.

Ōno, Taiichi (1978), *Toyota seisan hōshiki – datsu kibo no keiei o mezashite* (The Toyota production system – towards management beyond scale*),* Tokyo: Daiyamondosha.

Ōno, Taiichi and Yasuhiro Monden eds (1983), *Toyota seisan hōshiki no shintenkai* (New developments in the Toyota production system), Tokyo: Nihon Nōritsu Kyōkai.

Ōno, Takeshi (1997), 'X jidōsha ni okeru shokuba no jiritsusei to jiritsuseikanri no mekanizumu – X jidōsha ni okeru san'yo kansatsu no kekka kara' (Autonomy and control in the workplace in motor company X – from the results of participatory observation), *Shakaigaku hyōron* (Sociological review), 48 (2), pp. 143–57.

Ōno, Takeshi (1998), 'A. jidōsha no rōdō katei – A. jidōsha ni okeru san'yo kansatsu ni motozuite' (The labour process in motor company A – based on participatory observation), *Ōhara Shakai Mondai Kenkyūjo zasshi* (Journal of the Ohara Institute for Social Research), 470, pp. 14–40.

Parker, Mike and Jane Slaughter (1988), *Choosing Sides: Unions and the Team Concept*, Boston: South End Press. Japanese translation by Hideo Totsuka, *Beikoku jidōsha kōjō no henbō – 'sutoresu ni yoru kanri' to rōdōsha*, Ryokufū Shuppan, 1995.

Piore, Michael and Charles Sabel (1984), *The Second Industrial Divide*, New York: Basic Books. Japanese translation by Yasushi Yamanouchi et al., *Daini no sangyō bunsuirei*, Chikuma Shobō, 1993.

Roethlisberger, Fritz J. and William J. Dickson (1939), *Management and the Worker*, Cambridge: Harvard University Press.

Saga, Ichirō (1984), *Kigyō to rōdō kumiai – Nissan Jidōsha rōshiron* (The company and labour unions – on management and labour in Nissan Motor), Tokyo: Tabata Shoten.

Sakakibara, Kiyonori (1988), 'Seisan shisutemu ni okeru kakushin – Toyota no keesu' (Innovation in production systems – the case of Toyota), in Itami *et al.* eds (1988).

Sakolosky, Ron (1992), '"Disciplinary Power" and the Labor Process,' in Sturdy et al. eds (1992).

Saruta, Masaki (1995), Toyota shisutemu to rōmu kanri (The Toyota system and labour control), Tokyo: Zeimu Keiri Kyōkai.

Satake, Hiroaki (1998), *Toyota seisan hōshiki no seichō-hatten hen'yō* (Growth, development and change in the Toyota production system), Tokyo: Tōyō Keizai Shinpōsha.

Satake, Hiroaki (2000), 'Toyota seisan hōshiki to Nihonteki seisan shisutemu – sono kyōtsūsei to isshitsusei o megutte' (The Toyota production method and Japanese-style production systems – focusing on commonalities and differences), *Ōhara Shakai Mondai Kenkyūjo zasshi* (Journal of the Ohara Institute for Social Research), 498, pp. 1–18.

Sawada, Zentarō (1994), 'Rōdō to "jukuren" no henka' (Changes in work and 'skill'), in Shokugyō-Seikatsu Kenkyūkai ed. (1994).

Sewell, Graham and Barry Wilkinson (1992), 'Someone to Watch Over Me: Surveillance, Discipline and the Just-In-Time Labour Process,' *Sociology*, 26 (2), pp. 271–89.

Shi, Shi-Min (Shi, Semin) (1994), 'Toyota seisan hōshiki no aratana chōsen' (New challenges for the Toyota production system), in Ogawa ed. (1994).

Shimizu, Kōichi (1995), 'Toyota jidōsha ni okeru rōdō no ningenka (I), (II)' (The humanization of work in Toyota Motor Co.), *Okayama Daigaku Keizaigakkai zasshi* (Okayama economic review), 27 (1), pp. 1–24, 27 (2), pp. 293–315.

Shimizu, Kōichi (1999), 'Genba ga tsukuru kumitate rain (I), (II)' (How the workplace makes the assembly line), *Okayama Daigaku Keizaigakkai zasshi* (Okayama economic review), 30 (3), pp. 125–62, 30 (4), pp. 303–31.

Shimizu, Kōichi (2001), 'Kōdo jōhōka jidai no jidōsha kumitate shokuba – Toyota jidōsha no jirei'(The automobile assembly factory in the information age: Examples from Toyota Motor), in Odaka, Kōnosuke and Tsuyoshi Tsuru eds (2001).

Shimokawa, Kōichi and Takahiro Fujimoto eds (2001), *Toyota shisutemu no genten – kiipāson ga kataru kigen to shinka* (The source of the Toyota system – key people explain its origin and evolution), Tokyo: Bunshindō.

Shiomi, Fumimasa (1978–9), 'Kikankō taikenki (dai ikkai), A jidōsha kōjō' (Diary of a casual worker, Part 1, Car Factory A), '(dai nikai), Shinkeishitsu na honkō no moto de'(Part 2, Working under a temperamental full-time mechanic), '(dai sankai), Sawayaka undō no hamon' (Part 3, Ripples form the harmonious cooperation movement), '(dai yonkai), Furaisu sangōki to no tatakai' (Part 4, My battle with no. 3 milling machine), '(dai gokai), Kikai to jiyū to rentaikan' (Part 5, Machines, freedom and solidarity), *Gijutsu to ningen* (Technology and people), 7 (11), pp. 82–7, 7 (12), pp. 81–5, 8 (1), pp. 110–14, 8 (3), pp. 116–21, 8 (5), pp. 143–7.

Shokugyō Seikatsu Kenkyūkai ed. (Society for the study of work and lifestyle) ed. (1994), *Kigyō shakai to ningen* (Corporate society and people), Tokyo: Hōritsu Bunkasha.

Stewart, Paul and Philip Garrahan (1995), 'Employee responses to New Management Techniques in the Auto Industry,' *Work, Employment & Society*, 9 (3), pp. 517–36.

Sturdy, Andrew, David Knights and Hugh Willmott eds (1992), *Skill and Consent: Contemporary Studies in the Labour Process*, London and New York: Routledge.

Suzuki, Yoshiji (1994), *Nihonteki seisan shisutemu to kigyō shakai* (Japanese-style production systems and company culture), Sapporo: Hokkaidō Daigaku Tosho Kankōkai.

Suzuki, Yūzō (1983), 'Tanō kōka to jobu roteeshon ni yoru jūnan na shokuba-zukuri' (Creation of flexible workplaces through the move to multi-skilling and job rotation), in Taiichi Ōno, Yasuhiro Monden eds (1983).

Tanaka, Hirohide (1982), 'Rensai intabyū: Nihonteki koyō kankō o kizuita hitotachi (sono 2), moto Toyota Jidōsha Kōgyō senmu-torishimariyaku, Yamamoto Yoshiaki shi ni kiku (1), (2), (3) (Interview series: People who have created Japan's employment culture, part 2: Interview with Mr Yoshiaki Yamamoto, former executive director of Toyota Motor Industries), *Nihon Rōdō Kyōkai zasshi* (The monthly journal of the Japan Institute of Labour), 24 (7), pp. 38–55, 24 (8), pp. 64–81, 24 (9), pp. 25–41.

Tanaka, Hirohide (1983), 'Kūdōka suru jukuren – rōdō no genba de, ima, nani ga okotte iru no ka' (Deskilling: What's happening now in the workplace?) *Keizai hyōron* (Economic reports), 1983 (8).

Tanaka, Hirohide (1984), *Kaitai suru jukuren : ME kakumei to rōdō no mirai* (The breakdown of skill: the ME revolution and the future of work), Tokyo: Nihon Keizai Shinbunsha.

Thompson, Paul (1983), *The Nature of Work: An Introduction to Debates on the Labour Process*, London: Macmillan.

Tomita, Yoshinori (1998), *ME-kakushin to Nihon no rōdō shisutemu* (The ME reformation and the Japanese system of labour), Tokyo: Hihyōsha.

Totsuka, Hideo and Tsutomu Hyōdō eds (1991), *Rōshi kankei no tenkan to sentaku – Nihon no jidōsha sangyō* (Changes and options in labour-management relations – the Japanese automobile industry), Nihon Hyōronsha.

Toyota Jidōsha Kōgyō Kabushikigaisha (Toyota Motor Industries Co.) (1958), *Toyota Jidōsha nijūnenshi.* (The twenty-year history of Toyota Motor).

Toyota Jidōsha Kōgyō Kabushikigaisha (Toyota Motor Industries Co.) (1967), *Toyota Jidōsha sanjūnenshi* (The thirty-year history of Toyota Motor).

Toyota Jidōsha Kōgyō Kabushikigaisha (Toyota Motor Industries Co.) (1978), *Toyota no ayumi* (Tracing the footsteps of Toyota).

Toyota Jidōsha Kabushikigaisha (Toyota Motor Co.) (1987), *Sōzō kagiri naku – Toyota Jidōsha gojūnenshi* (Creativity unlimited – The fifty-year history of Toyota Motor).

Tsuji, Katsuji (1989), 'Jidōsha kōjō ni okeru "shūdanteki jukuren" no kinō keitai to sono keisei kikō – Toyotizumu to fōdizumu (jō), (chū), (ge)' (The functional formation and organizational structure of 'group skill' in automobile factories: Toyotism and Fordism, Parts I, II and III) *Ritsumeikan sangyō-shakai ronshū* (Ritsumeikan review of industrial society), 24 (4), pp. 29–57, 25 (2), pp. 1–33, 25 (3), pp. 107–44.

Tsuji, Katsuji (1998), 'Jidōsha rōdōron to "ryōsangata jukuren",' (The automobile labour debate and 'mass production skills), *Ritsumeikan sangyō-shakai ronshū* (Ritsumeikan review of industrial society), 34 (1), pp. 111–20.

Tsuji, Katsuji (2002), 'Jidōsha kōjō no shokuba kakushin to shin-rōdō soshiki – Toyota no shokuba, nijūnen no hensen' (Workplace reform and new labour organization in auto factories: 20 years of change in the Toyota workplace) *Ritsumeikan sangyō-shakai ronshū* (Ritsumeikan review of industrial society), 38 (1), pp. 91–109.

Tsunekawa, Masumi (2002), 'Kōdo ginō keisei to rōdōsha no kaisōsei – jidōsha sangyō A sha no jirei' (The formation of high levels of skill and the stratification of workers – actual examples from company A in the automobile industry), Nihon Rōdō Shakai Gakkai teirei kenkyūkai hōkoku (Reports of the regular meetings of the Japan Society for the Sociology of Labour), 27 July.

Tsuchiya, Naoki (1996), 'Tekkōgyō ni okeru sagyō soshiki to jinzai keisei – seizō-hozen no bungyō shisutemu no saihen' (The organization of work and staff development in the steel industry – reorganization of the separate production and maintenance systems), *Nihon rōdō kenkyū zasshi* (The Japanese journal of labour studies), 440, pp. 37–50.

Wardell, Mark, Thomas Steiger and Peter Meiksins eds (1999), *Rethinking the Labor Process*, New York: State University of New York Press.

Womack, James P., Daniel T. Jones and Daniel Roos (1990), *The Machine that Changed the World*, New York: Rawson Associates. Japanese translation by Hiroshi Sawada, *Riin seisan hōshiki ga sekai no jidōsha sangyō o kō kaeru*, Keizaikai, 1990.

Yamamoto, Kiyoshi (1981), *Jidōsha sangyō no rōshi kankei* (Labour and capital in the automobile industry), Tokyo: Tokyo Daigaku Shuppankai.

Yamamoto, Choku (1978), *Toyota yonjūnen no kiseki* (Toyota over the course of forty years), Tokyo: Daiyamondosha

Yamashita, Mitsuru (1995), 'Jukuren gainen no saikentō – jukurenron ni hitsuyō na shakaigaku teki shiten to wa nani ka' (Rethinking the concept of skill – what sociological perspectives are required?), *Nihon rōdō shakai-gakkai nenpō* (Annual review of labor sociology), 6, pp. 113–34.

Yoshida, Makoto (1993), 'A-sha tokusōsha kumitate kōtei no shokuba no sōbō – san'yo kansatsu ni motozuku ichi kōsatsu' (The face of the workplace in a special-purpose vehicle fit-out factory of company A – a view based on participatory observation), *Nihon rōdō shakaigakkai nenpō* (Annual review of labor sociology), 4, pp. 29–50.

Yumoto, Makoto (1989–90), 'Jidōsha rōdōsha no jukuren-ginō to kyariakeisei (jō), (ge)' (Skill and expertise of automobile workers and career development, parts I and II), *Ritsumeikan sangyō-shakai ronshū* (Ritsumeikan review of industrial society), 25 (3), pp. 145–69, 25 (4), pp. 67–104.

Yumoto, Makoto (1994), 'Gengyō rōdōsha no kigyōnai jukuren keisei' (On-the-job skill formation for currently-employed workers), in Shokugyō-seikatsu kenkyūkai (Society for the study of work and lifestyle), ed. (1994).

Yumoto, Makoto (1995), 'Nihongata seisan shisutemu to kigyō-shakai-ron – Nomura Masami shi no kincho o megutte' (Japanese-style production systems and the sociology of industry – focising on Masami Nomura's recent publication), *Nihon rōdōshakai gakkai nenpō* (Annual review of labor sociology), 6, pp. 81–102.

Zimbalist, A. ed. (1979), *Case Studies on the Labor Process*, London: Monthly Review Press.

Index

cleanliness 101

cleaning round 15, 21–2, 25–6, 28, 30, 33–5, 45, 49, 51–3, 57, 67, 72–3, 75–6, 78, 80, 82–4, 90, 92, 94, 99–101, 103–5, 107, 113, 116, 118, 147–50, 160

Clegg, S. R. 204

code

incorporated into technology 211

of the workplace 117–18, 145, 151–4, 191

coercion 99, 172, 202–4, 215

commitment 62, 129, 167, 174, 190, 216

competitive edge ix, 75, 176, 185, 187

competitive power x, 170, 184

competitiveness 166, 173, 175, 185

compliance xii, 118

concentration 28, 44, 46, 53, 55, 57, 62, 147, 189, 216

conception and execution 184, 215

conflict xiii, 62, 145, 146–7, 150, 154, 158–61, 178, 201, 203, 216

consensus 48, 112

consent 111, 143, 201

context of the workplace x, xiii, 68, 116–18, 159, 185, 187, 199, 213

contract (*See also* extension and worker) 1–2, 17, 23, 50, 83, 90, 105, 119, 121–3, 130, 132, 138, 140, 142, 144, 147, 149, 163–4, 187, 195, 197, 206, 212–13, 218

incomplete contract 105

length of period extended 192, 218

control (*See also* quality and management) xii–xiii, 5, 30, 36, 62, 66, 70–3, 86, 88–90, 95–7, 99–100, 102, 105–11, 113–17, 119, 144–6, 152, 155–7, 167–8, 171, 173, 183–4, 196, 203–6, 210, 216–17

controller 115

direct control 95, 100, 102, 103, 106, 156, 202

indirect control xii, 100, 102

through communication 111

through groups 167

through language 114

workers controlling fellow workers 116–17

cooperation 2, 174, 189

ability to cooperate (*kyōchōsei*) 211

Coriat, B. 215

Corolla 190

corporate society (*kigyō shakai*) 171–2

cost x, 11, 18, 25, 39, 41, 44, 78, 108, 130, 138–9, 141, 152, 187, 190, 200–1

cost-cutting plans 191

cost effectiveness 42

cost reduction (*See* Toyota terminology)

investment cost 10, 38

monitoring cost 94

salary costs 7

training costs 156

craftsman (*See also* artisan) 62, 171, 204, 210, 214

creative suggestion 5, 38, 64, 79, 80